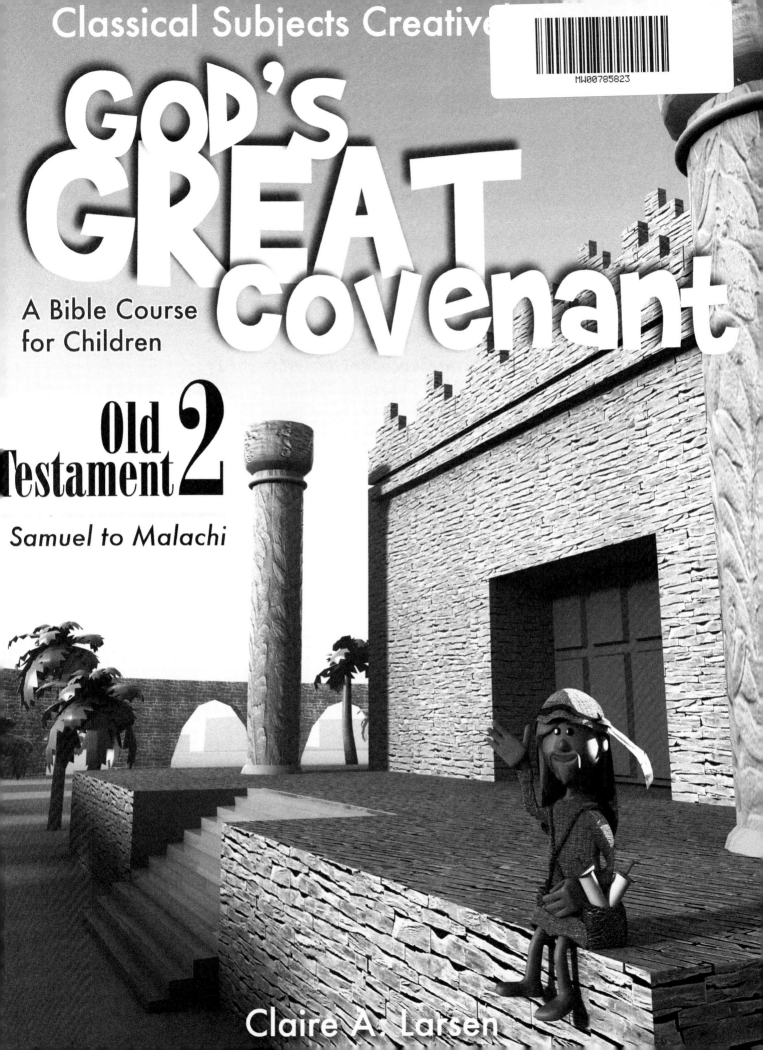

Classical Subjects Creative

GOD'S GREAT Covenant

A Bible Course
for Children

Old Testament 2

Samuel to Malachi

Claire A. Larsen

God's Great Covenant Old Testament 2:
A Bible Course for Children
© 2009, Classical Academic Press®
Version 2.0

Classical Academic Press
515 S. 32nd St.
Camp Hill, PA 17011

www.ClassicalAcademicPress.com

ISBN: 978-1-60051-049-6

Book cover and illustrations by:
Rob Baddorf

Book design by:
David Gustafson

In memory of Dr. John M. L. Young, beloved professor,
whose faithful teaching of God's Word changed many lives,
including mine.

Table of Contents

Appendices

Maps

"The king is coming! The king is coming!" All around you men, women, and children are shouting loudly. You are pushed and shoved, first this way and then that. Each person wants to be the first one to see the king's procession. The city is crowded, and everyone's excited. You are an Israelite child, and King David has come to your city!

God's people, the Israelites, didn't always have a king. Many centuries before King David ruled, God had made a covenant with a man named Abraham. "You will be the father of a great nation," the LORD promised. "I will be your God, and you will be My people."

The LORD kept his promise to Abraham. Abraham had a son named Isaac, who had a son named Jacob who had a very large family. Jacob's family moved to Egypt, and 400 years later there were so many descendents of Jacob living in Egypt that the pharaoh was afraid of them. He made Jacob's descendents, called Hebrews or Israelites, slaves so they wouldn't be a danger to his kingdom. The Israelites weren't a nation yet, and they certainly didn't have a king.

The LORD sent Moses to free the Israelites from Egypt. They spent forty years in the great and terrible wilderness, and then arrived at the Promised Land. The LORD appointed Joshua as Israel's commander. The people fought many battles, some mighty victories because they trusted the LORD and some terrible defeats because they disobeyed Him. Finally, they possessed the land that the LORD had promised to Abraham. Now the Israelites were a nation with their own land, but they didn't have a king.

The Israelites lived in the land and enjoyed all the good things that the LORD provided. Sometimes they obeyed the LORD and worshipped only Him. Many times, however, they disobeyed the LORD and worshipped Baal, Asherah, and the other Canaanite gods. The Israelites did what they wanted to do, not what God had commanded them to do.

Because of their idolatry, the LORD sent other nations to bring trouble to the Israelites. When the Israelites became miserable enough, they cried out to the LORD for help. Then the LORD sent men called judges to deliver them from their enemies. The judges ruled the land and saved the people from suffering and oppression. But the people continued to turn away from the LORD, and they didn't have a king.

Yet from the beginning the Israelites did have a king! God, creator of the world and King of all kings, was Israel's King. Because the LORD was Israel's King, they didn't need a human king.

God's Great Covenant, Old Testament 2: A Bible Course for Children continues the story that *God's Great Covenant, Old Testament 1* began. In the book of 1 Samuel, the Israelites asked God for a king. "We want a king like other nations," they demanded. So the LORD gave them a king. Over the next 500 years the people had many kings. A few of the kings were godly men who worshipped the LORD and ruled the nation well. However, most of the kings were wicked men who rejected the LORD and worshipped foreign gods. The kings' actions and the disobedience of the people eventually brought about the destruction of the nation.

God's Old Testament story would be a tragedy except for one thing: God's kingdom is greater than the nation of Israel. Israel's earthly kingdom was a picture of God's spiritual, eternal kingdom. Behind the scenes, God reigned supreme. He used even the disobedience of wicked kings to bring about His plan. He guided all of history toward its most important event—the coming of the Messiah.

Prophets prophesied about the Messiah, and their words became God's Scriptures. God's people prayed that the Messiah would come soon. Through the centuries, even when times were bleak and sin darkened men's hearts, the LORD's plan was right on schedule.

God's people had times of obedience and prosperity as well as times of disobedience and judgment. Through it all, God's kingdom remained secure because the LORD God was the Keeper of His Kingdom.

"Behold, He who keeps Israel Shall neither slumber nor sleep.
The LORD is your keeper." (Psalm 121:4-5a)

What is the Old Testament?

The Old Testament, God's holy Scripture, has thirty-nine books written over 1,200 years by more than 30 authors. It tells you how God created man, how sin entered the world, and how God made a covenant to be the God of His people. Beginning in Genesis 3:15, God hints that a Savior would come. This Savior, or Messiah, would die for His people's sin and then set up an eternal kingdom where He would rule forever. Everything in the Old Testament points to Jesus Christ—the Savior, the Messiah, the King of kings, and the Lord of lords.

Books of the Old Testament

Type	Old Testament Books	
Pentateuch: The Law (5 books) *History before entering the Promised Land*	<u>Five books of the Law:</u>	
	Genesis	Exodus
	Leviticus	Numbers
	Deuteronomy	
History (12 books) *History after entering the Promised Land*	<u>Nine books of history before the Exile:</u>	
	Joshua	Judges
	Ruth	1 and 2 Samuel
	1 and 2 Kings	1 and 2 Chronicles
	<u>Three books of history after the Exile:</u>	
	Ezra	Nehemiah
	Esther	
Poetry (5 books)	<u>Five poetry books:</u>	
	Job	Psalms
	Proverbs	Ecclesiastes
	Song of Solomon	
Major Prophets (5 books)	<u>Five books of the Major Prophets:</u>	
	Isaiah	Jeremiah
	Lamentations	Ezekiel
	Daniel	
Minor Prophets: The Twelve (12 books)	<u>Nine books of the Minor Prophets before the Exile:</u>	
	Hosea	Joel
	Amos	Obadiah
	Jonah	Micah
	Nahum	Habakkuk
	Zephaniah	
	<u>Three books of the Minor Prophets after the Exile:</u>	
	Haggai	Zechariah
	Malachi	

17 Historical Books + 5 Poetry Books + 17 Prophets = 39 Books in the Old Testament

UNIT 1

The Early Kingdom...The God Who Anoints

Theme: The Keeper of the Kingdom anoints those who lead His people.

Shalom. Let me introduce myself. I am Tobias, the royal chronicler, and I work in the king's palace. It's my job to record with utmost accuracy all the royal comings and goings. So with my expertise and wide experience (oh my, oh my, how humble I am!), I'm here, my friends, to retell this amazing story of how God faithfully keeps the promises of His great covenant. He is the keeper of His kingdom.

When the story begins, Israel is at the brink of historic changes. In only 100 years, the scattered tribes of Israel would become a mighty kingdom with a powerful army, a magnificent palace, and a world-renowned king. God made this happen through three men: Samuel, Saul, and David.

Until now, Israel's only King was God. When the Israelites demanded a king like other nations, they were rebelling against God. In the covenant, Israel had agreed that God would be their King and have authority over them. Samuel, the last judge and the first prophet, directed the people back to the LORD. It was because of Samuel that Israel's kingdom started out well. Samuel was godly and pleased the LORD.

Israel's first king, Saul, was tall, handsome, and strong. The people thought that he was the perfect king. Too soon, though, Saul's heart became proud. He disregarded the LORD's words and did things his own way.

Although Saul ruled Israel for more than twenty years, the LORD rejected him early in his reign. His sons would never rule after him. He was not a godly ruler. To everyone's surprise, the LORD chose David, a simple shepherd boy, to be the next king. Even though David was young and small, he was brave and mighty, and, most of all, his heart trusted in the LORD his God.

Each of these men—Samuel, Saul, and David—was specially chosen and anointed by God to serve Him. (Being anointed means being chosen by God and equipped by His Spirit to serve God in a particular job.) Now that I have introduced the main characters, let's go back in time to learn exactly how the early kingdom came about.

PSALM 23 A Psalm of David

1. The LORD is my shepherd;
   I shall not want.
2. He makes me to lie down in green pastures;
   He leads me beside the still waters.
3. He restores my soul;
   He leads me in the paths of righteousness
   For His name's sake.
4. Yea, though I walk through the valley of the shadow of death,
   I will fear no evil;
   For You are with me;
   Your rod and Your staff, they comfort me.
5. You prepare a table before me in the presence of my enemies;
   You anoint my head with oil;
   My cup runs over.
6. Surely goodness and mercy shall follow me
   All the days of my life;
   And I will dwell in the house of the LORD
   Forever.

David, the shepherd boy, wrote Psalm 23, which is commonly called the "Shepherd's Psalm." In this psalm, the LORD is the Shepherd, and His people are the sheep.

Sheep do not naturally know what they need. They will not lie down and rest if they are tired, bothered by nasty little insects, or frightened by other animals. When they are thirsty, they do not always choose the refreshing, cool water of the meadow streams. They will drink whatever water they find, even if the water is dirty or unsafe to drink.

A good shepherd takes care of his sheep, even if he must lead them through dark and dangerous valleys to reach the lush mountain pastures where good food and clear water are plentiful. With his rod, a symbol of his strength, and his staff, a symbol of his care, the shepherd protects and comforts his sheep.

In John 10, Jesus Christ is called the Good Shepherd. As the Shepherd, the LORD loves His people, protects them from all evil, and leads them carefully through all the circumstances of life. The LORD does only good things for His people, and His mercy goes with them all the days of their lives until they go to live in His house with Him forever.

Chapter 1

The Call of Samuel

LESSON SCOPE: 1 Samuel 1–3   **READ TO ME:** 1 Samuel 1–3

THEME: The Lord God calls His people to be holy.

MEMORY VERSE:

"In those days there was no king in Israel; everyone did what was right in his own eyes." (Judges 21:25)

KEY FACTS:

Samuel's Many Jobs

Judge	Priest	Prophet	Nazirite
1 Samuel 7:15	1 Samuel 7:9	1 Samuel 3:20	1 Samuel 1:11
He "judged Israel all the days of his life."	He offered sacrifices and prayed for God's people.	Everyone in Israel knew that God had made him a prophet.	His mother set him apart for the Lord before he was born.

Judge	= Person chosen by God to be a deliverer, peacemaker, and civil leader.
Priest	= Man in charge of offering sacrifices and offerings in the tabernacle.
Prophet	= Person called to speak for God.
Nazirite	= Person set apart for God; he could not drink wine, cut his hair, or touch a dead body.

THINGS TO REMEMBER:

Anoint	= Chosen by God and equipped by God's Spirit to serve the Lord in a particular job.
Covenant	= God's promise to be the God of His people forever.
Holy	= "Set apart by God" or "living in a way that pleases God."

MESSAGE FROM THE KING: The King wants *you* to be holy.

Even as a child, Samuel was holy. The Lord set him apart, and Samuel pleased God. What does it mean to be holy? Why is being holy so hard?

The Call of Samuel

Every year it was the same. The whole family walked through the hill country of Ephraim to the tabernacle at Shiloh to worship the LORD. Hannah dreaded these pilgrimages. Hannah loved the LORD, and she loved her husband, Elkanah. He was a good man, and she knew he loved her. But these trips always made her sad because Hannah had no children.

Elkanah's other wife, Peninnah, had many children. With gleeful pleasure, Peninnah would tease Hannah mercilessly about having no children until Hannah would weep in agony and could not enjoy the ceremonial meal.

> **Jesus in the OT**
>
> A prophet is a person called to speak God's words. How is Samuel, the prophet, like Jesus Christ, the Prophet?

This year Hannah stood before the LORD with a bitter soul and prayed in tears, "O LORD Almighty, see my misery and remember me. If you give me a son, I will give him back to you, and he will serve You his whole life. He will be a Nazirite, and he will never cut his hair."

Eli, the priest, saw Hannah's lips moving, but couldn't hear her words. He thought she was drunk, and rebuked her harshly. Quickly Hannah responded, "Oh, I am not drunk, my LORD, but I am deeply troubled. I was pouring out my heart to the LORD, hoping He would hear my plea." Eli comforted her, saying, "Go in peace. May God grant you your request."

The LORD did answer Hannah's prayer and gave her a son. "I will name him Samuel," she said, "because I asked the LORD for him."

For the next three years, Hannah stayed home when the family went to Shiloh to worship, and she nursed Samuel. Then came that special day when Hannah would dedicate her son to the LORD. Holding Samuel's small hand, she walked to the tabernacle with him. She took offerings of a young bull, a basket of flour, and a flask of wine along with her.

After the sacrifice, Hannah brought Samuel to Eli. "Remember me?" she asked. "In tears I prayed for this child, and the LORD answered my prayer. Now I give him to the LORD for his whole life." Hannah then sang a song of thanksgiving to the LORD, and when she left the tabernacle, Samuel stayed with Eli.

Although Eli was a godly man, his sons, Hophni and Phinehas, were wicked. The LORD was very angry with them because they treated His offerings with contempt. Samuel, on the other hand, grew up in the LORD's presence and served the LORD well. Every year, his mother would bring him a little robe; The LORD blessed Hannah with other children.

One day a man of God brought bad news to Eli, saying, "The LORD is angry because you honor your sons more than you honor Him. You didn't stop them when they sinned against Him. Both your sons will die on the same day, and the LORD will choose a faithful priest from a different family."

Years went by. Eli became old and blind. Samuel served the LORD under Eli's care. Unlike in the days of Moses and Joshua, the LORD did not often speak directly to people, but things were about to change.

One night, when Samuel was in bed, the LORD called him. Thinking it was Eli who had called, Samuel immediately ran to him. "You called me, Eli? Here I am," Samuel said. Eli was puzzled, and said, "Go back to bed, Samuel. I didn't call you." Samuel obeyed.

The LORD called Samuel a second time, and a second time Eli told Samuel to go back to bed. Samuel didn't know it was God who was calling him. When Samuel heard the voice a third time, Eli realized the LORD was calling Samuel. He told Samuel, "It's the LORD who is calling you. If He calls again say, 'Speak, for Your servant hears.'" The LORD did call again, and Samuel replied as Eli had instructed him.

The LORD's message to Samuel was frightening. The LORD said that He was going to judge Eli's family for their great sin against Him. No sacrifice would ever atone for their sin.

In the morning, Eli asked Samuel to tell him what the LORD had said. Samuel was afraid. How could he speak of God's judgment to Eli? After much urging, Samuel told Eli the sad news, and Eli accepted what God had spoken. "He is the LORD. Let Him do what He thinks is best," Eli said.

The LORD was with Samuel, and he grew up to be a godly man. The LORD revealed Himself to Samuel, and all Israel from the north to the south knew that Samuel was the LORD's prophet.

Review Worksheets

A. MEMORY VERSE:

"In those days there was no _____ in Israel; everyone did what was

_____ in his own _____." (Judges 21:25)

B. KEY FACTS: Put the answers to the questions in the boxes below.

1. Judge: How long did Samuel judge Israel?

2. Priest: What two things did Samuel do as a priest in the tabernacle?

3. Prophet: Who made Samuel a prophet over everyone in Israel?

4. Nazirite: Before Samuel was born, what did his mother do?

Samuel's Many Jobs

Judge	Priest	Prophet	Nazirite
1._____	2a. _____	3._____	4._____
_____	_____	_____	_____
_____	b._____	_____	_____
_____	_____	_____	_____

C. STORY FACTS: Fill in the blanks below.

1. Elkanah's family worshipped at the tabernacle at _____.

2. Hannah prayed that the LORD would give her a _____.

3. The LORD said Eli honored _____ _____ more than he honored God.

4. Hannah sang a song of _____ because God gave her a son.

5. Anoint means _____ by God and _____

   by God's Spirit to _____ the LORD in a particular job.

6. God's promise to be the God of His people forever is His _____.

D. WHAT'S THE RIGHT ANSWER?

Circle the word that completes the sentence correctly.

1. When Eli saw Hannah praying, he thought that she was _____.

    angry   drunk   depressed

2. One night the LORD called Samuel _____ times.

    two   three   four

3. Hannah named her son Samuel because she _____ God for him.

    asked   yelled at   cursed

4. The LORD's message to Samuel was about _____ for Eli's family.

    blessing   prosperity   judgment

E. WHAT DOES THIS PERSON DO? Match the job with the description of the job.

_____ Judge   1. Person called to speak for God

_____ Priest   2. Person set apart to serve God

_____ Prophet   3. Man who offered sacrifices

_____ Nazirite   4. Deliverer, peacemaker, and civil leader

F. HOW DID SAMUEL ANSWER THE LORD?

Circle every other letter and put the letters in the spaces below.

A S E P C E T A U K I F Y O K R

Q Y R O T U F R D S R E C R B V E A T N L T J H M E N A T R E S

___ ___ ___ ___ ___, ___ ___ ___   ___ ___ ___ ___

___ ___ ___ ___ ___ ___   ___ ___ ___ ___ ___

G. FIND OUT...

Who else did God call to serve Him? Look up the verses below to find out.

_____ Exodus 3:4,10   _____ Jeremiah 1:1-5

_____ Matthew 9:9   _____ Romans 1:1

What did the LORD call these men to do? _____

chapter 2

Samuel—The Last Judge

LESSON SCOPE: 1 Samuel 4–7   **READ TO ME:** 1 Samuel 4–7

THEME: The LORD God shows His power over idols.

MEMORY VERSE:

"Remember the former things of old, For I am God, and there is no other; I am God, and there is none like Me." (Isaiah 46:9)

KEY FACTS:

The Ark of the Covenant's Journey

From Shiloh	Where it sat in the tabernacle.
To the battlefield	Because Israel wanted victory over the Philistines.
To Ashdod	Where God destroyed Dagon in his temple, struck the Philistines with tumors, and sent rats to ravage the land.
To Gath and Ekron	Where God sent more tumors and rats to the Ekron and Gath Philistines.
To Israel	Where it stayed at Abinadab's house for twenty years.

THINGS TO REMEMBER:

Ark of the covenant	= Box that contained the Ten Commandments and reminded Israel that God was with them.
Ichabod	= Means "the glory [of the LORD] has departed from Israel."
Ebenezer	= Means "thus far has the LORD helped us."

MESSAGE FROM THE KING: Do you have an Ebenezer stone?

Samuel set up an Ebenezer stone to remember what the LORD had done for Israel. How can you set up an Ebenezer stone to remind you of what God has done for you?

Samuel—The Last Judge

The battle was over, and 4,000 Israelites were dead! How could the LORD let this happen? The elders of Israel shook their heads in disbelief, and said, "Maybe if we bring the ark from Shiloh, the LORD will protect us from the Philistines. If the ark is with us, the LORD will be with us, too."

So they sent for the ark of the covenant, which was in the tabernacle at Shiloh. When the ark entered Israel's camp, the Israelites shouted so loudly that the ground trembled. Hearing the deafening shouts, the Philistines exclaimed, "A god has come into the Israelites' camp. We're in trouble now. But don't give up. We must be strong and fight!" The Philistines attacked again and won another mighty victory over Israel.

Meanwhile, old Eli was sitting along the road near Shiloh, anxiously awaiting news. A messenger with ragged clothes and dust covering his head ran into town. "I've come from the battlefield and have dreadful news," he shouted. "Thirty thousand Israelites are dead, Hophni and Phinehas have been killed, and the Philistines have captured the ark!"

> **Jesus in the OT**
>
> What does a priest do? A priest makes sacrifices for sin. Samuel, as priest, offered a sacrifice for the people's sin, and the LORD forgave them. What does Jesus' sacrifice on the cross do for you?

Eli's grief over his sons' deaths was great, but to Eli the capture of the ark was the worst thing that could ever happen to Israel because it may have meant that the LORD's presence was gone from Israel. Unable to bear this, Eli fell backwards from his chair and died. Phinehas's wife was expecting a child. When she heard the news, she went into labor and had a son. In the last moments before she died, she named the baby Ichabod, meaning "the glory [of the LORD] has departed from Israel," because her husband and father-in-law were dead and the ark was captured by the Philistines.

What was happening? Israel wasn't supposed to lose battles. Wasn't the LORD stronger than the gods of the Philistines? The problem was that the Israelites thought the ark was a magic box that would always bring them good fortune. They had forgotten that God was holy and desired holiness from His people. They thought that they could do

whatever they wanted and that the priests could dishonor the LORD in the tabernacle and God would still do whatever they asked Him to do. They had forgotten that the LORD blessed those who obeyed and brought judgment on those who disobeyed.

The Philistines put the ark beside the statue of Dagon inside Dagon's temple at Ashdod. (Dagon was one of the chief gods of the Philistines.) The next morning, Dagon was on the floor bowing before the ark. They put the idol back on its seat, but the next day it was on the ground again. This time its hands and head had broken off.

At the same time, the LORD sent a plague of rats and tumors to the people at Ashdod. The people panicked and sent the ark to Gath and then to Ekron. Everywhere the ark went, the people got sick, and rats scurried through the fields, eating up the crops. The people cried out, "Send the ark back to Israel or it will kill all of us."

The Philistines met with their own priests and sorcerers to devise a strategy to return the ark to Israel. "Put the ark on a new cart pulled by two cows who just had calves. Send a guilt offering of five gold tumors and five gold rats," their advisors said. "Then send the cart down the road toward Israel. If the cows pull the cart toward Israel, leaving their calves behind, we will know that it was the LORD that brought this disaster upon us."

The Philistines did as they were advised, and the cows pulled the cart straight back to Israel, mooing in distress the whole way. The Israelites were harvesting wheat when they looked up and saw the cart with the ark beside a large rock. What a celebration they had! They chopped up the cart and killed the cows as a sacrifice to the LORD. They put the ark in Abinadab's house and asked Eleazar, his son, to guard it.

For twenty years the ark remained there. All that time, the Philistines continued to harass Israel, and Israel worshipped idols. Finally the people called out to the LORD, and He called Samuel, the last judge, to deliver them. Samuel assembled the people at Mizpah to confess their sins and sacrifice to the LORD. The Philistines took this opportunity

to attack Israel again. This time was different, however. With a thunderous voice, the LORD brought confusion on the Philistines, and they fled. At that place, Samuel set up a memorial stone and called it Ebenezer, which means "thus far has the LORD helped us." Then Samuel ruled over Israel as judge for the rest of his life, and Israel had peace from their enemies.

Unit I: The Early Kingdom...The God Who Anoints

Review Worksheets

A. MEMORY VERSE: "Remember the _____ _____

of old, For I am God, and there is no _____; I am God, and there is

_____ like Me." (Isaiah 46:9)

B. KEY FACTS: Use the words below to answer the questions. (Hint: One word is used twice.)

Shiloh   Battlefield   Dagon's temple   Ashdod   Gath   Ekron   Abinadab's house

1. Where was Dagon's temple located? _____

2. Where did the ark stay for twenty years? _____

3. Where was the tabernacle located? _____

4. Where did the Philistines put the ark after they captured it? _____

5. In what cities did the Philistines get tumors? _____,

_____, and _____

6. Where did the Israelites take the ark to give them good fortune? _____

Can you find Ashdod, Gath, Ekron, and Shiloh on Map 1?

C. STORY FACTS: Cross out the answer that is NOT correct.

1. When the Philistines heard the Israelites' loud shouts, they said, "_____."

  Don't give up   Be strong   Let's make a treaty

2. Eli was sad when he heard the news of _____.

  his sons' death   the ark's capture   the plague of rats

3. The Israelites forgot that God was holy and _____.

  judged sin   desired holiness   changed the rules

4. The Philistines' plan to send the ark back to Israel included _____.

  a new cart   a guilt offering   two mother donkeys

5. When Samuel assembled the Israelites at Mizpah, the people _____.

  sang songs   confessed sin   sacrificed to the LORD

D. DO YOU KNOW THE REASON? Circle the statement that completes each sentence.

1. The Israelites moved the ark from Shiloh to the battlefield because _____.

    a. they thought the ark would be safer there than at the tabernacle

    b. they thought the ark would protect them from the Philistines

    c. God commanded them to move the ark

2. The Philistines defeated the Israelites in battle because _____.

    a. the Philistines had a bigger and stronger army

    b. the Philistines' god Dagon was mightier than Israel's God

    c. the LORD was bringing judgment on Israel for their sin

3. The Philistines sent the ark back to Israel because _____.

    a. Israel threatened to burn up their wheat fields if they didn't

    b. they thought the ark would kill all of them if they kept it

    c. they wanted to make peace with the Israelites

E. IMPORTANT NAMES TO REMEMBER...

1. ____ ____ ____ ____ ____ ____ ____   Means "the glory [of the LORD] has departed."

2. ____ ____ ____ ____ ____ ____ ____ ____   Means "thus far has the LORD helped us."

F. FIND OUT...

Psalm 115 compares God, who is in heaven, with idols. Write down three things that Psalm 115 says about idols.

1. _____

2. _____

3. _____

How is our God greater than idols?

_____

_____

Chapter 3

Saul—The First King

LESSON SCOPE: 1 Samuel 8–15   **READ TO ME:** 1 Samuel 8–12, 15

THEME: The LORD God anoints and removes the rulers of His people.

MEMORY VERSE:

"Behold, to obey is better than sacrifice,
And to heed than the fat of rams." (1 Samuel 15:22b)

KEY FACTS:

Israel's Neighbors

Nation	Founder of Nation	Famous Events	Israelite Defenders
Amalek	Amalek: grandson of Esau	Israel defeated Amalek at Rephidim in the wilderness. King Saul defeated King Agag.	Moses Saul
Ammon	Ben-Ammi: son of Lot and his second daughter	Jephthah defeated Ammon. Saul defeated Ammon and was accepted as king by Israel.	Jephthah Saul
Edom	Esau: son of Isaac	Israel could not pass through their land on the way to Canaan.	
Moab	Moab: son of Lot and his first daughter	King Balak of Moab asked Balaam to curse Israel. Ehud defeated King Eglon.	Moses Ehud
Philistia	Sea People from Aegean Sea	The Philistines captured Samson. They captured the ark, but returned it after they got sick. They threatened Saul with chariots.	Samson Samuel Saul

Can you find these nations on map 1?

MESSAGE FROM THE KING: The King wants you to obey from your heart.

The LORD your King wants you to do the right thing for the right reason. What are some wrong reasons for doing the right thing? Why is obeying the LORD from the heart so important?

Saul—The First King

Samuel was old, tired, and discouraged. He had judged Israel well over the years, but his sons were wicked men, and the elders of Israel were now demanding that a king rule over them.

Samuel cried out to the LORD, and the LORD answered, "It's not you that the people are rejecting. They're rejecting Me as their King. They are again forsaking Me and the covenant. Let them have a king, but warn them what a king will do when he rules over them."

> **Jesus in the OT**
>
> Saul thought that because he was king he could do whatever he wanted. He forgot that God is the great King above all kings. In the New Testament, we learn that Jesus is the King of kings.

Samuel spoke frankly to the people, "A king will take your sons and make them go to war in chariots. Some will be commanders over thousands, and others will harvest the king's fields. A king will take your daughters to be bakers and cooks in his palace. He'll take the best of your fields and olive groves, your faithful servants, and your flocks and livestock. You will have to pay high taxes, and you will be his slaves. Is this what you want?" No matter what Samuel said, the people kept demanding, "We want a king like other nations to lead us and fight our battles."

One day a tall, handsome young Benjamite named Saul and his servant were out looking for his father's lost donkeys. After many unsuccessful days, Saul was ready to give up and go home. "No, don't stop now," said his servant. "A prophet named Samuel lives in this town. He's highly respected and what he says comes true. Let's ask him."

The day before, the LORD had spoken to Samuel, "Tomorrow a man will come to visit you. Anoint him to be king in Israel." Samuel met Saul, told him where the donkeys were, but more importantly, anointed Saul to be Israel's first king. Saul said he was from the smallest tribe, Benjamin, and the smallest family in the tribe. He thought he was not important enough to be the king. But Samuel assured him, "The LORD has chosen you to be king, and God will go with you."

Actually, Saul was anointed king three times. The first anointing happened privately at Samuel's house. Sometime later, Samuel gathered the people

Unit I: The Early Kingdom...The God Who Anoints

together at Mizpah to anoint Saul publicly, but Saul was shy. He was hiding behind some baggage. The people found him, and Samuel anointed him in front of everyone. Then they shouted, "Long live the king!"

Some Israelites doubted that Saul was the right man to be king, but soon all doubts were gone. The Ammonites besieged Jabesh Gilead in Israel. When Saul heard the cruel terms of the Ammonites' treaty, he was furious. God's Spirit came upon him, and he led Israel in an attack upon the Ammonites, killing most of them and scattering the few who had survived. Now all the Israelites gladly accepted Saul as their king, and he was anointed the third time.

After Saul's third anointing, Samuel made a farewell speech to the people, begging them to follow the LORD as their supreme King. The people repented of their sin in asking for a king and worshipping idols. They asked Samuel to pray for them.

Saul was king about two years when he committed his first big sin against the LORD. The Philistines were threatening Israel with thousands of chariots and soldiers. Saul's soldiers were hiding in caves and among the rocks, and Samuel had not arrived to offer the sacrifice asking for God's help in battle. Instead of waiting for Samuel, Saul offered the sacrifice himself. Out of fear, Saul had acted foolishly. He was not a priest and had no right to offer sacrifices to the LORD. The consequence for Saul's disobedience was severe: God decided to take the kingdom away from Saul and give it to a man with a godly heart!

Sometime later the LORD told Saul to attack the Amalekites because they had attacked Israel in the Sinai wilderness many years earlier. Saul ambushed the Amalekites and crushed their army, destroying everyone and everything just as God had commanded, except he took the best of the cattle and flocks to sacrifice to the LORD, and he didn't kill Agag, the Amalekite king, as God had instructed! When Samuel heard the bleating of the sheep, he confronted Saul, "Why did you disobey God? Don't you know that obedience is better than sacrifice? Because of your sin, the LORD has rejected you as king."

Saul was not repentant of his disobedience. By his actions, Saul had shown that he didn't want God to be the supreme King of Israel. The LORD was grieved that He had made Saul king, but there was no going back. Sadly, Samuel left Saul and that's the last time Samuel ever saw Saul.

Review Worksheets

A. MEMORY VERSE: "Behold, to _____ is better than sacrifice,

And to _____ than the fat of rams." (1 Samuel 15:22b)

B. KEY FACTS: Use the table on the **Memory Page** to answer the questions. The words can be used more than once.

Amalekites Ammonites Moabites Philistines

1. The nation that Israel defeated in the wilderness: _____

2. The nation that captured Samson and took away his strength: _____

3. The nation that Jephthah fought and defeated: _____

4. The nation that captured the ark in battle: _____

5. The nation ruled by King Eglon: _____

6. The nation that came to Canaan from across the sea: _____

C. STORY FACTS: Fill in the blanks.

1. The elders of Israel were demanding that God give them a _____.

2. Saul was looking for his father's _____ when Samuel anointed him to be Israel's king.

3. Saul was anointed as king _____ times by Samuel.

4. After the battle with the Amalekites, Saul refused to destroy two things:

_____ and _____.

5. Saul was not allowed to make sacrifices because he was not a _____.

6. _____ was the king of the Amalekites.

D. WHAT'S TRUE AND WHAT'S NOT?

Circle "T" if the sentence is true. Circle "F" if the sentence is false.

1. The people were rejecting Samuel when they demanded a king.   T   F

2. Saul disobeyed God when he offered a sacrifice.   T   F

3. The LORD was grieved that He made Saul the king.   T   F

4. Saul thought he was not important enough to be a king.   T   F

E. WHAT WOULD A KING BE LIKE? Write three things that God said a king would
do if he ruled over Israel.

1. _____

2. _____

3. _____

F. DO YOU KNOW THE ANSWER? Put the answers in the spaces on the left. Then
use the boxed letters to find the answer to the question below.

Eglon was king of _____.

Esau was founder of _____.

The people demanded to have a _____.

Eli's sons were _____.

Saul was looking for _____.

The Philistines had thousands of ____.

Saul was anointed _____ times.

What does the LORD say is better than sacrifice?

___ ___ ___ ___ ___ ___ ___ ___ ___

G. FIND OUT...

You can obey God with good motives or with selfish ones. In John 14:15, Jesus gives you a
good motive for obeying him. What does He say?

_____

Chapter 4

David Anointed as King

LESSON SCOPE: 1 Samuel 16, Psalms   **READ TO ME:** 1 Samuel 16

THEME: The LORD God looks at man's heart, not his outside appearance.

MEMORY VERSE:

"For the LORD does not see as man sees; for man looks at the outward appearance, but the LORD looks at the heart." (1 Samuel 16:7b)

KEY FACTS:

Types of Hebrew Poetry

Category	Definition	Example
Repeated	Second line has a similar meaning to the first line.	"The heavens declare the glory of God; And the firmament shows His handiwork." (Psalm 19:1)
Contrasted	Second line has an opposite meaning to the first line.	"He regards the lowly; But the proud He knows from afar." (Psalm 138:6)
Continuing	Second line adds meaning to or continues the thought of the first line.	"You who laid the foundations of the earth, So that it should not be moved forever." (Psalm 104:5)

Types of Psalms

Category	Definition	Examples
Hallelujah Psalms	Giving praise to God.	Psalms 146–150
Historical Psalms	Reminding Israel of who God is and what He has done.	Psalms 105–106
Judgment Psalms	Asking God to judge the wicked.	Psalms 35, 52, 55, 109
Messianic Psalms	Talking about the Messiah.	Psalms 2, 22, 45, 72
Passover Psalms	Sung during Passover meal.	Psalms 113–118
Pilgrim Psalms	Sung during journeys to Jerusalem.	Psalms 120–134
Repentance Psalms	Feeling sorry for one's sin.	Psalms 6, 32, 51, 130
Thanksgiving Psalms	Thanking God for His mercy and answers to prayer.	Psalms 18, 66, 107, 138
Wisdom Psalms	Giving wise counsel to the godly.	Psalms 1, 37, 49

MESSAGE FROM THE KING: The King says, "I have given you the psalms so that you can know how to pray and praise Me from the heart."

David Anointed as King

Upside down and backwards! Sometimes it seems that's the way God does things. In Isaiah 55:8, the LORD says, "For My thoughts are not your thoughts, nor are your ways My ways." Even when you don't understand what God is doing, He always has a plan, and it's always good.

Saul was tall, handsome, and courageous, but he refused to obey God, the real King of Israel. Who would the LORD choose to be Israel's next king? God's choice surprised everyone.

The LORD asked Samuel, "How long will you be sad that I have rejected Saul? Go to the family of Jesse, who lives in Bethlehem, and anoint one of his sons to be the next king."

"What if Saul hears about this and tries to kill me?" asked Samuel, who was afraid of what Saul would do when he learned that Samuel had anointed a new king. The LORD responded, "Take a calf for a sacrifice. Invite Jesse to the sacrifice, and I will show you what to do next."

Jesse came to the sacrifice with seven sons. Samuel saw the oldest son, Eliab, and thought, "Look how tall he is. Certainly he must be the LORD's choice to be king." But the LORD said to Samuel, "He's not the man I've chosen. Don't look at his outward appearance. Look at his heart as I do."

One by one all of Jesse's sons stood before Samuel, and one by one the LORD said, "He's not the one." Finally, Samuel asked Jesse, "Are these all your sons?" Jesse replied, "My youngest son is in the fields, watching the sheep." Samuel said, "Go, get him right away."

In the hills surrounding Bethlehem, Jesse's youngest son, David, spent many days by himself caring for his father's sheep. His days were long, and often lonely, but he amused himself with two things: a sling and a lyre.

Watching sheep in the deserted hills could be dangerous. Wild animals roamed the hills looking for their next meal. David spent hours practicing with his sling, ready to protect his sheep from preying animals. Once he killed a bear, shooting it with his sling and then wrestling it until it died. Another time he killed a lion the same way. During the quiet hours he played his lyre, a small stringed musical instrument, and sang praise songs that he wrote himself. These songs are called psalms.

> **Jesus in the OT**
> How is David, the shepherd, like the Lord Jesus? How is Jesus, the Good Shepherd, greater than David?

When David, handsome and ruddy from his days in the sun, stood before Samuel, the LORD said, "He's the one. Anoint him." That day, the Spirit of the LORD came upon David to equip him with power for his role as king.

Meanwhile, God's Spirit had left Saul, and a distressing spirit from the LORD troubled him. Saul's servants were concerned about him and suggested that Saul find someone to play music to calm his spirit. One servant suggested that Saul send for David. "This man is skilled at playing music, and he's brave and handsome as well. Not only that, but the LORD is with him." So Saul sent for David to come to his palace.

Immediately, Saul liked David very much, and David became one of Saul's armorbearers. From that time on, whenever Saul became distressed, David would play soothing music, and Saul would be refreshed.

David had been anointed to be the next king, but it wasn't time for him to take over the throne yet. David had many things to learn about trusting the LORD, and the LORD would bring much suffering into his life. Yet in God's time, David would rule over Israel as a king who served the LORD God as his King.

THE BOOK OF PSALMS

Right in the middle of the Bible is God's poetry book. Containing 150 chapters, Psalms is the biggest book of the Bible. The Hebrew title for Psalms is "Book of Praises." The hallelujah and thanksgiving psalms praise God for His greatness, His salvation, His Word, and His many blessings.

Even though Psalms is called the "Book of Praises," not all the chapters are songs of joy. The writers of Psalms expressed many different feelings and thoughts. Sometimes a writer was mournful because of his sin and begged for God's mercy and forgiveness. Other times a writer would be angry because of the wickedness he saw around him, and he would ask God to send judgment on those who hurt people and sinned against Him.

Some psalms were written for a specific purpose. The Israelites sang the pilgrim psalms as they walked to Jerusalem to worship. The Passover psalms were part of the annual Passover meal. Reading the historical psalms reminded Israel of all that their Lord had done for them in the past and that he had kept the covenants He made with them, His people. In the wisdom psalms, the psalmists gave wise counsel to those who were suffering or experiencing temptation. The Messianic psalms described present situations while at the same time pointed to Jesus, the Messiah.

Although David wrote more psalms than anyone else (seventy-three), other people (Moses, Asaph, Solomon, and the sons of Korah) also wrote some of the psalms. Many of the psalms do not tell you who wrote them.

Psalm 117, the shortest psalm, reminds us of God's faithfulness to the covenants He has made with His people. Psalm 119, the longest psalm, is a song of praise for God's Word. All but four verses (vs. 84, 121, 122, and 132) mention God's Word.

PSALMS WORD FIND

Find the words listed in the right column in this word find.

Jesus in the OT
David was anointed king, but it wasn't time for him to rule yet. How is this like the Lord Jesus' life?

P	H	A	L	L	E	L	U	J	A	H
O	M	I	R	G	L	I	P	U	S	I
M	O	D	S	I	W	P	I	D	A	S
C	N	A	O	P	I	A	L	G	P	T
N	O	D	L	S	S	S	E	M	H	O
O	C	I	N	A	I	S	S	E	M	R
M	P	V	D	L	L	O	K	N	E	I
O	E	A	U	M	B	V	O	T	S	C
L	N	D	J	P	O	E	T	R	Y	A
O	V	E	R	K	O	R	A	H	A	L
S	R	E	P	E	N	T	A	N	C	E

Asaph
David
Hallelujah
Historical
Judgment
Korah
Messianic
Passover
Pilgrim
Poetry
Psalm
Repentance
Solomon
Wisdom

Review Worksheets

A. MEMORY VERSE: "For the LORD does not see as _____ sees;

for man looks at the _____ _____, but the LORD looks at

the _____." (1 Samuel 16:7b)

B. KEY FACTS:

What type of poetry are the verses below (repeated, contrasted, or continuing)?

"The young lions lack and suffer hunger; But those who seek   _____
the LORD shall not lack any good thing." (Psalm 34:10)

"The LORD is high above all nations,   _____
His glory above the heavens." (Psalm 113:4)

"The LORD is my shepherd; I shall not want." (Psalm 23:1)   _____

Match the type of psalm with its definition.

_____ Psalm sung during the Passover meal   1. Hallelujah

_____ Psalm asking God to judge the wicked   2. Wisdom

_____ Psalm expressing sorrow over sin   3. Historical

_____ Psalm giving praise to God   4. Judgment

_____ Psalm sung on journeys to Jerusalem   5. Thanksgiving

_____ Psalm talking about the Messiah   6. Passover

_____ Psalm reminding Israel of what God did   7. Messianic

_____ Psalm giving wise counsel   8. Pilgrim

_____ Psalm thanking God for His mercy   9. Repentance

The Hebrew title for Psalms is …

___ ___ ___ ___ ___   ___ ___   ___ ___ ___ ___ ___ ___ ___

C. STORY FACTS: Fill in the blanks.

1. With his sling David killed a _____ and a _____.

2. God looks at the _____, not the outward appearance.

3. Samuel anointed David, Jesse's _____ son.

4. _____ is the longest psalm. It is a psalm of praise about

   _____ _____.

5. When a _____ _____ troubled Saul, David

   _____ _____ to calm him.

6. In addition to David, these men wrote Psalms: _____,

   _____, _____, and _____.

7. David and his family came from the town of _____.

8. The book of Psalms has a total of _____ psalms.

D. WHO AM I? Unscramble the names and then draw a line from the name to the description on the right.

SEJES   _____   I anointed David to be Israel's king.

VADDI   _____   I was Jesse's oldest son.

BEALI   _____   I was the father of David.

MELUSA   _____   I was a shepherd who wrote psalms.

E. WHAT'S THE REASON? In God's time, how would David rule Israel?
Write the answer below.

_____

_____

F. FIND OUT...
Psalm 119 gives nine words that mean God's Word. Can you find all nine?

_____ _____ _____ _____ _____

_____ _____ _____ _____ _____

chapter 5

David in Saul's court

LESSON SCOPE: 1 Samuel 17–20   **READ TO ME:** 1 Samuel 17–20

THEME: The LORD God is faithful to those who trust in Him.

MEMORY VERSE:

"In God I trust; I will not be afraid. What can mortal man do to me?" (Psalm 56:4b, NIV)

KEY FACTS:

The LORD's Faithfulness to David

By faith, David trusted the LORD…	The LORD was faithful to David.
He stood up to the giant in the LORD's name.	David killed Goliath with one stone, and the women sang about David.
He did whatever Saul told him to do.	The LORD gave him success.
He obeyed Saul and went to battle against the Philistines.	The LORD gave him victory over his enemy. All Israel loved David.
He played music to soothe Saul.	The LORD protected him from Saul's jealousy.
He made a covenant of friendship with Jonathan.	Jonathan helped David escape Saul's anger.

MESSAGE FROM THE KING: The King says, "Do not be afraid."

Who are the giants in your life? The King reminds you that you don't have to be afraid because He is more powerful than those who are against you, and He is always with you.

David in Saul's Court

The nine-foot giant was so tall that a man had to bend his head back and look up, up, up to see to the top of Goliath's bronze helmet. His threatening voice boomed out across the Valley of Elah, "I defy the army of Israel. Send out a man, and we will fight each other!"

By the time David arrived at the battlefield, bringing food supplies to his brothers, the giant had been making blasphemous threats against Israel and the LORD, day and night, for forty days. All of King Saul's army was terrified. When David heard Goliath's threats, he said, "Don't lose heart. I'll fight him. I killed a lion, and I killed a bear. This pagan Philistine will be like them because he has defied the armies of the living God."

King Saul dressed David in his armor and gave him his sword. But the armor was so heavy that David couldn't take a step. Instead, David chose five smooth stones from the stream and walked across the valley toward Goliath. David knew the LORD went with him. The giant scoffed when he saw this young lad accepting his challenge. Confidently, David said, "You come against me with sword and spear, but I come to you in the name of the LORD Almighty, whom you have defied."

Step by step, Goliath thundered toward David. David picked a stone from his pouch and, placing the stone in his sling, he flung it at the giant.

Z-i-n-n-g! The stone zipped through the air and hit Goliath in the middle of his forehead, the only spot on his body not covered by armor. Seeing their hero lying dead on the ground, the Philistines fled in terror. With a victorious shout, the Israelite army pursued them. Meanwhile, David cut off Goliath's head and held it up for all to see.

After this, David stayed with Saul, and whatever Saul told him to do, he did successfully. Women all over Israel sang, "Saul has slain thousands, but David, tens of thousands." Their praise of David made Saul jealous. One day, the troubling spirit came upon Saul while David was playing his lyre for him. Saul lifted up his spear and, whoosh, he hurled it at David. Twice Saul threw the spear, and twice David dodged it. Now Saul was afraid of David, because he knew that the LORD was with him.

Saul appointed David to be an army commander and sent him out to battle the Philistines, hoping David would be killed. To Saul's dismay, David had more military successes than any other commander, and his name was well-spoken of throughout the land. Because Saul knew that the LORD was with David, he became more and more afraid of him.

Saul had a son named Jonathan. He was a righteous man, and even though he knew David would someday take his place as king, he made a covenant with David to be loyal friends. Jonathan warned David, "My father is trying to kill you. Go into hiding and be on guard."

Jonathan rebuked his father about his hatred of David, and Saul replied, "As the LORD lives, David will not be put to death." But Saul's promise didn't last long. A short time later after returning from another battle, David was once again playing music for Saul. Saul was fingering his spear when, in a fit of intense jealousy, Saul tried to pin David to the wall with his spear. David jumped sideways, and the spear sunk deep into the wall. David fled.

David's wife, Michal (she was Saul's daughter), said, "If you don't run for your life today, my father will kill you." Michal helped David escape. She put an idol in David's bed and covered it, making it appear that David was asleep. By the time Saul's soldiers realized that David was not at his house, David had safely run away.

David and Jonathan devised a plan. David would not attend the New Moon festival and would hide out in the field behind a large stone. If Saul got angry about David's absence from the festival, Jonathan would shoot three arrows beyond David's hiding place. If not, he would shoot the arrows to the side. The next day at the festival, Saul flared up in anger, and shouted, "David must die!" Jonathan followed through with the plan and warned David of Saul's intention to kill him. Then the two friends sadly parted.

David's troubles with Saul were not over yet, but through each difficulty and danger, the LORD would be faithful to David, who had put his trust in Him.

Review Worksheets

A. MEMORY VERSE: "In God I _____; I will not be _____.

What can mortal _____ do to me?" (Psalm 56:4b, NIV)

B. KEY FACTS: Answer the questions below.

What are two ways that David trusted in the LORD?

1. _____

2. _____

What are two ways that the LORD was faithful to David?

1. _____

2. _____

C. STORY FACTS: Circle "T" if the sentence is true and "F" if the sentence is false.

1. David went to the battlefield to take food to his brothers. T F

2. David was angry because Goliath insulted King Saul. T F

3. Goliath threatened the Israelite army for twenty days and nights. T F

4. David was confident because he had great skill with a sling. T F

5. Whatever Saul told him to do, David did successfully. T F

6. Saul sent David into battle so that David would be killed. T F

7. Saul threw a spear at David because David married his daughter. T F

8. David chose ten stones from the stream for his sling. T F

9. Women sang, "David has slain tens of thousands." T F

The LORD was faithful to David, who had put his

____ ____ ____ ____ ____ ____ ____ ____ ____ ____ ____.

D. DO YOU KNOW THE ANSWERS? Complete the crossword puzzle.

Across:

1. The Philistine giant was named _____.
6. David's wife was named _____.
7. The Philistine giant was _____ feet tall.
11. Saul was afraid because the _____ was with David.

Down:

2. Saul's son was named _____.
3. Jonathan knew he would never be _____.
4. David put his _____ in the Lord.
5. David killed a bear and a _____.
8. Michal put an _____ in David's bed.
9. David met Goliath in the Valley of _____.
10. Jonathan shot three _____ to tell David that Saul wanted to kill him.

E. WHO SAID IT? Draw a line from the quote to the person who said it.

Saul   David   Goliath   Jonathan

I come in the name of the Lord.

As the Lord lives, David will not be put to death.

My father is trying to kill you.

Send out a man and we will fight each other.

F. FIND OUT...

In Proverbs 3:5-6, King Solomon wrote about trusting in the Lord. What did he say about how you should trust in the Lord?

_____

What will happen when you trust the Lord?

_____

Chapter 6

David—The Fugitive

LESSON SCOPE: 1 Samuel 21–31
1 Chronicles 10

READ TO ME: 1 Samuel 24, 26, 30

THEME: The Lord God's plan for His kingdom is right, just, and good.

MEMORY VERSE:

"For the word of the Lord is right, And all His work is done in truth. He loves righteousness and justice; The earth is full of the goodness of the Lord." (Psalm 33:4-5)

KEY FACTS:

David's Pictures of God

These are some of the word pictures that David used to describe God.

Picture	Verse	Description
Fortress	Psalm 62:2	He is a strong, safe place in trouble.
King	Psalm 5:2	He has power and controls everything that happens in the world.
Light	Psalm 27:1	He shows His people the right thing to do.
Rock	Psalm 28:1	He is unchangeable and unmovable.
Shepherd	Psalm 23:1	He perfectly cares for all His people.
Shield	Psalm 3:3	He protects His people from their enemies.
Strength	Psalm 18:2	He strengthens His people when they are weak.

THINGS TO REMEMBER:

Medium = Person who talks to the spirits of people who have died.

MESSAGE FROM THE KING: The King's plan is always right and good.

Sometimes God's plan doesn't make sense to us. Sometimes people ask, "What is God doing?" Remember, even if God's plan seems confusing, everything He does is good, because He is good.

David—The Fugitive

This wasn't the way a king was supposed to live—running for his life, living in caves, scrounging for enough food to feed himself and his small band of men. David had been anointed king, but his life was more like that of a common bandit than a king. What was the LORD doing?

David left Saul's court and fled to Nob, the town of priests. (The tabernacle had been at Nob ever since the Philistines stole the ark many years earlier.) David begged Ahimelech, the priest, to give him some food. The only food Ahimelech had was the bread from the tabernacle, so he gave five loaves of consecrated bread to David and his men. Ahimelech also gave David Goliath's sword, which had been safely kept in Nob since David had killed the giant. As David left, he saw Doeg the Edomite, Saul's head shepherd, watching him. That could mean only trouble!

David went to Gath in Philistia, but, fearing for his safety, he pretended to be insane and escaped from the city to the hillside caves of Adullam. All who were distressed, in debt, or discontented went to David, and he became the leader of a little army of 400 men.

Meanwhile, Doeg was ready to cause trouble. He told Saul that Ahimelech and the priests at Nob had helped David. Saul sent for Ahimelech, and said to him, "How dare you give David food and a sword! Because you have aided this rebel, you and your family will die!" Saul ordered his guards and Doeg to kill all eighty-five priests in Nob along with all their women, children, and animals. Only Abiathar, son of Ahimelech, escaped. He fled to David's camp and became one of his men. David was grieved because he felt responsible for the massacre at Nob.

David continued to move from place to place. He protected the city of Keilah from the Philistines, but soon after, that city became unsafe. David and his band of men, which had grown in number to 600, hid in rocky strongholds in the desert and in the hills in the Desert of Ziph. Saul pursued David relentlessly, but God prevented Saul from discovering David's hiding places. In the Wilderness of Maon, Saul abruptly called off his search to fight the Philistines who were raiding Israel's countryside.

Once, David and his men were hiding deep within a cave when Saul and his soldiers entered the cave. David crept stealthily to the front of the cave and cut off a corner of Saul's robe. As Saul left the cave, David came out, and said to him, "Why do you listen to the men who say I want to kill you?" David showed Saul the piece of robe, and continued, "Look! I could have killed you, but I spared your life."

Another time, David and Abishai crept into Saul's camp at night. While Saul slept, David stole his spear and water jug, but he refused to kill Saul, even though Abishai told him to do so. David sneaked back to his own camp, and then yelled to Saul, "Why are you still pursuing me? What have I done wrong? Once again I could have killed you, but I didn't."

Both times, Saul admitted his sin of chasing after David, but Saul's sorrow was not from the heart. He continued his evil plan to kill David. Why didn't David kill Saul when he had the opportunity? David's response was the same each time: "God forbid that I should kill the Lord's anointed." David knew that the Lord had a plan, and even though the plan wasn't clear to David, he wasn't going to rush God's timing by killing Saul. He knew that God's plan was right and good. He just had to wait patiently.

While Saul was still pursuing David, Samuel the prophet died, and all Israel mourned for him. Around that time, the Philistines gathered together to make war on Israel once again. Saul was terrified, and when the Lord didn't answer his cries for help, he became even more terrified. Saul then did something strictly forbidden by God. He disguised himself and went to the medium at Endor.

> **Jesus in the OT**
> Rejected, homeless, hated by authorities—there are so many ways in which David's life as a fugitive was like Jesus' life.

At Saul's request, the medium called up the spirit of Samuel to talk with Saul. Samuel gave Saul the worst possible prophecy: God would give the kingdom to David, Saul's enemy, and Saul and his sons would die in the battle with the Philistines. The next day, the battle was fierce. The Philistines killed three of Saul's sons, including Jonathan. Then an archer shot an arrow and critically wounded Saul. In fear and despair, Saul asked his armorbearer to kill him, but the man refused. So Saul took his own sword, fell on it, and died.

Thus ended the reign of Saul, and thus began the reign of David, who had waited patiently for the Lord's will to happen.

Review Worksheets

A. MEMORY VERSES: "For the word of the LORD is _____, And

all His work is done in _____. He loves _____ and

_____; The earth is full of the _____ of the LORD." (Psalm 33:4-5)

B. KEY FACTS: Using the information on the **Memory Page**, draw a line from the phrase
on the left to the matching description of God.

David's Names for God

1. When you feel weak and helpless…   God is your Shield.

2. When you're confused and don't know what to do…   God is your King.

3. When you need a safe place from danger…   God is your Fortress.

4. When everything around you is changing…   God is your Shepherd.

5. When you need tender care and comfort…   God is your Light.

6. When enemies are attacking you…   God is your Rock.

7. When you need to know that someone   God is your Strength.
   is in charge of the world…

C. STORY FACTS: Fill in the blanks.

1. Ahimelech gave David consecrated bread from the _____.

2. _____ told Saul that Ahimelech had helped David.

3. David stole Saul's _____ and _____ _____ while he slept.

4. David knew that the LORD's plan was _____ and _____.

5. Saul sinned by going to a _____ in Endor for advice.

6. Saul's armorbearer refused to _____ Saul.

D. WHAT HAPPENED HERE? Unscramble the words on the left and then draw a line from the word to its description.

BON   _____   A dangerous city for David and his men

PHIZ   _____   Where David pretended to be insane

THAG   _____   City where eighty-five priests were killed

HAKLIE   _____   Hills where David and his men hid

E. WHAT HAPPENED NEXT? Put the story boxes in order.

____ Saul was killed in battle with the Philistines.	____ David hid in caves, and Saul pursued him.	____ Samuel died, and all Israel mourned.
____ David fled to Nob and got bread from the tabernacle.	____ David had a chance to kill Saul, but he didn't.	____ Saul visited a medium to get advice.

F. WHY DIDN'T DAVID KILL SAUL?

Circle every other letter below to find the answer. (Start with the second letter.)

A S T A C U S L A W M A T S Y G B O R D V S Z A S N K O N I Y N O T D E F D

___ ___ ___ ___ ___ ___ ___ ___ ___ ___'___ ___ ___ ___ ___ ___ ___ ___ ___.

G. FIND OUT...

The Bible gives you many pictures of what the LORD is like. Find some other pictures of God in the verses below. Using the **key facts** table as an example, write your own description of one of the word pictures you find in these verses.

Psalm 18:1-2 _____   _____   _____

Psalm 46:1 _____   _____

Description:

_____

Chapter 7

Looking Backwards...Looking Ahead

LESSON SCOPE: 1 Samuel 1-31   **READ TO ME:** Psalm 21
Psalms, 1 Chronicles 10

"Who's in charge here? Who's the boss?"

Were you ever in a situation in which everyone was running around doing his own thing, and the result was that nothing got done and everyone was unhappy? That's what was happening in Israel when God's story opened in 1 Samuel. There was no king in Israel, and everyone was doing what he or she thought was right. Actually, God was the King, but nobody was listening to Him!

In Unit I you learned that the Israelites had forgotten who they were—God's people! The LORD had made a covenant with them at Mt. Sinai and had promised to be their God. They, in turn, had promised to worship Him.

The Israelites hadn't totally forgotten about the LORD, but they didn't love Him from their hearts. They thought the ark was a magic box that would give them success in battle. They only prayed to Him when they were in trouble or were afraid. But the LORD wanted more from His people than outward worship; He wanted them to worship and obey Him out of love.

Because they asked, Israel got their king, but Saul wouldn't let the LORD be his King. Saul died in disgrace on the battlefield. In Unit II, you will learn how the next king, David, took his rightful place on the throne. The LORD renewed the covenant with David and promised to bless David if he loved and honored Him. During the reign of David and of David's son, Solomon, the LORD did bless the kingdom of Israel, and it became a kingdom of power and wealth.

IMPORTANT THINGS TO KNOW:

Word	Meaning of the Word
Anoint	Chosen by God and equipped by God's Spirit to serve the LORD in a particular job.
Priest	Man in charge of offering sacrifices and offerings in the tabernacle.
Holy	Means "set apart by God" or "living in a way that pleases God."
Covenant	God's promise to be the God of His people forever.
Medium	Person who talks to the spirits of people who have died.
Prophet	Person called to speak for God.
Psalms	"Book of Praises."

The BOSS

Review Worksheets

A. MEMORY VERSE REVIEW—VERSE SCRAMBLE: Put the words in the boxes in the right order and then write the memory verse phrase on the line beside the boxes.

1. _____ _____
   _____
   _____
   (1 Samuel 15:22b)

obey	Behold	fat
than	sacrifice	better
to	to	than rams
heed	of is	And the

2. _____
   _____
   _____
   (Psalm 56:4b, NIV)

afraid	God	I be
man	trust	What
me In	to	will I
not	can	do mortal

3. _____
   _____
   _____
   (Judges 21:25)

everyone	days	what
in Israel	king	no
In	his	eyes right
own	those	in was
	was there did	

B. MEMORY VERSE REVIEW—FILL IN THE BLANK: Answer the questions below using your memory verses.

1. What are two things that God says about Himself in Isaiah 46:9?

_____

2. The LORD does not see as man sees. How does He see differently?

"Man looks at the _____ _____, but the LORD looks at the

_____." (1 Samuel 16:7b)

3. According to Psalm 33:4-5, what does the LORD love?

_____ and _____

C. WHAT WAS THE THEME OF UNIT I? Answer the questions in the blanks beside them. Then take the first letter of each answer to complete the phrase below.

___ ___ ___ ___   Who was the king that Saul didn't kill?

___ ___ ___ ___   How many feet tall was the giant Goliath?

___ ___ ___ ___ ___ ___ ___ ___ ___   What is better than sacrifice?

___ ___ ___ ___ ___ ___ ___ ___   What name means "the glory [of the LORD] has departed from Israel"?

___ ___ ___   In what town were eighty-five priests killed?

___ ___ ___ ___ ___ ___   What plague did God send on the Philistines?

___ ___ ___ ___ ___ ___   In what town did Eli serve in the tabernacle?

The theme for Unit I

The God who ___ ___ ___ ___ ___ ___ ___.

D. WHERE DID THE ARK GO ON ITS JOURNEY? Follow the ark of the covenant from the tabernacle at Shiloh back to Israel.

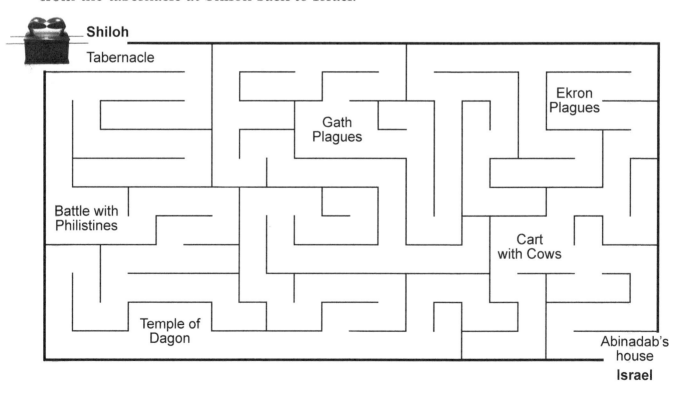

E. WHAT DO YOU REMEMBER ABOUT THE TYPES OF PSALMS?

Match the type of psalm to its definition.

_____ Hallelujah   1. Psalm sung during the Passover

_____ Historical   2. Psalm thanking God for His mercy and answers to prayer

_____ Judgment   3. Psalm sung on journeys to Jerusalem

_____ Messianic   4. Psalm giving good counsel

_____ Passover   5. Psalm praising God

_____ Pilgrim   6. Psalm reminding Israel of who God is

_____ Repentance   7. Psalm talking about the Messiah

_____ Thanksgiving   8. Psalm expressing sorrow over sin

_____ Wisdom   9. Psalm asking God to judge the wicked

What are the three types of Hebrew poetry?

_____ _____ _____

F. WHAT'S THE REASON? Circle the **correct** answer.

1. Samuel set up the Ebenezer stone so that Israel would _____.

    remember that God had helped them   have victory in battle

2. The LORD rejected Saul as king because Saul didn't _____.

    pray for the people   obey God as supreme King

3. The Israelites wanted a king so that they could _____.

    be like other nations   worship the LORD better

4. David refused to kill Saul when he found him in the cave because _____.

    Saul was his friend   Saul was God's anointed

5. The LORD gave David protection and good success because _____.

    by faith David trusted God   David was a kind person

6. David killed the Philistine giant because Goliath had _____.

    killed many Israelites   defied the LORD

G. WHAT THINGS GO TOGETHER?

Draw a line from the word on the left to the word on the right that describe it.

Covenant	Man who offered sacrifices
Prophet	Loyal friend of David
Ebenezer	Weapon used to kill a giant
Psalms	Priest at the tabernacle in Shiloh
Spear	God's promise to His people
Gath	Means "Book of Praises"
Sling	Weapon stolen from King Saul
Samuel	Person called to speak for God
Jonathan	Means "thus far has the LORD helped us"
Eli	Town where God sent a plague
Priest	Last judge in Israel

UNIT **II**

The Glorious Kingdom...The God Who Blesses

Theme: The Keeper of the Kingdom brings blessing to His people.

Shalom. It's I, Tobias, again. Oh, what a busy man I've been, trying to record with utmost accuracy all of David's many adventures in and out of caves. Isn't the LORD amazing, keeping David safe from King Saul's wicked schemes? Now Saul is dead, and David will take his place as king over all of Israel.

But wait, it isn't quite that simple, my friends. For years David had trusted the LORD by faith, believing in God's promises and waiting patiently as the LORD worked out His plan. David's waiting wasn't done yet. But although it didn't happen all at once, and it didn't happen quickly, eventually David did indeed become the king of Israel.

The years of David's reign and, later, the reign of Solomon, were good years. In so many ways the LORD blessed Israel. David's military successes over the Moabites, Edomites, and other neighboring nations expanded Israel's territory in every direction. Israel became prosperous, and Solomon's palace and temple became known far and wide for its glorious splendor. The LORD blessed David with mercy and forgiveness when he sinned greatly, and He gave Solomon the wisdom that made him the wisest man who ever lived.

Yet greater than all these things was the blessing of the covenant. Through the prophet Nathan the LORD renewed the covenant with David. The covenantal blessings—a son, a land, and a great name—had a familiar sound. This is what the LORD had promised to Abraham. The covenant to David, however, had one big difference: the LORD promised to establish David's kingship forever!

David knew that there was a King greater than he was, a King who demanded to be worshipped exclusively and obeyed completely. This greater King promised David, "I will be your God. I will be with you, bless you, and make your kingdom great."

Covenant and kingship linked together—this was the LORD's plan for His people. Now let's see what the glorious kingdom looked like.

PSALM 51:1–6 A Psalm of David

1. Have mercy upon me, O God,
    According to Your lovingkindness;
    According to the multitude of Your tender mercies,
    Blot out my transgressions.
2. Wash me thoroughly from my iniquity,
    And cleanse me from my sin.
3. For I acknowledge my transgressions,
    And my sin is always before me.
4. Against You, You only, have I sinned,
    And done this evil in Your sight—
    That You may be found just when You speak,
    And blameless when You judge.
5. Behold, I was brought forth in iniquity,
    And in sin my mother conceived me.
6. Behold, You desire truth in the inward parts,
    And in the hidden part You will make me to know wisdom.

"Have mercy on me!" That was the cry from David's heart.

David had sinned greatly. A man was dead, and many people were suffering because of David's selfishness and greed. Not until Nathan, the prophet, confronted David with God's truth did David take responsibility for his sin and repent from his heart. Psalm 51 is what David said to the LORD in repentance.

Psalm 51 teaches you two truths about sin. The first truth is that all sin is against the LORD. When you steal candy from a drugstore or tell lies about your friend, you are sinning against a person. At the same time, you are also sinning against God. Whenever you sin, you are actually saying, "What I want to do is more important to me than doing what God wants me to do."

The second truth taught in Psalm 51 about sin is that sinning is as natural as breathing. We sin against God because we were born with a sinful nature. It's only by God's grace that anyone can be holy and please Him.

Just like David, you can ask for God's mercy when you sin. And, because of the tender mercies of the LORD, you, too, can be forgiven.

Chapter 8

The Covenant with David

LESSON SCOPE: 2 Samuel 1–7
1 Chronicles 11–17

READ TO ME: 2 Samuel 2, 5–7

THEME: The LORD God remembers His promises and renews His covenant.

MEMORY VERSE:

"I have made a covenant with My chosen, I have sworn to My servant David: 'Your seed I will establish forever, And build up your throne to all generations.'" (Psalm 89:3-4)

KEY FACTS:

God's Covenant with David: 2 Samuel 7

David's covenant was like the covenant with Abraham because…	
God Promised:	A son to succeed David on the throne of Israel (7:12).
	A land that was peaceful (7:10-11).
	A great name among the men of the earth (7:9).
	The blessing of God's love and presence (7:9,15).
David's covenant was greater than the covenant with Abraham because…	
God Promised:	That David would be the first in a line of kings (7:12).
	That David's son would build God a temple (7:13).
	That David's son would rule after him (7:12b).
	That David's kingdom would endure forever (7:16).
	That the Messiah would be born from David's line (7:16).
The everlasting kingdom is the kingdom of Jesus Christ.	

MESSAGE FROM THE KING:

The King says, "I will never stop loving you."

Just as He promised to love David, the LORD promises to always love you. Every day this week, write down one way that the LORD shows His love to you. You'll be surprised by what you learn.

The Covenant with David

How does an anointed king become the ruling king? Do you say, "Here I am! I'm your new king!"? Do you wait until the people ask you to be king? This was David's dilemma. He was the anointed king, but he wasn't sitting on the throne yet. David waited for the LORD's time, and then the LORD said, "Go to Hebron." So David did, and the men anointed him king over Judah.

Meanwhile, Abner, commander of Saul's army, made Ishbosheth, Saul's son, the king over all Israel except Judah. Soon a civil war broke out. The Israelites in Judah, led by Joab, fought against all the other Israelites led by Abner. God's people were fighting against each other. How sad it was!

One day, at the end of the day's fierce fighting, Asahel, Joab's brother, took off after Abner, determined to chase him down and kill him. Abner repeatedly asked Asahel to stop chasing him. Asahel, swift as a wild gazelle, wouldn't give up. Finally, Abner stopped running and speared Asahel right through the stomach. Asahel died in the hills of Gibeon.

Then Abner had a quarrel with Ishbosheth and turned against him. "May God deal with me severely," Abner threatened, "if I don't try to make David king over all Israel." Ishbosheth was now afraid of Abner.

Joab, still angry because Abner had killed his brother Asahel, didn't trust Abner. Joab pretended to talk with Abner, but then killed him because Abner had killed Asahel. David rebuked Joab for killing Abner, and David and his people mourned Abner's death. Not long after, two men crept into Ishbosheth's house while he was sleeping, killed him, and brought his head to David. Although these murders made it possible for David to be king over all Israel, David was angry about the deaths. He didn't want other men murdered so that he could be king. David executed the men who killed Ishbosheth. David was thirty years old when he was crowned king. He reigned for seven-and-a-half years in Hebron and for thirty-three years over all Israel.

Now that he was king, David did three important things. First, he established a capital city. Hebron was too far south to unite the nation as one people, so he moved the capital to Jerusalem. Jerusalem was the perfect choice because it was a

well-fortified city built on a hill more centrally located in Israel. The only problem was that the Jebusites still lived there. But, David conquered this seemingly unconquerable city easily because the LORD God Almighty was with him.

> **Jesus in the OT**
> Jesus Christ is the fulfillment of God's covenant promises to David. He is the Son of David who rules forever and whose kingdom will never fail.

Second, David conquered the Philistines who had been continually attacking Israel for many years. Third, David sent for the ark of the covenant to be brought from Abinadab's house, where it had sat for twenty years. The men put the ark on a new cart with Abinadab's sons, Uzzah and Ahio, to guide it. The people danced in front of it, singing songs and playing lyres, tambourines, and cymbals. Along the way, the oxen stumbled, and Uzzah reached out to steady the ark. Instantly, the LORD struck him down, and he died. All celebration stopped, and David put the ark in Obed-Edom's house.

Why did God kill Uzzah? The ark was holy to the LORD, and David had not followed the LORD's instructions on moving the ark. Three months later, David tried again, this time following God's rules. The Levites carried the ark between two poles all the way to Jerusalem. David and the people danced before the LORD with loud singing and blasts of trumpets. The ark then rested in the tent in Jerusalem that David had pitched for it.

Sitting in his palace, contented after subduing all his enemies, David said to Nathan the prophet, "It's not right that I have this beautiful palace while the ark of God remains in a tent. I want to build a temple for the ark."

That night the LORD spoke to Nathan, "Go and tell My servant David: you are not the one to build Me a house." David wasn't to build the LORD's temple, but the LORD had wonderful promises for David. The LORD was renewing His established covenant with David.

The covenant with David was like the one with Abraham. Through the prophet Nathan, the LORD told David that David's son would rule after him and build a temple for the LORD, the land would have peace with its enemies, and David's name would be great among the nations. The covenant was also greater. The LORD said David's throne would endure forever; the Messiah would someday be born from David's line. No matter what happened, the LORD would be his God and never take away His love.

When David heard the words of God's covenant, he humbly thanked the LORD for His mercy and grace.

Review Worksheets

A. MEMORY VERSE: "I have made a covenant with My _____, I have

sworn to My _____ David: 'Your _____ I will establish forever,

And build up your _____ to all generations.' " (Psalm 89:3-4)

B. KEY FACTS: Answer the questions below.

1. What four things about the covenant with David were like the covenant

   with Abraham? _____ _____ _____ _____

2. What are some of the ways in which the LORD's covenant with David was greater than
   His covenant with Abraham?

   a. David's son would _____.

   b. David's kingdom would _____.

   c. The Messiah would _____.

What is the everlasting kingdom? _____

C. STORY FACTS: Unscramble the words. Then fill in the blanks.

David was first anointed king in _____. He was _____
                                   HONBER   HIRTTY

years old when he became king in Judah. After _____ and
                                         BREAN

and Ishbosheth were murdered, David became king over all _____.
                                                  LARESI

David conquered the Jebusites and made Jerusalem his _____.
                                               PILATAC

He conquered the Philistines who had attacked Israel for many _____.
                                                 ARESY

When David brought the ark to Jerusalem, _____ touched it and died.
                                         HAZUZ

The LORD made a _____ to make David's kingdom eternal.
                     TOVENCAN

D. WHAT DO YOU KNOW? Circle the names in the word find. Then match the names with the descriptions below.

1. Abner 5. Hebron 9. Nathan
2. Ahio 6. Ishbosheth 10. Obed-Edom
3. Asahel 7. Joab 11. Temple
4. David 8. Judah 12. Uzzah

A	H	A	O	T	T	D
J	O	A	B	E	E	A
I	N	L	E	M	U	V
S	H	E	D	P	Z	I
H	E	H	E	L	Z	D
B	B	A	D	E	A	L
O	R	S	O	I	H	A
S	O	A	M	W	E	B
H	N	A	H	T	A	N
E	D	O	J	H	T	E
T	J	U	D	A	H	R
H	U	O	N	V	A	D

_____ Saul's commander

_____ David's commander

_____ Killed by Abner

_____ Prophet

_____ King in Israel for a short time

_____ Touched the ark and died

_____ City in Judah

_____ Kept the ark in his house

_____ What David wanted to build   _____ Crowned king in Hebron

_____ Brother of Uzzah   _____ David was first anointed king of this part of Israel

E. WHAT HAPPENED TO UZZAH? Answer the question below.

The LORD struck down Uzzah when he touched the ark because the ark was…

___ ___ ___ ___   ___ ___ ___ ___ ___   ___ ___ ___ ___

F. FIND OUT…

The LORD promised that the Messiah would come from David's line. What do the verses below tell you about the Messiah?

Isaiah 7:14 _____

Isaiah 53:3, 5 _____

Micah 5:2 _____

chapter 9

David's Kindness & David's Sin

LESSON SCOPE: 2 Samuel 8–12
Psalm 32

READ TO ME: 2 Samuel 11–12
Psalm 32

THEME: The LORD God gives grace and forgiveness to those who repent.

MEMORY VERSE:

"Blessed is he whose transgression is forgiven,
   Whose sin is covered." (Psalm 32:1)

KEY FACTS: David's Sin and God's Forgiveness

David's fall into sin

1. David stayed home while his army went to war.

2. David loved another man's wife, whose name was Bathsheba.

3. David plotted to kill Uriah, Bathsheba's husband.

4. David married Bathsheba and they had a son.

4. David had to bear the consequences of his sin. His son died.

3. David repented and had God's peace.

2. God sent Nathan to confront David with his sin.

1. David had a stubborn heart.

God's grace to David

THINGS TO REMEMBER:

Blessed   = Contented because God is pleased with you.
Transgression   = The breaking of one of God's laws.

MESSAGE FROM THE KING:

The King says, "Whatever controls your heart controls your actions."

When sinful desires control your heart, you will sin. Anytime you say, "I want what I want, and I want it *now*," your desire is sinful. Ask the LORD to help you want to please Him.

David's Kindness & David's Sin

Unusual kindness one day and dreadful sin another day—that was the life of King David. When he lived by faith, trusting the LORD, David acted in kindness when other people would have taken revenge. When sinful desires controlled his heart, however, David loved another man's wife and plotted the man's murder.

David had peace from his enemies. The Edomites, Moabites, Philistines, and Amalekites were defeated by David's army. David's kingdom expanded from the border of Egypt to the middle of Syria, from the Mediterranean Sea to the edge of the Eastern Desert.

One day, David asked, "Is there anyone alive from Saul's family to whom I can show kindness?" Ziba, a servant of Saul's household, answered, "Yes, Mephibosheth, a son of Jonathan. He is crippled in both feet." (Mephibosheth was injured as a child when he and his nurse were fleeing after the death of Saul and Jonathan.)

David sent for Mephibosheth. "Don't be afraid," he said. "I want to show kindness to you because of my covenant of friendship with your father, Jonathan. I will give you back the land that belonged to your grandfather, Saul, and you can live in my palace and eat at my table always." As king, David had the power of life and death. Just a word from him and a person would be executed. Yet David was a man after God's heart. He chose to show kindness to the grandson of his enemy, King Saul.

In the spring, when kings go off to war, David ordered Joab, his chief commander, to go to battle against the Ammonites. David should have led the army himself, but he stayed at home in his palace in Jerusalem.

Restless and bored one evening, David climbed to the roof of the palace and leisurely walked around. Looking down from the rooftop, he saw in the distance a woman taking her evening bath. She was very beautiful, and David wanted to love her as only

> **Jesus in the OT**
> What did Mephibosheth do to merit kindness from King David? Absolutely nothing. What do you do to merit salvation from Jesus? Absolutely nothing. It's all by grace.

a husband should. At this time, David had several wives, and this woman, Bathsheba, was married to Uriah, one of David's mighty soldiers. What David wanted was against God's law, but he didn't turn away from his own desires. The temptation was strong, and David sinned.

A short time later, Bathsheba sent a message to David, saying, "I'm going to have a baby." Since Uriah was still fighting the Ammonites with Joab, David knew that he was the father of Bathsheba's baby. He panicked and immediately sent for Uriah. He ordered Uriah to go home and spend time with his wife. Uriah, a loyal soldier, refused to enjoy the pleasures of his home while his fellow soldiers were fighting and dying on the battlefield.

David's plan had failed. He sent a letter to Joab, who was still at the battlefield, and plotted a wicked plan. "Put Uriah at the front of the army where the fighting is the fiercest. Then withdraw the rest of the men. I want Uriah to die in battle," David told Joab in his note.

Joab obeyed David, and Uriah died. Bathsheba mourned for her husband, and after the time of mourning was over, David brought her to his palace to be his wife. In time, she had a son. But all was not well, because the LORD was not pleased with David.

David knew he had sinned against the LORD. His body became sick and his soul was in distress, but he still refused to repent of his sin. The LORD had mercy on David and sent Nathan, the prophet, to visit David. "Listen to this sad story," Nathan said. "There were two men, a rich man with many flocks, and a poor man who had but one sheep, which was kept as a family pet. One day a traveler came to the rich man's house. The rich man took the poor man's one sheep and served it as dinner for his guest."

David was enraged when he heard the story. "This is wrong!" he shouted. "Bring this rich man to me at once. He deserves to die." Nathan, looking straight at David, said, "You are the man."

By his own words, David had condemned himself. The LORD opened David's eyes, and David realized he was the rich man in the story. He who had many wives had taken the one wife of his loyal soldier, Uriah. In great sorrow, David repented, and the LORD forgave him. However, a great consequence of David's sin would soon follow: the son born to Bathsheba would get sick and die. From that time forward, David experienced many troubles in his kingdom.

Review Worksheets

A. MEMORY VERSE: "Blessed is he whose _____ is forgiven, Whose

_____ is covered." (Psalm 32:1)

B. KEY FACTS: Circle "T" if the answer is true and "F" if the answer is false.

1. The Lord told David to stay home from war.   T   F

2. David loved Bathsheba in a way that pleased the Lord.   T   F

3. David had a stubborn heart and refused to repent for a long time.   T   F

4. David's sin was too great for the Lord to forgive.   T   F

5. David repented after he heard Nathan's story about the rich man.   T   F

6. Because David repented, there were no bad consequences for him.   T   F

C. STORY FACTS: Circle the **correct** answer.

1. David showed kindness to Mephibosheth because _____.

   of his friendship with Jonathan   of his great respect for Saul

2. In the spring, when the kings went off to war, David _____.

   led his army to battle   stayed home in his palace

3. When David was tempted to love Bathsheba in the wrong way, he _____.

   resisted and obeyed God   sinned and displeased God

4. When Uriah refused to go home to be with his wife, David _____.

   praised him for his loyalty   plotted to have him killed

5. When David refused to repent of his great sin, _____.

   his soul was in distress   God stopped loving him

6. After David heard Nathan's story, he _____.

   sent Nathan away in anger   repented of his sin

D. WHAT WAS IN DAVID'S HEART? Sometimes David pleased God and sometimes David sinned. What controlled his heart when he did right and when he did wrong?

When David showed kindness

When David plotted murder

E. WHAT HAPPENED WHEN NATHAN TALKED TO DAVID?

Nathan's Story

There was a _____ man with many _____. There was a

_____ man with one _____. A _____ visited

the _____ man. The _____ man took the poor man's

_____ _____ and served it as dinner for his _____.

When David got angry about the rich man's actions, what did Nathan say?

_____ _____ _____ _____

How did David condemn himself? _____

Who opened David's eyes to see his sin? _____

F. FIND OUT...

Read 1 John 1:9. What happens when you confess your sin?

_____

_____

Why does God forgive you when you confess your sin?

_____

Chapter 10

Troubles in the Kingdom

LESSON SCOPE: 2 Samuel 12–24
1 Chronicles 18–27
Psalm 3

READ TO ME: 2 Samuel 15–18, 22
Psalm 3

THEME: The LORD God is present with His people even when they suffer the consequences of their sin.

MEMORY VERSE:

"But You, O LORD, are a shield for me, My glory and the One who lifts up my head…. I lay down and slept; I awoke, for the LORD sustained me." (Psalm 3:3, 5)

KEY FACTS: David's Troubles

These **events** resulted in these **reactions**.

When…	Then…
Amnon sinned against his sister.	David was angry, but didn't punish him.
Absalom killed Amnon.	David was sad, but did nothing.
Absalom plotted against David.	David was rejected as king and fled from Jerusalem.
Joab killed Absalom in battle.	David mourned Absalom's death and returned to Jerusalem to be king.
Sheba revolted against David, and eleven tribes rejected David as king.	David made Amasa commander in order to win back the people's loyalty.
Joab killed Amasa, and the people in Aram killed Sheba.	David made Joab commander again, and David was once again accepted as king.
David ordered a census.	The LORD punished David and sent sickness to Israel.

MESSAGE FROM THE KING:

The King wants you to know the truth about consequences.

Even when the Lord forgives you, you may still suffer natural consequences. Continue trusting God even when consequences are difficult, because the Lord still loves you.

Troubles in the Kingdom

Troubles, troubles, there were troubles in the kingdom. Ever since David had sinned with Bathsheba, all kinds of troubles happened in David's family and in the kingdom. The LORD had forgiven David, but David was God's anointed king, so the ripples of his sin reached far and wide.

It began with the death of David and Bathsheba's son. After Nathan's visit to David, the child became ill. For seven days David fasted and prayed, pleading for the child to live. When the child died, David went to the LORD's house to worship. "Can I bring him back?" he asked. He knew this was impossible. "I will go to him, but he will not return to me." David accepted his child's death as from the LORD. Soon after, David and Bathsheba had a second son. They named him Solomon, meaning "peace."

Time passed. Amnon, one of David's sons, fell in love with his own half-sister, Tamar. Instead of loving her properly, Amnon sinned against her and hurt her badly. David was furious at Amnon, but didn't punish him. Tamar's brother, Absalom, hated Amnon for what he did to Tamar.

Two years later, David had still not punished Amnon. Absalom decided to take action. Absalom invited Amnon to a feast, and after Amnon got drunk, Absalom's men killed him. Then Absalom fled to the country of Geshur. David was sad that Amnon was dead and that Absalom had fled, because he loved both Amnon and Absalom, but he did nothing. Though David yearned to see his son, he didn't tell Absalom to come home. After three years, David told Joab to bring Absalom back to Jerusalem, but David refused to talk to Absalom for two more years.

Absalom was handsome and charming. He sat at the city gate and talked with people as they entered Jerusalem. He listened to all their problems, and said, "If I were judge in the land, I would hear your complaints, and everyone would get justice." So the people all loved him.

Meanwhile, Absalom was plotting how to steal the kingdom from his father David. More and more people turned away from David to follow Absalom. Soon David realized that Jerusalem was not safe for him. As David, his men, and his

Unit II: The Glorious Kingdom...The God Who Blesses

household escaped from the city, David wept. His son had turned against him, and his people had rejected him.

David's men and Absalom's men fought each other fiercely. When Joab killed Absalom, the battle ended. David mourned Absalom's death and returned to Jerusalem. Then Sheba, a Benjamite, incited the men of Israel against David, and everyone except those from Judah deserted David again.

Without asking counsel from the LORD, David then appointed Amasa, Absalom's chief commander, to be commander of his army, replacing Joab. This was not a just way to treat Joab, who had been David's loyal commander for many years, but David did this to win back the loyalty of the northern tribes. However, it wasn't that easy.

When David told Amasa to squelch Sheba's rebellion, Amasa delayed. Frustrated with Amasa, David told Joab's brother to take Joab's men and capture Sheba. Two sad things then happened. Joab pretended to be Amasa's friend and killed him. Sheba fled to a city in Aram, and the people in that city killed him. The people gave Amasa's head to Joab, and Joab returned to Jerusalem. All Israel once again accepted David as their king.

At the end of David's life, he committed another serious sin. David told Joab, "Go throughout the land and count all the fighting men." Reluctantly, Joab obeyed. Nine months later, Joab returned with the count. Immediately David knew that he had sinned. By taking a census, he had stopped trusting God and was trusting instead in the strength of his army.

> **Jesus in the OT**
> David was a good king, but his son, Absalom, plotted against him and the people turned against David. Jesus Christ is the perfect King, yet people refused to allow Him to rule over them.

David asked the LORD for forgiveness, but the result of David's sin of taking a census was great. The prophet, Gad, came to David, and said he had to choose a consequence: three years of hunger, three months of fleeing from his enemies, or three days of sickness. He chose sickness, and all over Israel people died—70,000 people!

Second Samuel ends with David building an altar and making a sacrifice to the LORD. David sinned many times during his life, and often he sinned greatly. But David pleased the LORD because he never forgot that the LORD was the real King of Israel. And, the LORD never deserted David.

Review Worksheets

A. MEMORY VERSE: "But You, O LORD, are a _____ for me,

My _____ and the One who lifts up my _____.... I

_____ _____ and _____; I _____,

for the LORD sustained me." (Psalm 3:3, 5)

B. KEY FACTS: Match the **event** with the **reaction**.

When...	Then...
Amnon sinned against Tamar	The LORD sent sickness
Joab killed Amasa	David made Joab commander again
Absalom killed Amnon	David mourned Absalom's death
Eleven tribes followed Sheba	David had to flee from Jerusalem
David ordered a census	David was sad, but did nothing
Absalom plotted against David	David didn't punish Amnon
Joab killed Absalom in battle	David told Amasa to squelch Sheba

C. STORY FACTS: Unscramble the names & match the name to the person's description.

BOJA	_____	David and Bathsheba's son
DAG	_____	Commander who replaced Joab
NAMON	_____	Man who killed Absalom
LASBAMO	_____	Man killed by Absalom
ONMOLSO	_____	David's son who plotted against him
SMAAA	_____	Prophet who spoke to David

When David sinned and ordered the census, Gad, the prophet gave David the choice of three consequences. What were they?

1. _____

2. _____

3. _____

D. WHAT WAS THE REASON? Circle the **correct** answer.

1. David had many troubles in his family and in his kingdom because _____.

   a. the LORD was angry with David

   b. the effect of his sin brought many consequences

   c. David refused to repent of his sin after Nathan confronted him

2. David sinned when he decided to count his fighting men because _____.

   a. he was trusting in the strength of his army, not in the LORD

   b. he lied to Joab about the reason for the census

   c. commanding that a census be taken was against God's law

3. Despite his sin, David was a king that pleased God because _____.

   a. he helped many people and all the people loved him

   b. he remembered that the LORD was the real King of Israel

   c. he prayed and offered sacrifices to the LORD

E. HOW DID DAVID WORSHIP GOD? Unscramble the words to find the answer.

David did two things to worship the LORD...

TILUB NA TARAL

___ ___ ___ ___ ___ ___ ___ ___ ___ ___ ___ ___

FREDOFE A CAFRICIES

___ ___ ___ ___ ___ ___ ___ ___ ___ ___ ___ ___ ___ ___ ___ ___ ___

F. FIND OUT...

Psalm 139:7-10 says that the LORD is always present with you. Write down some times when you especially feel God's presence with you.

God is present with me when I _____

_____.

Chapter 11

The Wisdom of Solomon

LESSON SCOPE: 1 Kings 1–4, Proverbs 1–31   **READ TO ME:** 1 Kings 2–4
Ecclesiastes 1–12, Song of Songs 1–8

THEME: The LORD God gives holy wisdom to those who ask.

MEMORY VERSE:

"The fear of the LORD is the beginning of wisdom, And the knowledge of the Holy One is understanding." (Proverbs 9:10)

KEY FACTS: Old Testament Poetry Books

Book	Primary Author(s)	Theme
Job	Unknown Israelite	Trusting God during suffering.
Psalms	David, Asaph, sons of Korah, other unknown authors	Praising and worshipping the LORD in all circumstances.
Proverbs	Solomon, Agur, Lemuel	Being wise through the fear of God and by making godly choices.
Ecclesiastes	"The Preacher" (maybe Solomon)	Finding purpose in the fear of God, not earthly pleasures.
Song of Songs	Solomon	Celebrating God's gift of love.

THINGS TO REMEMBER:

Fear God   = Be in awe of God so that you respect and obey Him.

MESSAGE FROM THE KING:

The King says, "To be wise, fear God and obey His commands."

What makes a person wise? Old age and gray hair? Years of going to school? Absolutely not! Long life and years of schooling simply make a person old and educated, not wise. You will be wise if you fear the LORD and obey what He says. Are you becoming a wise person?

The Wisdom of Solomon

"Mirror, mirror, on the wall. Who's the wisest of them all?"

In 970 BC, the answer to that question would have been, "Solomon, King of Israel." He was wiser than all the sages in the East. The greatest wisdom in Egypt couldn't compare to his, and his fame spread throughout the known world. He spoke 3,000 proverbs and composed over 1,000 songs. He wrote about plants, animals, and creatures of all kinds. Men from all over the world came to sit at his feet and listened to him speak. But how did Solomon become king of Israel?

In his old age, David was feeble in mind and body, and his son Adonijah decided to take advantage of his father's weakness. He invited important men in the kingdom, including Joab and Abiathar, the priest, to a sacrificial meal. His intention was that at the end of the meal, these men would proclaim him to be the new king of Israel.

Nathan, the prophet, heard of the plot and told Bathsheba. She went to David, and asked, "Isn't my son, Solomon, to be the next king? Why is Adonijah scheming to be king?" While she was speaking, Nathan approached David, and asked, "Have you heard that Adonijah plans to be king by the end of the day?" Then David told Nathan and Zadok, the priest, to anoint Solomon as king immediately. They obeyed quickly, and soon all the people were playing flutes, and shouting, "Long live King Solomon!" so loudly that the ground shook.

David had learned that justice must be done if there was to be peace in the land. He told Solomon to remove Abiathar from his office as priest and banish him. Adonijah, Joab, and others who revolted were executed.

At that time there was no central place to worship. The tabernacle and altar of burnt offerings were at Gibeon, and the ark was in Jerusalem in the tent that David had prepared for it. People offered sacrifices to the LORD in many high places throughout the land. King Solomon went to Gibeon to make an enormous sacrifice. He desired to begin his reign by seeking the LORD.

> **Jesus in the OT**
> Was Solomon really the wisest man of all? In Colossians 2:2-3, the Apostle Paul said that all the treasures of wisdom and knowledge are found in Jesus Christ.

While in Gibeon, the LORD appeared to Solomon in a dream. "Ask for whatever you want, and I'll give it to you," the LORD said. Solomon replied, "Give me a discerning heart to rule my people well and to make right choices." The LORD was pleased with Solomon's request for wisdom and fulfilled it.

Soon all Israel knew about Solomon's great wisdom and respected him. One day two women came to him, bringing a young baby with them. The women shouted at each other, "This is my son. My son is alive and your son is dead." How would Solomon know which woman was telling the truth? Solomon said, "Bring me a sword. We'll cut the child in half and give half to one and half to the other." One woman cried out, "Please, no! Don't hurt the baby! Give the baby to her." Solomon then knew that the woman who was willing to give up the child to save its life was the real mother. By God's grace, Solomon could discern the motives of men's hearts and give sound judgments. The wicked were afraid of such wisdom, and the righteous felt safe under the care of a king who feared God.

OLD TESTAMENT POETRY BOOKS

In the middle of the Old Testament, there are five books of poetry: Job, Psalms, Proverbs, Ecclesiastes, and Song of Songs. Written by many different people, some unknown by name, these books show you how to trust God when you are suffering, how to praise and worship the LORD at all times and in all circumstances, and how to be a wise person.

The book of Job tells the story of Job, an Edomite who lived during the days of Isaac and Jacob. (Genesis 21-50 gives the stories of the lives of Isaac and Jacob.) He was a righteous man who trusted God and prayed faithfully for his children. God allowed Satan to bring trouble into Job's life, taking his children, his riches, and finally his health away from him. Satan was certain that when Job had nothing left, he would curse God.

Job never cursed God, but he didn't understand why he was suffering so much. His friends said it was because he had sinned. When Job asked God, "Why am I suffering?" the LORD turned the conversation around and asked Job question upon question until Job was overwhelmed by God's greatness. The LORD never answered Job's "why" question, but instead taught Job to trust in His goodness and love in the midst of suffering.

The book of Psalms is God's "Book of Praises." David wrote about half of the 150 psalms. Most of the psalms were written during one of three times in Israel's history: 1) during Moses's life; 2) during the time of David and Solomon; or 3) after God's people returned from exile. The book of Psalms is like a hymnbook, giving you songs to sing no matter what circumstances you might be experiencing. In the Psalms we learn about who God is and how He wants us to trust and put our hope in Him. (Chapter 4 describes the different types of psalms.)

The book of Proverbs gives practical advice about how to be a wise and godly person. Wisdom begins with fearing God. (To fear God means to be in awe of God in such a way that you respect Him and obey His commands.) God's children don't have to be terrified of God, but they should take their sin seriously and confess it quickly.

In Proverbs 1–8 Solomon used the words "my son" many times as he wrote about the beauty and value of wisdom. Later he compared the "wise man" to the "foolish man," explaining the blessings that happen when a person listens to instruction and the hardship that happens when wise words are rejected or ignored. Proverbs gives general principles of life, not absolute promises. In other words, if a person chooses to act in a particular way (either wisely or foolishly), generally speaking, a particular result will occur. Proverbs does not guarantee happiness to those who do the right things (because bad things often happen to righteous people), but it does promise God's blessing to those who fear Him. Even though the wicked may prosper for a time, in the end they will die and stand before God their Judge.

Proverbs has the same types of Hebrew poetry that are found in Psalms (repeated, contrasted, and continuing). One of the most well-known chapters is Proverbs 31, a description of the virtuous wife. This woman of noble character cares for her family, has the respect of her husband, is a successful businesswoman, and is industrious and wise. Most important, the virtuous woman is beautiful and should be praised because she fears the LORD.

Ecclesiastes, written by "The Preacher," tells you to find purpose in fearing God and obeying His commands, not in earthly pleasure, fame, and possessions. Over and over, The Preacher said, "Vanity of vanities," exclaiming over the hopelessness of looking for joy in anything but God.

Song of Songs, also referred to as the Song of Solomon, celebrates God's gift of love. Some people think the book describes the love that a man and a woman have for each other. Other people think this book is a beautiful picture of God's love for His people.

Review Worksheets

A. MEMORY VERSE: "The _____ of the LORD is the beginning of

_____, And the knowledge of the _____

_____ is _____." (Proverbs 9:10)

B. KEY FACTS: Match the theme with the Old Testament book.

_____ Job   1. Celebrating God's gift of love.

_____ Psalms   2. Being wise and making good choices.

_____ Proverbs   3. Trusting God during suffering.

_____ Song of Songs   4. Finding purpose in the fear of God.

_____ Ecclesiastes   5. Praising and worshipping the LORD.

1. Who wrote Psalms? Give three names:

_____, _____ and _____

2. Who wrote Proverbs? Give three names:

_____, _____ and _____

3. What book did The Preacher write? _____

4. During what three times in Israel's history were most of the Psalms written?

_____, _____ and

_____

C. STORY FACTS: Cross out the **wrong** word.

1. David's son (Amnon/Adonijah) tried to make himself king in Israel.

2. Solomon asked the LORD for (wisdom/strength) when he became king.

3. Job's friends said he was suffering because he was (righteous/sinful).

4. Proverbs 31 describes the (wise man/virtuous woman).

5. Proverbs 1–8 describe the (beauty of wisdom/goodness of God).

6. Wisdom begins with (seeking knowledge/fearing God).

7. Proverbs gives (absolute promises/general principles) about daily living.

D. WHAT ARE THE ANSWERS? Complete the crossword puzzle.

Across:

1. The _____ wrote Ecclesiastes.

3. Solomon was a king who feared _____.

5. Solomon asked God for_____.

6. Song of Songs celebrates God's gift of ____.

7. Zadok, the _____, anointed Solomon as king.

9. Psalms is the "Book of ____."

10. _____ wrote some of the Psalms, but not as many as David.

11. The Old Testament has _____ books of poetry.

12. Solomon was the _____ man.

Down:

1. _____ is a book about wisdom.

2. Satan said that Job would _____ God.

4. ____ learned to trust God when he suffered.

7. _____ has 150 chapters.

8. The Preacher said, "____ of vanities."

E. WHAT DOES IT MEAN TO FEAR GOD? Write the definition.

_____

_____

F. FIND OUT...

James 1:5 tells you what to do if you want wisdom. What should you do?

_____

_____

chapter 12

The Reign of Solomon

LESSON SCOPE: 1 Kings 5–11   **READ TO ME:** 1 Kings 8–10
1 Chronicles 28, 2 Chronicles 1–9

THEME: The LORD God brings blessing even when His people are unfaithful.

MEMORY VERSE:

"Praise be to the LORD, who has given rest to his people Israel just as he promised. Not one word has failed of all the good promises he gave through his servant Moses."
(1 Kings 8:56, NIV)

KEY FACTS:

God's Covenant with Solomon

If...	Then ...
Your heart is upright before Me AND you obey all I command…	I will establish your throne over Israel forever as I promised.
You or your sons turn away from Me AND you disobey My command and worship idols…	I will cut Israel off from this land AND I will reject this consecrated temple AND other nations will laugh at Israel.

MESSAGE FROM THE KING:

When the King says, "Worship only Me," He means what He says.

Idols can be made of gold or silver. Idols can also be desires of the heart that cause you to disobey God. Every time you sin, you are worshipping an idol. What idols do you worship?

The Reign of Solomon

Peace and prosperity settled over the land of Israel. King Solomon was wise and just, and the people felt safe and secure under his rule.

Solomon remembered the words of the LORD's covenant with his father David: "Your son will build a house for my Name." Because David had been a warrior, the LORD wanted Solomon, whose name means "peace," not David, to build His temple. Before he died, David made preparations for the building of the temple. He gathered together gold, silver, bronze, wood, and precious stones. He wrote down all the detailed plans for the temple building and furnishings that God's Spirit had given to him and gave them to Solomon. Then David charged Solomon, "Be strong and courageous. Don't be afraid to build this temple because the LORD will not fail you."

Solomon sent a message to Hiram, king of Tyre, saying, "Give me cedars of Lebanon to build the LORD's temple, and in exchange I'll give you wheat and olive oil." Solomon raised up a force of Israelites to transport timber from Tyre and large stones from quarries in Israel. Skilled craftsmen fashioned elaborate, carved cherubim and covered the cherubim and the inner walls of the temple with gold.

Solomon hired Huram, a highly skilled craftsman from Tyre, to create two decorated bronze pillars for the portico of the temple. The pillar to the south he called Jachin (meaning, "He establishes"), and the northern pillar he called Boaz (meaning, "in Him is strength").

For seven years, hundreds of thousands of stonecutters, craftsmen, and laborers worked to build the magnificent temple. When it was completed, Solomon called the leaders of Israel together. The priests and Levites carried the ark and all the furnishings to the temple and arranged them inside. As the priests withdrew from the Holy Place, the cloud of God's presence filled the temple. Then Solomon stood before the people and dedicated the temple. His prayer, the longest prayer in Scripture, blended

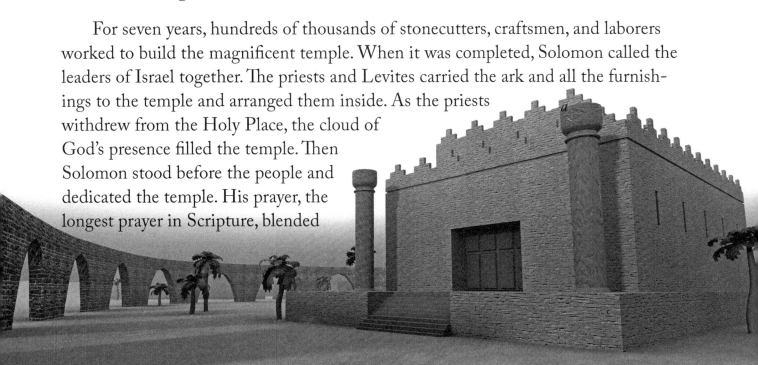

together in a perfect way the greatness of Elohim, God the Creator, and the closeness of Yahweh, God of the covenant.

The LORD appeared to Solomon and renewed the covenant. The LORD promised that if Solomon and his sons worshipped and obeyed the LORD, his kingdom would stand firm. But serious consequences would follow if they forgot the LORD and worshipped idols.

> **Jesus in the OT**
>
> "I will establish your throne forever." These were God's words to Solomon. Who would be on Solomon's throne forever? Jesus Christ!

After Solomon finished the temple, he built his own palace. It took thirteen years to build it. His throne was inlaid with ivory and overlaid with gold, with six steps leading up to it. Lions stood on either side of the throne, and lions sat on either side of the six steps. He built ships that sailed far and wide, bringing gold and treasures, as well as apes and baboons to the kingdom. In Solomon's kingdom, silver was as common as stone and cedar wood as plentiful as sycamore. He imported horses from Egypt and had thousands of chariots. His wealth, as well as his wisdom, was known throughout the world, and kings and wise men came to sit at his feet and hear him speak.

One day, the queen of Sheba, having heard of his fame and his God, visited Solomon. In her caravans she brought spices, gold, and precious stones as a gift. She talked about everything on her mind, and Solomon answered all her questions. Then she said, "In my country I heard about your achievements and wisdom, and I didn't believe that what I heard could be true. Now I have seen with my eyes and what I see far exceeds the report. Praise to the LORD who put you on the throne of Israel." Solomon gave the queen all that she asked for and more.

Yet all was not right in the kingdom. Solomon married women from many foreign nations. These women brought with them their foreign gods—Chemosh of the Moabites, Molech of the Ammonites, Ashtoreth of the Sidonians—yet Solomon continued to love these wives. As he grew older, his wives turned his heart from the LORD. He built altars on the high places so they could worship their gods. The LORD was angry with Solomon. Twice He had appeared to Solomon, yet Solomon forgot the covenant.

In the kingdom was a hard-working man named Jeroboam. Solomon put him in charge of the laborers from Ephraim and Manasseh. One day, Ahijah, the prophet, met Jeroboam in the countryside. Ahijah took his new robe and tore it into twelve pieces. He gave ten pieces to Jeroboam, and said, "Take these pieces. Because of Solomon's disobedience, the LORD will give you ten tribes to rule after Solomon's death. His son will rule over only the people of Judah and Benjamin." Solomon, the wisest man, became foolish. He worshipped idols, and at his death the nation of Israel, the glorious kingdom, split in two.

Review Worksheets

A. MEMORY VERSE: "Praise be to the LORD, who has given _____

to his people Israel just as he _____. Not _____

_____ has failed of all the _____ _____

he gave through his servant _____." (1 Kings 8:56, NIV)

B. KEY FACTS:

God's Covenant with Solomon

IF...Solomon had an...

_____

_____

AND _____ God...

THEN...God said,

"I will establish your

_____

as I promised."

BUT IF Solomon turned from God and worshipped idols THEN...

1. _____

2. _____

3. _____

C. STORY FACTS: Fill in the blanks.

1. David couldn't build the temple because he had been a _____.

2. Hiram of Tyre gave Solomon _____ of Lebanon for the temple.

3. The names of the two temple pillars were _____ and _____.

4. It took _____ years to build the temple and _____ years to build the palace.

5. The _____ heard of Solomon's fame and visited him.

6. The prophet Ahijah told _____ he would rule ten tribes.

7. The LORD was angry with Solomon because he forgot the _____.

D. WHAT DOES NOT BELONG?

Cross out the word(s) that do(es) **not** belong with the other words.

1. Names of idols:

   Chemosh   Sheba   Molech   Ashteroth

2. Materials for the temple:

   gold   sycamore wood   precious stones   bronze

3. Animals that Solomon brought to Israel:

   baboons   apes   Egyptian horses   elephants

4. Ways that Solomon sinned against the LORD:

   married foreign wives   built altars on high places

   built a large palace   forgot the covenant

5. Wealth that Solomon possessed:

   many sailing ships   robes trimmed with diamonds

   thousands of chariots   lions standing beside his throne

E. SOLOMON'S PRAYER: Solomon used two names for God in his prayer.
Write a description of each one.

Elohim: _____

Yahweh: _____

When the priests withdrew from the Holy Place, what happened?

_____

F. FIND OUT... What promises did the LORD give to Moses? Be prepared to discuss with
the teacher how the LORD fulfilled them.

Exodus 6:7a _____

Exodus 6:8 _____

Deuteronomy 28:7 _____

Deuteronomy 28:8-9 _____

Chapter 13 Looking Backwards...Looking Ahead

LESSON SCOPE: 2 Samuel 1–24, 1 Kings 1–11, **READ TO ME:** 2 Chronicles 6–7
1 Chronicles 1–28, 2 Chronicles 1–9   Psalm 72
Proverbs 1–31, Ecclesiastes 1–12
Song of Songs 1–8

So many blessings from God! The LORD blessed the Israelites with an upright man, David, to be their king. The LORD gave them peace from their enemies and forgiveness for their sins. He promised to be present with His people, even after they had sinned greatly. Most importantly, the LORD remembered His promise to be Israel's God.

The LORD blessed Solomon with great wisdom and wealth, and Solomon became renowned for the decisions he made and the magnificent palace he inhabited. After years of hard work and skilled craftsmanship, Solomon's temple was finished. The LORD's presence filled the temple just as it had filled the tabernacle in the wilderness. Israel's territory had expanded. No longer was Israel a small nation of loosely allied tribes. As we learned in Unit II, Israel had become the glorious kingdom that attracted royalty and sages from faraway countries to see its wealth and learn from its wisdom.

In Unit II, you learned how the LORD blessed His people. Israel reached the height of its glory as a nation. But the hearts of Israel turned from the worship of Yahweh to the pagan gods of the nations surrounding them, and tragedy was soon to come.

In Unit III, you will learn about the split of Israel into two kingdoms. Solomon's son, Rehoboam, would rule one tribe because the LORD had promised that David's line would endure. The ten other tribes would rebel against Rehoboam and set up Jeroboam as their king. How sad, how tragic, that the glorious kingdom would be divided in two because of Israel's unfaithfulness to the LORD. Yet, despite Israel's sin, the Almighty King reigned supreme in Israel. His will could not be thwarted! He was the Keeper of His Kingdom.

IMPORTANT THINGS TO KNOW:

Word	Meaning of the Word
Blessed	Contented because God is pleased with you.
Covenant	God's promise to be the God of His people forever.
Fear God	Be in awe of God so that you respect and obey Him.
Prophet	Person called to speak for God.
Psalms	"Book of Praises."
Transgression	The breaking of one of God's laws.

Review Worksheets

A. MEMORY VERSE REVIEW: Cross out the **wrong** word(s) in the memory verse phrases. You will find one wrong word in each line. Write the **correct** word in the blank.

1. "Blessed is he whose wickedness is forgiven…" _____

2. "But you, O LORD, are a protection for me, _____

   My glory and the One who lifts up my heart." _____

3. "I have made a covenant with My people… _____

   'Your family I will establish forever, _____

   And build up your kingdom to all generations." _____

4. "The love of the LORD is the beginning of wisdom, _____

   And the knowledge of the Holy One is truth." _____

5. "Praise be to the LORD, who has given hope to his people… _____

   Not one word has failed of all the just promises he gave…" _____

6. "I lay down and cried; _____

   I awoke, for the LORD helped me." _____

What are three things David asked the LORD to do in Psalm 51:1-6?

1. _____

2. _____

3. _____

B. RHYMING STORY FACTS: Write the rhyming story facts in the blanks below.

Curse	Health	Fame	Lyre	Name	Nurse
One	Sacrifices	Son	Spices	Tyre	Wealth

1. **What Solomon gained**   **what Job lost**

_____   rhymes with   _____

2. **What God promised to make great**   **what spread abroad**

David's _____   rhymes with   Solomon's _____

3. **What instrument David played**   **where cedar wood came from**

_____   rhymes with   _____

4. **Who fled with Mephibosheth**   **what Satan said Job would do**

_____   rhymes with   _____

5. **What the Queen of Sheba brought**   **what were made on high places**

_____   rhymes with   _____

6. **Number of sheep the poor man had**   **relation of Absalom to David**

_____   rhymes with   _____

C. WHAT WAS THE THEME OF UNIT II? What is God's blessing like? Fill in the blanks below to find out.

R __ M __ __ B __ __ __   God _____ His promises.

           L __ __ __   God never takes His _____ away.

G __ __ __ E   God gives mercy and _____.

    P __ __ S __ __ T   God promised to be ____ with us.

M __ __ S __ __ __   The _____ will be born.

      W I __ __ __ __   God gives _____ to those who ask.

C __ __ __ N __ __ __   God renews His _____.

    F __ __ G __ __ __ __ __ __   God gives _____ for sins.

D. WHAT DO YOU KNOW ABOUT THESE PEOPLE? Match the person to the
words that describe him.

_____ Absalom

_____ Uzzah

_____ Ishbosheth

_____ Nathan

_____ Abner

_____ Joab

_____ Mephibosheth

_____ Solomon

_____ Molech

_____ Uriah

_____ Asaph

_____ Hiram

1. Man who wrote several Psalms

2. King who built the temple

3. God of the Ammonites

4. Commander of Saul's army

5. Son of Jonathan who couldn't walk

6. King of Tyre

7. Man who touched the ark and died

8. Husband of Bathsheba killed in battle

9. Commander of David's army

10. Prophet who spoke to David

11. David's son killed by Joab

12. Saul's son who was king for a brief time

E. THE RENEWED COVENANT: Unscramble the words and use them to fill in the
blanks in the paragraph below.

God renewed the _____ with David. He said that David's son
VOCENTAN

would build the _____ and David's kingdom would _____
MELTEP   ERENUD

forever. He said He would never take away His _____. When David
VELO

heard these words, he thanked the LORD for His _____ and
CYMER

_____. God renewed the covenant with Solomon, but
ACREG

Solomon turned away from _____ and worshipped _____.
HET ROLD   SLOID

F. WHAT'S THE REASON? Circle the **correct** answer.

1. Uzzah died when he touched the ark because the ark _____.

   was holy to the LORD   fell on top of him

2. David sinned by loving Bathsheba because _____.

   she was an idol worshipper   she was another man's wife

3. The LORD forgave David of his sin because _____.

   David was a good king   David repented in sorrow

4. The LORD was pleased with David because David never _____.

   forgot that God was King   was frightened in battle

5. Solomon was the wisest of all men because _____.

   he asked God for wisdom   he had wise teachers

6. Solomon sinned when he married many foreign wives because _____.

   he made many enemies   he started worshipping idols

G. WHAT DO YOU KNOW ABOUT THE BOOKS OF POETRY?

Cross out the **wrong** word in the sentences below.

1. The Old Testament has (five/six) books of poetry.

2. Job's friends said he was suffering because he was (righteous/sinful).

3. After God asked Job question upon question, Job was overwhelmed by

   God's (anger/greatness).

4. Psalms is the Old Testament ("Book of Praises"/"Book of God's Law").

5. Proverbs says that wisdom begins with (fearing God/making good decisions).

6. Proverbs gives (absolute promises/general principles) about life.

7. The Preacher wrote the words ("my son"/"vanity of vanities") many times.

8. Song of Songs celebrates God's gift of (love/wisdom).

UNIT III

The Divided Kingdom...The God Who Reigns

Theme: The Keeper of the Kingdom rules over the kingdom of men.

Oh my, oh my, I can't believe this is happening! It is I, Tobias, the royal chronicler, and things are looking bad. How can I record with utmost accuracy the events of the kingdom when my heart is so heavy with sadness? Yet, I promise to record the story with confident faith, because the LORD is King, and He is keeping His kingdom safe.

What a glorious kingdom Israel was in the days of King Solomon! Wealth, fame, wisdom, and many blessings came from the LORD, the King of kings. The tragedy was that Solomon forgot that the LORD blesses those who fear His name and punishes those who sin. God's people cannot sin without enduring the consequences. Turning from the worship of the one true God to pagan idols made the wisest man in the world become a foolish man, and after his death, the glorious kingdom split in two.

Solomon's son, Rehoboam, also was a foolish man. He threatened the people with higher taxes. His harshness caused the ten northern tribes that King Jeroboam ruled to split apart from Judah and Benjamin and form their own country. Rehoboam was not wise enough, powerful enough, or godly enough to win back the allegiance of these tribes, and the nation was permanently divided in half.

Jeroboam, king of the northern tribes, set up his capital at Shechem. He built worship centers at Dan and Bethel because he didn't want people going to Jerusalem to worship. His actions made the split between the two kingdoms politically and religiously unsettled. In years to come, he would be known as "the son of Nebat, who had made Israel sin" (1 Kings 22:52).

In the next eighty years, the northern kingdom of Israel would have eight kings, none of whom served the LORD, and the southern kingdom of Judah would have four kings, two of whom worshipped the LORD. The story of the divided kingdom started out sad and became even sadder as years went by. But in the darkness, some light shone. Prophets spoke God's truth, and the LORD, the Keeper of His Kingdom, directed all events by His sovereign hand. Even in the divided kingdom, the LORD reigned supreme.

PSALM 121 A Song of Ascents

1. I will lift up my eyes to the hills—
     From whence comes my help?
2. My help comes from the LORD,
     Who made heaven and earth.
3. He will not allow your foot to be moved;
     He who keeps you will not slumber.
4. Behold, He who keeps Israel
     Shall neither slumber nor sleep.
5. The LORD is your keeper;
     The LORD is your shade at your right hand.
6. The sun shall not strike you by day,
     Nor the moon by night.
7. The LORD shall preserve you from all evil;
     He shall preserve your soul.
8. The LORD shall preserve your going out and your coming in
     From this time forth, and even forevermore.

Isn't it comforting to know that the LORD, Creator of heaven and earth, the Maker of the majestic mountains that reach high and sturdy into the skies, is the One who keeps you safe? Who can move a mountain, even an inch? No one. Just think, the LORD's protection is as secure as the highest, unshakable mountain.

In the darkness, when the lights are out and you are alone, sometimes you can feel afraid. But remember, the LORD never goes to bed at night. All night long He stays awake, never sleeping even for a minute, keeping you safe and secure.

When the burning heat of the sun or the chill of the moonlit night surrounds you, the LORD stays by your side. He keeps you safe from evil and safeguards your soul from enemies. Each day and in everything you do, the LORD's protection never fails.

The LORD is Keeper of His Kingdom, but He is also the Keeper of you, His precious child and heir to the eternal Kingdom of Almighty God.

chapter 14

A Nation Divided

LESSON SCOPE: 1 Kings 12–16
2 Chronicles 10–16

READ TO ME: 1 Kings 12
2 Chronicles 15–16

THEME: The LORD God rules even when kings are wicked and turn against Him.

MEMORY VERSE:

"[They] exchanged the truth of God for the lie, and worshiped and served the creature rather than the Creator, who is blessed forever. Amen." (Romans 1:25)

KEY FACTS: The Divided Kingdom—The First Eighty Years

	Judah	Israel
Kings	Four kings: Evil—Rehoboam, Abijah Godly—Asa, Jehoshaphat	Eight kings: All eight kings did evil in God's eyes—Jeroboam, Nadab, Baasha, Elah, Zimri, Tibni, Omri, Ahab
Capitals	Jerusalem	First: Shechem, Second: Samaria
Tribes	Two tribes: Judah and Benjamin	Ten tribes: Reuben, Simeon, Dan, Naphtali, Gad, Asher, Issachar, Zebulun, Ephraim, Manasseh
Religion	Worship at temple in Jerusalem; priests were Levites	Worship at high places in Dan and Bethel; priests were not Levites; use of images of golden calves
Prophets	Azariah, Hanani	Ahijah, Jehu, Elijah

MESSAGE FROM THE KING: The King says, "Worship Me in a holy way."

Psalm 96:9 says, "Worship the LORD in the splendor of his holiness!" (NIV). God wants you to be joyful but respectful in your worship. What are some right and wrong ways to worship the LORD?

Unit III: The Divided Kingdom...The God Who Reigns

A Nation Divided

What makes a man a wise king? A wise king desires to bring well-being and prosperity to his people and heeds the advice of wise, godly men. Rehoboam, Solomon's son, did neither of these things.

The people cried out to Rehoboam, "Your father, Solomon, made us pay high taxes and do harsh labor. Lighten our burdens, and we will serve you." The older men who had served Solomon urged Rehoboam to listen to the people, but Rehoboam was stubborn. He listened to the young men, who said, "Make the burden on the people even heavier!" The people rebelled, and all the tribes but Judah and Benjamin proclaimed Jeroboam to be their king. This was the fulfillment of Ahijah's prophecy to Jeroboam several years earlier. Now there were two nations: Israel and Judah.

> **Jesus in the OT**
> Rehoboam promised to put heavy burdens on the people. In contrast, King Jesus' "burdens" are not hard to carry. In fact, Jesus said, "My yoke is easy, and My burden is light."

In Israel, Jeroboam set up his capital in Tirzah. Because he wanted his people to be loyal to him, he created his own way of worshipping God. He built high places in Dan and Bethel as worship centers and made golden calves to help the people worship. This was wrong because the LORD had commanded that everyone worship at the temple in Jerusalem and had strictly forbidden the use of images for worship. Jeroboam also let men who were not Levites become priests, even though God had said that only Levites were to be priests. All of these things angered the LORD. Even after a prophet warned Jeroboam of his sin and the altar at Bethel split apart, Jeroboam continued in his wicked ways.

When Jeroboam's son became ill, Jeroboam sent his wife in disguise to Ahijah, the prophet, to ask for healing. Ahijah, though blind, was not fooled by the disguise, and the LORD told him to say, "Because Jeroboam has done more evil in Israel than anyone who lived before him, the LORD will bring disaster to his family. One day a king in Israel will kill everyone in Jeroboam's family." Jeroboam's wife returned home, and the young boy died.

Jeroboam's son, Nadab, ruled after Jeroboam's death and was just as evil as Jeroboam, his father. After two years, a man named Baasha plotted against Nadab and killed him and all the rest of Jeroboam's family. This was the fulfillment of the LORD's prophecy against Jeroboam by the prophet Ahijah.

Baasha ruled for twenty-four years. Like Nadab and Jeroboam before him, Baasha displeased the LORD with his constant sin. The word of the LORD came to Baasha through the prophet Jehu, saying, "I made you leader of my people Israel, but you walked in the ways of Jeroboam and caused My people to sin. So I am about to consume you and all your house. (This prophecy would be fulfilled after Baasha's death, during the rule of his son, Elah.)

Baasha remained king until he died of natural causes. After Baasha died, his son, Elah, became king. But after only two years, Zimri, one of Elah's officials who had command of half of Elah's chariots, plotted against Elah, killed him, and became king. After murdering Elah, Zimri immediately killed all of Baasha's family, every single male, in accordance with the LORD's words spoken by Jehu the prophet to Baasha. The LORD used Zimri, wicked as he was, to bring about the fulfillment of His justice.

Jesus in the OT

The king was the representative of the covenant between God and the people. Isn't it sad that most of the kings forgot the covenant and led their people far from the LORD? Jesus, the King, is the representative of the covenant with you. Following Him brings you closer to your heavenly Father.

When the Israelite soldiers encamped near the Philistine town of Gibbethon heard how Zimri had murdered Elah and set himself up as king, they revolted against Zimri, and that very day they proclaimed Omri, commander of Israel's army, to be king of Israel.

With Omri in charge, the army then marched to Tirzah, and laid siege to the city. When Zimri saw that Omri's army had taken the city, he lost hope. He went to the citadel of the palace, set the palace on fire all around himself, and died. Zimri had been king in Israel for only seven days.

The northern kingdom of Israel was now in turmoil. Two men, Omri and Tibni, fought to gain control of the kingdom. The people of Israel were split: Half of them supported Omri and half of them supported Tibni. It was a confusing, uncertain, and violent time, but in the end, Omri's army was stronger than Tibni's army. No one knows exactly how, but Tibni died during the struggle between the two groups of Israelites, and Omri was crowned king in Israel.

While he was king, Omri stabilized the government and moved Israel's capital to Samaria. Within Israel and among neighboring nations, Omri was respected as an impressive ruler. In God's eyes, Omri was an idolater who hurried his nation closer to the day of judgment. After Omri's death, Ahab, Omri's son, became Israel's eighth king.

In Judah, when Rehoboam died, his son, Abijah, became king in Judah. Abijah's heart wasn't devoted to the LORD, and he did evil in God's eyes. He ruled only three years. When he died, his son, Asa, became king in Judah.

Asa commanded that the people of Judah seek the LORD and obey His commands. He smashed the foreign altars and cut down the Asherah poles. He was fully committed to the LORD, and the kingdom was at peace because the LORD gave rest to the land.

The Spirit of God came upon the prophet Azariah, and he said to Asa, "The LORD is with you. Be strong. Don't give up. You will be rewarded." So Asa took courage and removed all the detestable idols from Judah. He even removed his grandmother from her position as queen because she had an Asherah pole. Asa's heart was committed to the LORD all his life.

Off and on throughout these years, Israel and Judah fought against each other. Late in Asa's life, he made a treaty with Ben-Hadad, king of Aram, to ally with him against Baasha, king of Israel. Hanani, the seer, warned Asa, "You were foolish because you trusted Ben-Hadad instead of the LORD. You will be at war from now on." Asa was so angry at Hanani that he put him in prison and brutally oppressed some people who agreed with Hanani. Then Asa got a severe foot disease and sought help from doctors, not from the LORD. Because of this disease, his son Jehoshaphat ruled alongside him for his last few years.

How sad that the first eight kings of Israel and two of Judah's first four kings (Rehoboam and Abijah) refused to acknowledge the LORD as King. When the kings and the people forgot God's covenant, they were ignorant of the blessing that worshipping God could bring to them.

Review Worksheets

A. MEMORY VERSE: "[They] exchanged the _____ of God for the

_____, and worshiped and served the _____ rather than the

_____, who is _____ forever. Amen." (Romans 1:25)

B. KEY FACTS: If the word(s) below describe(s) Judah, write "Judah" in the blank. If the word(s) describe(s) Israel, write "Israel" in the blank.

Eight evil kings _____   Prophet Ahijah _____

Temple at Jerusalem _____   Golden calves _____

Two godly kings _____   Capital at Samaria _____

Ten tribes _____   King Jeroboam _____

Levites as priests _____   Two tribes _____

King Rehoboam _____   King Asa _____

Prophet Azariah _____   King Omri _____

C. STORY FACTS: Circle **all** the **correct** answers.

1. When Rehoboam became king, the people got upset about the _____.

     high taxes   bad roads   harsh labor

2. Rehoboam took the advice of the _____.

     young men   older wise men   priests

3. Jeroboam built worship centers in the cities of _____.

     Dan   Shechem   Bethel

4. Because Asa was committed to the LORD, he _____.

     built a new temple   smashed foreign altars   removed idols

5. Tribes that made up the kingdom of Judah were _____.

     Ephraim   Benjamin   Judah

D. HOW WELL DO YOU KNOW THE KINGS? Find the kings' names in the Word
Find. Then in the blank beside each name put a "J" if he was king in Judah and an "I" if he was king in Israel.

Ahab _____   Tibni _____

Elah _____   Omri _____

Asa _____   Zimri _____

Abijah _____   Baasha _____

Jeroboam _____

Rehoboam _____

Jehoshaphat _____

Nadab _____

One king is found twice in the Word Find.

Who is it? _____

T	I	B	R	I	M	O	A	H
A	R	B	E	H	A	H	T	O
H	T	A	H	A	B	A	I	P
P	Z	D	O	J	A	J	B	H
A	I	A	B	A	A	I	N	A
H	M	N	O	H	S	B	I	T
S	A	S	A	S	H	A	L	E
O	I	R	M	O	A	A	T	L
H	A	J	I	T	U	S	E	A
E	I	R	M	I	Z	H	N	P
J	E	R	O	B	O	A	M	O

E. GODLY AND EVIL KINGS:
1. What are two things that King Jeroboam did to change worship in Israel?

_____

_____

2. What are two godly things that King Asa of Judah did?

_____

_____

3. What is one thing that King Asa did that displeased the LORD?

_____

F. FIND OUT... Jeroboam disobeyed God in his worship. What did the LORD say about
correct worship in the Scripture passages below?

Images (Exodus 20:4-6) _____

Priests (Numbers 3:5-12) _____

Place of sacrifices (Exodus 29:42-43) _____

Chapter 15

Elijah—God's Voice of Judgment to a Wicked King

LESSON SCOPE: 1 Kings 16:29–19:18   **READ TO ME:** 1 Kings 16–19

THEME: The LORD God proves He is God over nature, kings, and foreign gods.

MEMORY VERSE:

"The steps of a good man are ordered by the LORD, And He delights in his way. Though he fall, he shall not be utterly cast down; For the LORD upholds him with His hand." (Psalm 37:23-24)

KEY FACTS: God Shows His Sovereign Power

During Elijah's life, the LORD showed...

His power over...	When He...
Weather	...stopped the rain and dew in Israel for several years.
Daily Food	...provided flour and oil for the widow and her son.
Death	...brought the widow's son back to life.
Pagan Idols	...showed that He was God, not Baal.
Enemies	...helped Elijah escape from wicked Queen Jezebel.
Discouragement	...took away Elijah's discouragement and helped him serve faithfully.

MESSAGE FROM THE KING:

The King says, "Listen to my gentle whisper of encouragement."

Isn't it strange that Elijah became so discouraged after his big victory on Mt. Carmel? Discouragement often happens after great spiritual triumphs. But God hasn't changed. If you listen to His gentle voice, He'll remind you of how much He loves and cares for you.

Elijah—God's Voice of Judgment to a Wicked King

A large black bird hovered overhead and then glided down, landing on the flat rock beside the brook. A few seconds passed before the bird dropped the chunk of meat in its beak onto the rock and flew off. Elijah, God's prophet, thanked the LORD for the food and ate his evening meal.

The ravens had provided food for Elijah—bread and meat in the morning and evening—ever since the drought began. Elijah had warned Ahab, Israel's wicked king, saying, "As the LORD lives, no rain or dew will fall in the next few years except at my word." There at the Kerith Ravine, the LORD provided food and water for Elijah while famine stalked the rest of Israel.

Ahab, son of Omri, did more evil in God's eyes than any king before him, even Jeroboam. He married Jezebel, a worshipper of Baal, and rejected the LORD to serve Baal. He built a temple to Baal in Samaria and told the people to worship Baal. Because of his sin, there was no rain in Israel for several years.

When the brook dried up, the LORD sent Elijah to Zarephath. "I have commanded a widow to take care of you," the LORD said. Elijah met the widow at the city gate and asked for bread. "I have no bread," she replied. "I have only a little flour and oil to make my last meal. After we eat that, my son and I will die."

Elijah encouraged her not to be afraid, saying, "Feed me from what you have, and the LORD promises that your flour will not be used up nor your oil run dry until the LORD sends rain." She did as Elijah said, and from that day, she cared for Elijah and always had plenty of flour and oil.

One day, the widow's son got sick and died. "What do you have against me? What sin have I done that my son must die?" she cried out. Elijah took the son in his arms and carried him to his bed. Three times he stretched himself out on top of the boy, and prayed, "O LORD God, let this boy's life return to him!" The LORD answered Elijah's prayer, and the boy came back to life. The widow exclaimed, "Now I know that you are a man of God and that God's words from your mouth are truth."

Some time later, King Ahab set out to meet Elijah, and asked him, "Is that you, troublemaker?" Elijah answered, "By worshipping Baal, you have brought trouble to Israel." Elijah challenged Ahab to a contest: the 450 prophets of Baal against Elijah, the prophet of the LORD.

Everyone gathered at the top of Mt. Carmel. Elijah shouted aloud, "If the Lord is God, follow Him, but if Baal is god, follow him." Two altars were built and sacrifices laid on top of them. Elijah said, "You call upon Baal, and I will call upon the Lord. The god who answers by fire, he is God."

The prophets of Baal shouted prayers from morning to noon, but no fire ignited their sacrifice. "Shout louder," Elijah urged. "Maybe Baal is sleeping or on a trip." The prophets danced, cut themselves with swords, and shouted louder, but nothing happened. Then it was Elijah's turn. He told the people to pour water over the sacrifice until the offering was all wet and the water ran down the sides of the altar into the trench. Three times they poured water on the sacrifice. Then Elijah prayed, "O Lord, let everyone know You are God in Israel, and I am your servant." Immediately, fire fell from heaven, burning up the sacrifice, the altar, and all the water in the trench. The people fell on their faces, and cried, "The Lord is God."

Elijah commanded, "Seize the prophets of Baal and put them to death." Meanwhile, the sky darkened, the clouds gathered, and a strong wind arose. For the first time in years, there was rain in Israel.

Jezebel hated Elijah, and sent a message to him that she planned to kill him the next day. Discouraged and afraid, Elijah fled into the desert. "I've had enough. I am worthless. Take my life, Lord," he said in despair. But the angel of the Lord provided him with food and Elijah was able to go on.

Elijah traveled forty days to a cave at Mt. Horeb, the mountain of God, and there the Lord appeared to him. The Lord sent a powerful wind, then an earthquake, and finally a fire, but He was not found in any of those things. After the fire, Elijah heard a gentle whisper, that said, "What are you doing here, Elijah?" Elijah replied to God, "I am the only one left, and Jezebel is going to kill me." The Lord encouraged Elijah, saying, "You are not alone as a worshipper of Yahweh, and I still have work for you to do."

No longer discouraged, Elijah believed God. In the strength of God's words, Elijah got up and continued serving the Lord faithfully.

Jesus in the OT

Even when Elijah was discouraged and ready to die, the Lord was with him, speaking in a gentle, encouraging voice. Jesus, your Lord, is always with you. He promises, "I will never leave you nor forsake you."

Unit III: The Divided Kingdom...The God Who Reigns

Review Worksheets

A. MEMORY VERSE: "The steps of a _____ _____

are ordered by the _____, And He _____ in his way.

Though he _____ , he shall not be utterly _____

_____; For the LORD upholds him with His _____."
(Psalm 37:23-24)

B. KEY FACTS: Fill in the blanks.

The Life of Elijah

BY GOD'S POWER… Elijah spoke the words from God and the _____

and _____ stopped for several years. He promised the widow she would

always have _____ and _____ to make bread, and he

brought her _____ back to life. Elijah showed the people that the LORD, not

_____, was God. He escaped from wicked Queen _____.

God spoke to him in a whisper, and Elijah was no longer _____. He

continued to _____ God faithfully all his life.

C. STORY FACTS: Circle the **correct** answer.

1. The LORD sent _____ to bring food to Elijah.

    eagles   ravens   pigeons

2. Ahab was more wicked than Jeroboam because he _____.

    built a temple for Baal   killed prophets   fought many wars

3. There were _____ prophets of Baal on the top of Mt. Carmel.

    40   450   7,000

4. When Elijah was discouraged, God spoke to him _____.

    by a strong wind   by an earthquake   in a gentle whisper

5. After the LORD spoke to Elijah in the cave at Mt. Horeb, Elijah _____.

    served God faithfully   built an altar to God   went to the desert

D. WHO SAID THIS? Draw a line from each quote to the person who said it. Some of them said more than one thing.

Ahab   Elijah   Widow   God's People   The LORD

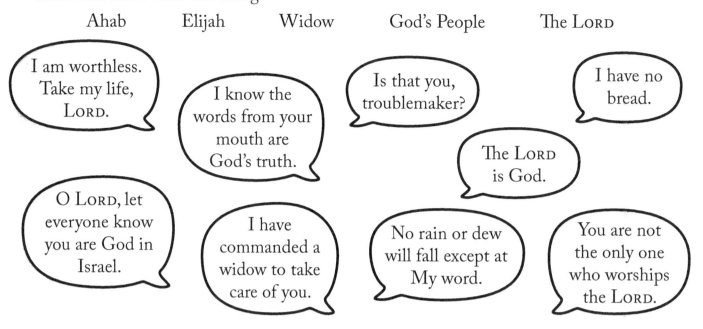

I am worthless. Take my life, LORD.

I know the words from your mouth are God's truth.

Is that you, troublemaker?

I have no bread.

The LORD is God.

O LORD, let everyone know you are God in Israel.

I have commanded a widow to take care of you.

No rain or dew will fall except at My word.

You are not the only one who worships the LORD.

E. WHAT HAPPENED ON MT. CARMEL? Put the story boxes in order.

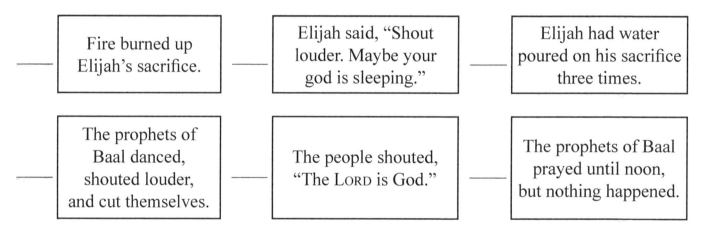

____ Fire burned up Elijah's sacrifice.

____ Elijah said, "Shout louder. Maybe your god is sleeping."

____ Elijah had water poured on his sacrifice three times.

____ The prophets of Baal danced, shouted louder, and cut themselves.

____ The people shouted, "The LORD is God."

____ The prophets of Baal prayed until noon, but nothing happened.

F. FIND OUT... Read Psalm 42. Then circle every other letter and put the letters in the blanks to find out what to do when you are discouraged. (Start with the second letter.)

A P O U S T E Y R O T U M R I H E O S P O E N I K N W G L O S D

—— —— —— —— ——   —— —— —— ——   —— ——   —— —— ——

Chapter 16

Ahab & Jehoshaphat—Two Very Different Kings

LESSON SCOPE: 1 Kings 20–22
2 Kings 1–2
2 Chronicles 17–21

READ TO ME: 1 Kings 20–22

THEME: The Lord God controls the course of history.

MEMORY VERSE:

"Many are the plans in a man's heart, but it is the Lord's purpose that prevails."
(Proverbs 19:21, NIV)

KEY FACTS: Two Very Different Kings

King Jehoshaphat: Judah	King Ahab: Israel
Turned people back to the Lord.	Turned people away from the Lord.
Worshipped at Jerusalem's temple and instructed people in the fear of God.	Built a temple to Baal and encouraged idol worship.
Walked in the ways of godly King David.	Walked in the ways of wicked King Jeroboam.
Jehu prophesied God's blessing on him.	Micaiah prophesied his death.
Neighboring nations were at peace.	Aram attacked Israel several times.
Prayed before battle.	Ignored a prophet's advice and put that prophet in prison.

MESSAGE FROM THE KING:

The King says, "Nothing happens by accident. I am sovereign!"

How often do you say, "That was an accident! It wasn't supposed to happen that way!"? Since the whole world is under God's sovereign control, there can't really be accidents. Isn't it comforting to know that the world isn't spinning out of control?

Ahab & Jehoshaphat—Two Very Different Kings

Arising from the shambles of Solomon's glorious kingdom were two very different kingdoms with two very different kings. What made these kingdoms so different? Each king's reaction to the covenant, that's what!

King Ahab of Israel rejected God's covenant, and disobeyed the LORD's commands. While Ahab was king, Ben-Hadad, king of Aram, along with thirty-two other kings, besieged the city of Samaria. "Give me your silver, gold, and the best of your wives and children," Ben-Hadad demanded.

At first, Ahab agreed to give Ben-Hadad what he wanted, but when Ben-Hadad demanded more, the elders of the people told Ahab, "Don't listen to him or agree with his demands."

Then a prophet came to Ahab, and said, "Start the battle against Ben-Hadad. God will give you victory, and then you will know that He is the LORD."

Ahab attacked Ben-Hadad, and a drunken, defeated Ben-Hadad escaped with his army. Undaunted, Ben-Hadad returned the next spring to fight Israel. With God's help, Israel again conquered the Arameans. When Ben-Hadad begged for his life, Ahab disobeyed the LORD and let him live. He made a treaty with Ben-Hadad. A prophet then confronted Ahab, saying, "Because you set free a man that the LORD had determined should die, you will die." (Ben-Hadad was to die because he had dishonored the name of the LORD and had attacked God's people.)

Near Ahab's palace was a well-groomed, fruitful vineyard belonging to Naboth. Ahab wanted this vineyard, and when Naboth refused to sell it to him, Ahab pouted like a little child. Seeing her husband so sullen, Jezebel rebuked Ahab, "Is this how a king acts? If you want something, you should have it because you are the king! I'll get it for you." Jezebel plotted a wicked scheme. She hired two men to lie about Naboth, saying he had blasphemed God. When the elders of Naboth's town heard that Naboth had blasphemed, they dragged him outside the city and stoned him to death. (This was the penalty for anyone who blasphemed God.)

> **Jesus in the OT**
> When Ahab refused to kill Ben-Hadad, he was not a faithful king. He wasn't defending the honor of the LORD and wasn't protecting his people from enemies who wanted to destroy them. Jesus, as King, always honors God the Father and protects His people from those who would destroy them.

The LORD sent Elijah to Ahab. "Because you have murdered a man, you and your sons will die, every last one, and the dogs will lick up your blood." Hearing this, Ahab humbled himself, and the LORD delayed the destruction of Ahab's whole household until the days of his son.

Three years later, Ahab asked Jehoshaphat, king of Judah, to go to war with him against Aram. Jehoshaphat replied, "Let's seek counsel from the LORD." Instead, Ahab got advice from 400 false prophets. They told him that he'd have victory, which was just what he wanted to hear. When the prophet Micaiah warned Ahab against this, Ahab scoffed, "Why don't you ever say anything good about me?" He sent Micaiah off to prison, and he and Jehoshaphat went off to war against the king of Aram.

Ahab knew the king of Aram wanted to kill him, so he disguised himself to look like an ordinary soldier. But God is never fooled, and events always happen just as He plans. An Aramean soldier drew his bow and shot a random arrow into the air. The arrow hit the king between the sections of his armor, and Ahab died. His blood spilled from his chariot into a pool in Samaria, and dogs came by to lap up his blood, just as the LORD had said.

Jehoshaphat, king of Judah, respected God's covenant and turned his people back to the LORD, walking in the ways of his ancestor, King David. At the beginning of his reign, he removed the high places of idol worship and cut down the Asherah poles. He appointed wise judges to settle disputes, warn people of sin, and administer God's law. He reminded them, "Fear the LORD and judge carefully." He built strong, fortified cities with large storehouses and had great wealth. Jehu, the seer, promised God's blessing on him if he continued to set his heart on seeking the LORD.

One day, Jehoshaphat received word that a vast army of Moabites and Ammonites was approaching Judah. Frightened people came from every town in Judah to seek the king's help. Jehoshaphat assembled the people, and prayed, "O LORD, power and might are in Your hand. If calamity comes upon us, we will stand in Your presence and cry to You. You will hear us and help us. By ourselves, we have no power to face this vast army. We don't know what to do, but our eyes are on You."

The prophet, Jahaziel, said, "Don't be afraid. You will not have to fight this battle. Go to the battlefield and see the deliverance that God will provide."

Early in the morning, Jehoshaphat led his people to the battlefield. He ordered them, "Sing to the LORD. Give thanks to Him, for His love endures forever." At the top of the ridge they looked down on the desert plain, and surprise! They saw only dead bodies. The LORD had set ambushes, and the enemy armies had destroyed each other. No one had escaped. The men of Judah went home rejoicing, and God gave Judah peace from war.

Jehoshaphat continued to seek the LORD, but some high places remained, and all Judah did not turn from idols to serve the LORD.

Review Worksheets

A. MEMORY VERSE: "Many are the _____ in a man's

_____, but it is the LORD's _____ that prevails."
(Proverbs 19:21, NIV)

B. KEY FACTS:

Two Very Different Kings

Jehoshaphat served the LORD. Ahab served Baal and other idols. The god they served made a difference in what their kingdoms looked like. Using the **key facts** table, describe these two different kingdoms in the blanks.

Kingdom of Jehoshaphat	Kingdom of Ahab
_____	_____
_____	_____
_____	_____
_____	_____
_____	_____

C. STORY FACTS: Fill in the blanks.

1. When Ahab worshipped Baal, he was rejecting God's _____.

2. Ahab disobeyed God when he refused to kill _____.

3. Ahab wanted to buy Naboth's _____, but Naboth wouldn't sell it.

4. Two men lied, and said that Naboth had _____ God.

5. Jehoshaphat wanted to seek advice from _____ _____.

6. Ahab was killed by a _____ _____ shot into the air.

7. Jehoshaphat walked in the ways of his ancestor _____.

8. The prophet _____ told Jehoshaphat not to be afraid.

9. When Judah arrived at the battlefield, they saw only _____ _____.

D. JEHOSHAPHAT'S WISE JUDGES: Cross out all the I's, P's, and S's to discover
what Jehoshaphat told his wise judges.

FIESPARISTIHSPELIOSIRID
JISUPSIDGSECISPARSESPFIULILSPY

_____ _____ _____ _____   _____ _____ _____   _____ _____ _____ ____ AND

_____ _____ _____ _____ _____   _____ _____ _____ _____ _____ _____ _____ _____ _____ .

What three tasks were Jehoshaphat's judges told to do?

1. _____   2. _____

3. _____

E. JEHOSHAPHAT'S PRAYER: Unscramble the words and then use them to
complete Jehoshaphat's prayer.

"O LORD, _____ and _____ are in Your hand. If
            ROPEW   THIMG

_____ comes upon us,..._____ and _____ us....
      TAILAMCY   REAH   LEPH

We have no power to face this vast _____.... Our _____ are on You."
                                          MYRA   YESE

F. FIND OUT... What is a prophet?

A prophet is a person who speaks for God. The three different Hebrew words for a prophet
are translated into English as "prophet" or "seer."

1. How does a person become a prophet? (Jeremiah 14:14, NIV)

_____

2. How did the people know whether a prophet spoke God's words or lied?

(Deuteronomy 13:1-3) _____

(Deuteronomy 18:22) _____

Chapter 17

Elisha—God's Voice to Rulers & Ordinary People

LESSON SCOPE: 1 Kings 19:19–21
2 Kings 1–8

READ TO ME: 2 Kings 2, 5–7

THEME: The LORD God controls the destiny of rulers and ordinary people.

MEMORY VERSE:

"[The Most High] does according to His will in the army of heaven And among the inhabitants of the earth. No one can restrain His hand Or say to Him, 'What have you done?'" (Daniel 4:35b)

KEY FACTS: God's Sovereignty and Elisha's Ministry

God is sovereign over…	By God's power Elisha was able to…
Nature	Divide the Jordan River and heal the bad waters.
Ordinary People's Lives	Make the widow's oil fill up many jars.
Life and Death	Bring the Shunammite woman's son back to life.
Disease	Heal Naaman from leprosy.
Enemies and Nations	Know the battle plans of the king of Aram.
Disaster and Good Fortune	Prophesy the end of the Aramean siege.
Rulers	Prophesy the future actions of Hazael of Aram.
How big is God?	
God is **sovereign**.	God controls all things.
God is **omnipotent**.	God is all-powerful.
God is **omniscient**.	God knows all things.

MESSAGE FROM THE KING: The King says, "Don't fret and worry. I've got everything under control."

What do you worry about? Most of the things you worry about probably won't ever happen. Psalm 37:8 says, "Do not fret—it only causes harm." You can trust God because today, tomorrow, and forever are under His control.

Elisha—God's Voice to Rulers & Ordinary People

One minute the two prophets were walking side by side, chatting together. The next minute, a fiery chariot pulled by flaming horses swooped down from heaven and parted the men, just before a twirling, swirling whirlwind wrapped around one of them and swooshed him into the clouds.

Elisha stared heavenward at the spot where his teacher had vanished from sight. Elijah, the prophet of judgment, was gone, and Elisha, the prophet of mercy, received a double portion of Elijah's spirit. Elisha was now God's messenger to Israel and the neighboring nations. Picking up Elijah's discarded cloak, Elisha struck the Jordan River with it and passed through the divided water to the other side. This was the first of many miracles that Elisha would do to show God's mercy or to proclaim His absolute control over heaven and earth.

As God's prophet, Elisha walked from town to town. In Jericho, the men of the city said, "The water here is bad, and the crops won't grow. Can you help us?" Elisha asked for a new bowl filled with salt. He sprinkled the salt into the spring water, saying, "This is what the LORD says, 'I have healed this water.'" Instantly, the water was pure and healthy.

In another town, a poor widow begged him, "My husband is dead, and I have nothing but a little oil. If I don't pay my creditor, he will make my two sons his slaves." Elisha had compassion on her, and said, "Find as many jars as you can. Pour the oil into the jars, and keep pouring until all the jars are filled." She did as Elisha said, and one by one she filled jar after jar after jar. When all the jars were filled from her tiny supply of oil, she sold the oil and had plenty of money to provide for her sons.

A rich woman from Shunem showed hospitality to Elisha whenever he passed through her town. The woman grieved because she had no son. In gratitude for her kindness and to show God's power, Elisha promised that in a year

God would give her a son, and He did. Several years later, this son died. The woman immediately sent for Elisha. Arriving at her house, Elisha lay on top of the son once, and then again. The boy sneezed seven times and opened his eyes. The LORD had brought him back to life.

Naaman, a valiant commander in Ben-Hadad's army, had the dreadful disease of leprosy. A young Israelite slave girl in his household said, "God's servant, Elisha, could cure you." When Naaman told Ben-Hadad what the girl said, Ben-Hadad sent Naaman to the king of Israel. In panic, Israel's king tore his robe. "How can I cure leprosy?" he exclaimed. Hearing this, Elisha told the king to send Naaman to him.

When Naaman arrived at Elisha's house, Elisha sent a messenger to Naaman with the strangest instructions: He said, "Go wash seven times in the dirty Jordan River." Naaman was furious. He was an important man! Why couldn't Elisha talk to him in person? Aren't the rivers of Aram better than the Jordan River? What a ridiculous thing to ask him to do! Naaman left in a rage, but his servants gave him good advice. "If the prophet had given you some great thing to do, wouldn't you have done it? Why not do this simple thing?" So Naaman bathed seven times in the Jordan River, and immediately upon rising up the seventh time, his skin became perfectly healthy. Naaman praised God, saying, "Now I know that there is no God in the world except Israel's God."

Once again, Ben-Hadad, the king of Aram, fought against Israel. Yet each time he moved his army, Israel's king was aware of his plans and evaded his attack. Ben-Hadad called his officers together, and demanded, "There is a spy among us. Which one of you is telling Israel's king what our battle plans are?" One of the officers replied, "It's not us! It's the prophet Elisha!" for through the LORD's revelation, Elisha knew all about Ben-Hadad's military strategy.

In response, Ben-Hadad and his army marched to Dothan where Elisha was staying. In the morning, Elisha and his servant saw a mighty army of horses and chariots surrounding the city. "What shall we do?" the frightened servant exclaimed. "Don't be afraid," Elisha replied. "Those that are with us are more than those that are with them." Then he prayed, "LORD, open my servant's eyes so he can see." The LORD opened the servant's eyes, and in the hills he saw horses and chariots of fire—God's heavenly host—protecting the city.

As the Aramean army advanced toward the city, Elisha prayed, "Strike the army with blindness." Then Elisha led the blinded soldiers into the city of Samaria. When the LORD opened their eyes again, the enemy soldiers were standing in the middle of

Israel's capital city. Israel's king fed them and sent them back to their own country. For a time, no Arameans invaded Israel's territory.

The threat from the Arameans wasn't over, however. Ben-Hadad strengthened his army and planned for a grand siege of Samaria. Weeks and weeks passed with Ben-Hadad's men lying in wait outside the city walls. Inside, the people became desperate. Food and water became more and more scarce, until there was no food at all. The people were thirsty, hungry, and scared. The king of Israel tried to encourage his people, but was helpless to do anything. The king finally blamed the siege on Elisha and threatened his life.

In the presence of the city elders, Elisha answered the messenger from the king, "In twenty-four hours the siege will end, and flour and barley will sell for only a shekel."

> **Jesus in the OT**
> Elijah introduced the ministry of Elisha as John the Baptist introduced the ministry of Jesus. In what other ways was Elijah like John the Baptist and Elisha like Jesus?

The next day, a miracle happened. The Arameans had completely deserted their camp outside the city walls. At first the king thought it was a trick. Yet, sure enough, all the Aramean soldiers were gone, leaving behind their tents, horses, donkeys, clothing, and food. The people in the city plundered the camp. Food was cheap, and there was plenty for everyone. Elisha's words from God, as unbelievable as they had seemed, happened just as he predicted they would.

Later, the LORD sent Elisha to Damascus, capital of Aram. While Elisha was there, Ben-Hadad, king of Aram, became ill. When Hazael, one of Ben-Hadad's officers, asked Elisha what would happen to his king, Elisha stared Hazael straight in the eyes, and prophesied, "Ben-Hadad will recover, but then he will die. You will be king of Aram and do many wicked things." A day later, the king did recover, but Hazael smothered him with a thick cloth. Hazael then became king of Aram.

Six different kings of Israel reigned during Elisha's lifetime. In simple ways, such as healing a village's spring water, and in dramatic ways, such as rescuing besieged Samaria, Elisha demonstrated to ordinary people and great rulers that the LORD God was King. The sovereign God reigned supreme, and nothing could stop His hand of mercy or His rod of judgment.

Review Worksheets

A. MEMORY VERSE: "[The Most High] does according to His will in the

_____ of _____ And among the _____

of the _____. No one can restrain His _____ Or say to Him,

"_____?" (Daniel 4:35b)

B. KEY FACTS:

God's Sovereignty and Elisha's Life

How big is God?
Match the words with their definitions.

Sovereign   God **knows** all things.

Omnipotent   God **controls** all things.

Omniscient   God has **all power**.

How was God sovereign in these people's lives?

_____ Shunammite woman   1. Made her oil fill many jars.

_____ Naaman   2. Told him about Aram's war plans.

_____ Hazael   3. Made her son come back to life.

_____ Poor widow   4. Blinded his army's eyes.

_____ Ben-Hadad   5. Predicted he would be king.

_____ Elisha   6. Healed him of leprosy.

C. STORY FACTS: Fill in the blanks.

1. Elisha received a double portion of Elijah's _____.

2. Elisha used Elijah's _____ to divide the Jordan River.

3. The siege was over after the Arameans _____ their camp.

D. WHAT DO YOU REMEMBER? Fill in blanks in the spaces beside the sentences.

S __ __   Elisha raised the widow's _____ to life.

__ __ __ __ O __ __   Naaman had the disease of _____.

__ __ V __ __   Naaman washed _____ times in the river.

__ __ E __ __   A _____ chariot parted Elijah and Elisha.

__ __ __ R __ __ __ __ __   Elijah went to heaven in a _____.

__ E __ __ __   Elisha was the prophet of _____.

__ I __ __   Elisha said Hazael would be _____.

__ __ __ G __   Ben-Hadad laid _____ to Samaria.

__ __ __ N __ __ __ __ __   God struck the Aramean army with _____.

E. ELISHA AT DOTHAN: Elisha was not afraid of Ben-Hadad's army.

Why was Elisha not afraid? _____

_____

_____

Who was protecting Elisha and his servant? _____

_____

_____

F. FIND OUT...

Elijah went to heaven without dying. The Scripture tells us about one other person who went to heaven without dying first. Read Genesis 5:22–24 and Hebrews 11:5–6.

Who was this person? _____

What do these verses say about this person? _____

_____

Chapter 18 — Three Prophets of Judgment

LESSON SCOPE: Hosea 1–14
Amos 1–9
Jonah 1–4

READ TO ME: Hosea 11, Amos 3–4, Jonah 1–4

THEME: Through His prophets, the LORD God warns of judgment to come.

MEMORY VERSE:

"Those who cling to worthless idols forfeit the grace that could be theirs."
(Jonah 2:8, NIV)

KEY FACTS:

What is a prophet?

Definition: A prophet…
- is called by God.
- receives messages from God.
- speaks God's messages to kings and ordinary people.

Themes: Sin, Punishment, Repentance, and Forgiveness

Message:
- Worship only the LORD.
- Remember God's covenant.
- Sin brings punishment.
- Repentance brings God's mercy.

Test of a Prophet:
- His words must be true.
- His words must agree with God's law.

THINGS TO REMEMBER:

Idol = Anything we trust in rather than God; any desire or fear that controls our behavior.

MESSAGE FROM THE KING: The King says, "Listen to the words of my prophets."

The messages of God's prophets speak to you today, telling you that sin has consequences, the LORD will always love you, and salvation is a gift you can't earn.

Three Prophets of Judgment

Amos—Prophet of Justice

Amos was not a learned prophet, yet God called this herdsman and sycamore tree farmer from Judah to be His spokesman to Israel. From the rugged wilderness Judean village of Tekoa, where cries of jackals and the bleating of sheep echoed in rocky canyons, this stern man of God traveled northward to Israel to rebuke the self-righteous people of Israel for their greed, injustice, and idolatry.

The name Amos means "bearer of burdens." During the prosperous reign of Jeroboam II, the LORD sent Amos to bring the burden of judgment to God's people. The wealthy oppressed the poor, the merchants cheated their customers, and the leaders took bribes and did immoral things. The people were extravagantly religious, but they weren't devoted to the LORD. They worshipped the golden calves set up by Jeroboam I many years earlier.

Amos pronounced God's judgment on eight nations. He started with nations far away like Philistia, Phoenicia, and Aram. Judgment came closer to Israel when he spoke against Edom, Ammon, and Moab. After accusing Judah of rejecting God's law, Amos gave the longest sermon to Israel, threatening that not even the fastest or bravest warrior would escape God's judgment. These judgments had two things in common. Eight times Amos said the words "for three sins, even for four," meaning that God had been patient for a very long time. Amos used the symbol of fire to tell the people that terrible sin must bring terrible consequences. The theme verse in the book of Amos could be "let justice roll on like a river" (Amos 5:24a, NIV).

Amos warned that God would judge His people for injustice and idolatry, but that one day He would bless Israel again. Through Amos, His prophet of justice, God showed that He could speak through anyone, even a simple herdsman who was willing to serve the LORD faithfully.

Hosea—Prophet of the Broken Heart

During the years of Israel's prosperity, the people worshipped Baal and the golden calves. Hosea (whose name means "salvation") proclaimed the message of God's loving-kindness to His unfaithful people. Unlike stern Amos, Hosea spoke with tenderness and compassion. He said that Israel's love

> **Jesus in the OT**
> Hosea loved a woman who was unfaithful to him. The Lord Jesus loved you and died for you when you were unfaithful to Him.

for the LORD was like the morning mist that quickly vanished when the sun got hot, but God, in His love, would never let go or give up.

The LORD gave Hosea a strange command. He was to marry Gomer, a woman who would not love him faithfully, and even after she betrayed him, he was to forgive her and continue to be her husband. Gomer's unfaithfulness was a picture of Israel's unfaithfulness to the LORD. The names of his children, which meant "not my people" and "not loved," were to warn Israel that the God who made a covenant to be Israel's God and to love the Israelites forever was righteously angry about their idolatry and sin.

Because of Gomer's unfaithfulness to him and Israel's unfaithfulness to God, Hosea was the prophet with a broken heart. He urged the people, "Come, let us return to the LORD." Because of His love, God forgives repentant people and promises to make them fruitful like a green pine tree.

Jonah—Prophet of Salvation

Although many of the prophets didn't really want to be prophets, they obeyed God and spoke His words. (Being a prophet was a difficult job, and usually meant being hated by people and suffering hardship.) Unlike the other prophets, however, Jonah refused to obey God and took a ship in the other direction from where the LORD God wanted him to go.

The LORD told Jonah to go to Nineveh, the capital of Assyria, and preach judgment upon it for its wickedness. Because Jonah hated the Ninevites, he didn't want them to repent and be forgiven, so he took a ship to Tarshish. No one, though, can run away from God. The LORD sent a violent storm, and the ship going to Tarshish nearly sank in the raging waves. Realizing he was the cause of the storm, Jonah asked the sailors to throw him into the sea. They did, and God sent a great fish to swallow Jonah.

Inside the belly of the fish, Jonah repented of his stubbornness. He realized, "Salvation comes from the LORD." On the third day, the fish spit Jonah out onto the shore, and Jonah walked through the city of Nineveh, preaching a simple message to the Ninevites: "In forty days Nineveh will be destroyed." The LORD had saved Jonah from the fish, and then through Jonah's message, He saved the Ninevites from judgment.

Nineveh's repentance angered Jonah. He sat under a vine and pouted. When the vine died, Jonah was so depressed that he wanted to die. The LORD rebuked Jonah, saying, "You have more compassion for this vine than for all the people in Nineveh upon whom I had mercy."

Jonah, the prophet of salvation, learned two things. The first was that salvation is a gift from God, and no one can save himself. (Jonah could not save himself from the fish's belly). The second was that God gives salvation to those He chooses. (God gave salvation to the repentant Ninevites.)

THE MESSAGES OF THE PROPHETS

(Prophets who wrote books of the Old Testament)

Prophet	Description	Audience
Isaiah	Prophet of Comfort	Judah
Jeremiah	Prophet of Tears	Judah
Ezekiel	Prophet of Visions	Jews in exile
Daniel	Prophet of God's Sovereignty	Jews in exile
Hosea	Prophet of a Broken Heart	Israel
Joel	Prophet of God's Grace	Judah
Amos	Prophet of Justice	Israel
Obadiah	Prophet of Edom's Disaster	Edom
Jonah	Prophet of Salvation	Assyria
Micah	Prophet of Hope	Judah
Nahum	Prophet of God's Wrath	Assyria
Habakkuk	Prophet of Faith	Judah
Zephaniah	Prophet of Total Destruction	Judah
Haggai	Prophet of Encouragement	Jews returned from exile
Zechariah	Prophet of Future Glory	Jews returned from exile
Malachi	Prophet of Preparation	Jews returned from exile

Review Worksheets

A. MEMORY VERSE: "Those who cling to _____ _____

forfeit the _____ that could be theirs." (Jonah 2:8, NIV)

B. KEY FACTS:

What is a prophet?

A prophet must be _____ by God. Prophets tell people to

_____ only the LORD and to _____ God's covenant.

They remind people that sin brings _____, but repentance brings God's

_____.

Tests of the true prophet: His words must be _____, and his words must

_____.

Four themes of the prophets:

S _____   P _____   R _____   F _____

C. STORY FACTS: Cross out the **wrong** words.

1. During the days of Amos, the Israelites were (humble/unjust).

2. Amos came from the village of Tekoa in (Judah/Israel) and went to preach to the people in (Judah/Israel).

3. The name of the woman Hosea married was (Jezreel/Gomer).

4. Hosea said Israel's love for God was like (morning mist/rising smoke).

5. Inside the great fish, Jonah (was angry with God/repented of his sin).

6. When the vine died, Jonah wanted to (die/preach judgment to Nineveh).

7. The religious Israelites to whom Hosea spoke (were devoted to God/worshipped golden calves).

8. Being a prophet meant that most people (hated/respected) you.

Memory Page • Story Time • **Worksheets** • Quiz

D. HOW WELL DO YOU KNOW THE PROPHETS? Use the first letter of each

prophet's name and match the statements to the correct prophet.

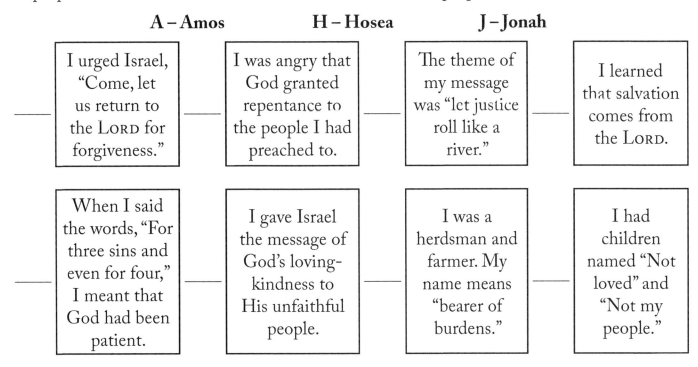

A – Amos   H – Hosea   J – Jonah

____ I urged Israel, "Come, let us return to the LORD for forgiveness."

____ I was angry that God granted repentance to the people I had preached to.

____ The theme of my message was "let justice roll like a river."

____ I learned that salvation comes from the LORD.

____ When I said the words, "For three sins and even for four," I meant that God had been patient.

____ I gave Israel the message of God's loving-kindness to His unfaithful people.

____ I was a herdsman and farmer. My name means "bearer of burdens."

____ I had children named "Not loved" and "Not my people."

E. WHAT WAS GOD'S MESSAGE?

Prophet of Justice: God would judge His people for _____

and _____, but He would one day _____ Israel again.

Prophet of a Broken Heart: Because of His _____, God

_____ repentant people and promises to make them _____.

Prophet of Salvation: Salvation is a _____ from God, and

God gives salvation to those He _____.

F. FIND OUT... Salvation is a gift from God.

Read Ephesians 2:8-9. What does Paul say about your salvation?

_____

_____

Salvation is God's gift to you. Discuss with your teacher what this means to you.

Chapter 18: Three Prophets of Judgment   113

Chapter 19 — Looking Backwards...Looking Ahead

LESSON SCOPE: 1 Kings 12–22
2 Kings 1–8, 2 Chronicles 10–21
Amos 1–9, Hosea 1–14, Jonah 1–4

READ TO ME: Psalms 93, 97, 99

"The LORD reigns, He is robed in majesty; and is armed with strength" (Psalm 93:1, NIV).

Sometimes it certainly didn't seem like the LORD was reigning in Israel and Judah! In the first eighty years after the kingdom split, all the kings of Israel and Judah, except Asa and Jehoshaphat, reigned as though they were the ultimate authority and the Great King didn't exist. They worshipped Baal or golden calves or they simply ignored the LORD. They killed each other for power and glory, and oppressed the people in their pursuit of wealth and fame. What was the LORD doing when this was happening?

In Unit III, you learned how the LORD is the God who reigns. He reigned even when wicked men ruled. He sent fire from heaven on Mt. Carmel and blindness upon Israel's enemies at Dothan. Through miracles, the King proved to great rulers and ordinary people that He was not absent. Through prophets' words of judgment, the King showed He was not silent.

In Unit IV, you will learn that the God who reigns is also the God who judges when His authority is disregarded and His warnings are ignored. None of Israel's kings worshipped God, and after 200 years, the LORD sent Assyria to destroy Israel. Some of Judah's kings were faithful to God's covenant, but eventually God judged Judah, too, and Babylon attacked and conquered Judah.

The LORD, the Mighty King, is also the Just Judge. The Keeper of the Kingdom protects the kingdom, even though man attempts to destroy it through wickedness and idolatry.

IMPORTANT THINGS TO KNOW:

Word	Meaning of the Word
Idol	Anything we trust in rather than God; any desire or fear that controls our behavior.
Prophet	Person called to speak for God.
Sovereign	Possesses supreme power; controls all things.
Omnipotent	Has all power.
Omniscient	Knows all things.

Review Worksheets

A. MEMORY VERSE REVIEW: Match the description to the memory verse words.

_____ Truth of God

_____ Worthless idols

_____ The LORD's purpose

_____ Army of heaven

_____ Creator

_____ Steps of a good man

_____ Creature

_____ Grace from God

_____ No one

1. What an idolater forfeits

2. What prevails

3. What is exchanged for a lie

4. Who is blessed forever

5. What an idolater clings to

6. Where God does His will

7. Who can restrain God's hand

8. What are ordered by the LORD

9. Who is served instead of God

B. WHAT WAS THE THEME OF UNIT III? Cross out all the A's, B's, and C's below and write the remaining letters in the blanks.

T A B H E C A G B C O B A C D A C W A C C H A O B R E A B A I C G A N C S

____ ____ ____   ____ ____ ____

____ ____ ____   ____ ____ ____ ____ ____ ____

C. WHO AM I? Beside each name identify what job the person had.

Write "K" for **king**, "P" for **prophet**, or "M" for **military officer**. If the person was a king or prophet in Judah, circle the name. If the person was a king or prophet in Israel, draw a square around the name.

_____ Ben-Hadad	_____ Rehoboam	_____ Elisha	_____ Ahab
_____ Abijah	_____ Jehoshaphat	_____ Naaman	_____ Omri
_____ Elijah	_____ Baasha	_____ Hosea	_____ Amos
_____ Jahaziel	_____ Jonah	_____ Micaiah	_____ Asa

Bonus: Which prophet was born in Judah but prophesied in Israel? _____

D. WHAT'S THE REASON? Circle the **correct** answer.

1. The people rebelled against Rehoboam because he wouldn't _____.

      make their burdens lighter   destroy the altars of Baal

2. Jeroboam was not a godly king because he _____.

      made the people pay high taxes   didn't worship God's way

3. Elijah challenged the prophets of Baal because he wanted people to _____.

      know that Israel's God was the true God   kill all Baal's prophets

4. The king of Israel knew all about Ben-Hadad's battle plans because _____.

      Ben-Hadad had a spy in his army   God revealed them to Elisha

5. Naaman didn't want to wash in the Jordan River because he thought _____.

      it was a ridiculous idea   the river was too deep

6. Jonah ran away to Tarshish because he didn't want the Ninevites to _____.

      capture and kill him   repent and be forgiven by God

7. Hosea's marriage to Gomer was a picture of God's _____.

      love toward His unfaithful people   anger at His people's sin

8. God stopped the rain when Ahab was king of Israel because _____.

      Ahab was worshipping Baal   Ahab put Elijah in prison

E. HOW GOOD IS YOUR MATH? Find the answer to the math problem. Then draw a line from the answer to the description that matches.

1. $175 + 315 - 40 =$ _____   Tribes in Israel.

2. $8 + 6 + 6 - 18 =$ _____   Days Nineveh had to repent.

3. $1,642 - 1,634 =$ _____   Prophets of Baal on Mt. Carmel.

4. $17 + 13 + 13 - 3 =$ _____   Altars on Mt. Carmel.

5. $651 - 423 - 218 =$ _____   Nations Amos warned.

F. HOW MUCH DO YOU REMEMBER?

Across:

2. The raven brought _____ to Elijah to eat every morning and evening.
4. Elisha put _____ in the water to make it pure and healthy.
5. Jeroboam built golden _____ to worship.
6. Elijah heard God's gentle whisper in a _____ at Mt. Horeb.
8. God healed Naaman of the disease of _____.
9. Elisha raised the Shunammite woman's _____.
12. At Dothan God struck the Aramean army with _____.
17. Ahab put the prophet Micaiah in _____.

Down:

1. Jehoshaphat removed the high _____ where people worshipped idols.
2. Elijah challenged the prophets of Baal on the top of _____.
3. Naaman washed in the Jordan River _____ times.
7. Two _____ were built on the top of Mt. Carmel.
10. After he washed in the river, Naaman had healthy _____.
11. Jeroboam didn't want his people to worship at the _____ in Jerusalem.
13. God said not to worship worthless _____.
14. When Jonah went to Tarshish, God sent a violent _____.
15. The widow filled all the _____ with oil.
16. The northern kingdom had _____ tribes.

Chapter 19: Looking Backwards...Looking Ahead

G. WHAT DID YOU LEARN ABOUT THE PROPHETS?
Three Prophets of Judgment

Amos	Hosea	Jonah
Prophet of	Prophet of	Prophet of

_____. _____. _____.

Spoke to the nation of   Spoke to the nation of   Spoke to the nation of

_____. _____. _____.

                             "Come, let us

"Let _____   _____   " _____
    flow like a river."   to the Lord."   comes from the Lord."

The message of the prophets:

1. _____ only the Lord.   2. _____ God's covenant.

3. _____ brings punishment.   4. _____ brings God's mercy.

H. KINGDOM AND COVENANT: Unscramble the words and fill in the blanks.

Israel: The first _____ kings of Israel worshipped _____
                      HIGET   DILOS

and _____ the covenant. They didn't remember that the Lord was the
         GROOFT

supreme _____ in Israel. **Judah:** Two of Judah's kings did evil in God's
              GINK

_____, but Asa and Jehoshaphat _____ the people back to
        YESE   UNDERT

the Lord. **Prophets:** Men who were _____ by God and warned people:
                                      LACDEL

" _____ and God will _____."
        PERTEN   VEFOGIR

UNIT IV

The Remnant Kingdom...The God Who Judges

Theme: The Keeper of the Kingdom brings judgment when people refuse to worship Him.

Why don't they learn? Oh, why don't these stubborn kings learn? As I, Tobias, the royal chronicler, write down with utmost accuracy the chronicles of the kings, I am furious! How can these kings continue to do evil in the eyes of the LORD? Don't they understand that God is holy? Don't they fear the judgment of the just Judge of all the earth?

The glorious kingdom that became the divided kingdom will now become the remnant kingdom. (Oh, by the way, the word "remnant" means, "the part left after the rest has been lost.") God who blesses His faithful people and reigns supreme is also the God who judges righteously.

Without exception, all of Israel's kings did evil in God's sight. Jeroboam, Israel's first king, made golden calves and set up his own worship centers, discouraging the people from worshipping at the LORD's temple in Jerusalem. Every king after him "did evil in the eyes of the LORD by following the sins of Jeroboam, son of Nebat." It only got worse when Ahab built a temple to Baal. In 722 BC, after 200 years of Israel's idolatry and wickedness, the LORD sent Assyria to conquer and destroy Israel. Then only the two tribes in Judah, the remnant, were left.

Several of Judah's kings followed in the footsteps of righteous Asa and Jehoshaphat, yet their devotion to the LORD was not wholehearted. They didn't destroy all idol worship from their nation, and they often strayed away from the LORD in their old age. By 586 BC, Judah's kings were lost in idolatry. The mighty kingdom of Babylon swept over Judah, destroying Jerusalem and taking God's people into captivity.

Behind the suffering and judgment, God still showed mercy. The nation would one day be restored, and the Messiah, promised by so many prophets, would someday come. God was still King, and He would not forget His covenant. There was still hope!

PSALM 99:1–5, 8–9, NIV

1. The LORD reigns,
      let the nations tremble;
      he sits enthroned between the cherubim,
      let the earth shake.
2. Great is the LORD in Zion;
      he is exalted over all the nations.
3. Let them praise your great and awesome name—
      he is holy.
4. The King is mighty, he loves justice—
      you have established equity,
      in Jacob you have done
      what is just and right.
5. Exalt the LORD our God
      and worship at his footstool;
      he is holy.

* * * * * * * *

8. O LORD our God,
      you answered them;
      you were to Israel a forgiving God,
      though you punished their misdeeds.
9. Exalt the LORD our God
      and worship at his holy mountain,
      for the LORD our God is holy.

Can't you just picture it? The Mighty God sits on a throne too majestic to describe with words. Winged cherubim surround Him, protecting His absolute holiness. His awesomeness is so great that the entire earth shakes in His presence as if in a massive earthquake! All nations are to praise His awesome name!

Have you ever shouted, "That's not fair!" when someone treated you unjustly? Our mighty God loves justice—He only does what is right and just. His throne sits on a solid foundation of righteousness and justice. Not one sin escapes His watchful eyes, and He judges all men fairly.

The LORD God is also a forgiving God. He doesn't hold a grudge. When you call to Him with a repentant heart, He hears you and forgives you quickly, even though sometimes He must punish you when you sin.

God is perfectly holy in everything He does. Thanking God for the just and righteous things He does is one way to fear God and worship Him.

Chapter 20 Israel Falls & Judah Remains

LESSON SCOPE: 2 Kings 17–19
2 Chronicles 21–28

READ TO ME: 2 Chronicles 22–26

THEME: The LORD God's patience with idolatry does not last indefinitely.

MEMORY VERSE:

"For the LORD knows the way of the righteous, But the way of the ungodly shall perish." (Psalm 1:6)

KEY FACTS: Kings and Chronicles

Some of the stories in the books of Kings and Chronicles are the same. How are these books different from each other?

	Kings	Chronicles
Time period	970 BC—From the reign of Solomon to the fall of Judah (stories about Israel and Judah).	1010 BC—From the reign of David to the fall of Judah (stories about Judah only).
Author	Unknown prophet.	Unknown priest.
Theme	God's blessing and judgment.	God's presence and holiness.
Content	1. History of both Israel and Judah.	1. History of Judah only.
	2. Personal stories of kings' lives.	2. No strictly personal stories.
	3. Stories of Elijah and Elisha.	3. Details about how the temple was built.
		4. Emphasis on worship.
		5. Genealogies.

MESSAGE FROM THE KING: The King says, "Remember My covenant."

"I will be your God and you will be My people"—those are the words of God's covenant. The LORD promises never to take His presence from you.

Israel Falls & Judah Remains

ISRAEL FALLS

Like a mighty army, God's judgment was coming! Israel's kings refused to obey the LORD as their King. Judgment was coming, but no one was paying attention. Wicked King Ahab died, and his son, Ahaziah, became king of Israel. Ahaziah fell from his upstairs room, but instead of praying to the LORD for healing, he prayed to Baal-Zebub, a Philistine idol. So, after ruling only two years, he died, and his brother, Joram, became king for twelve years.

One day, while Joram was still Israel's king, the LORD said to one of His prophets, "Go anoint Jehu to be king in Israel." Then, newly anointed Jehu went to visit Joram, who was recovering from battle wounds. Jehu pretended to come as a friend, but instead of bringing peace, he killed Joram. Jehu then went to Jezreel, where he killed wicked Queen Jezebel and everyone in Ahab's family, including Ahaziah. By doing this, Jehu fulfilled the LORD's prophecy that every last person in Ahab's house would perish, and Jehu ensured that there would be no one left to threaten his rule as king.

To rid Israel of idolatry, Jehu demolished Baal's temple and killed all its prophets. These actions destroyed Baal worship in Israel. Because of what Jehu did, the LORD promised him that the next four generations of his family would be king. However, even though Jehu was zealous against idolatry, he did not carefully obey God's law and didn't turn away from the sins of Jeroboam. Israel's next four kings (Jehoahaz, Jehoash, Jeroboam II, and Zechariah), who were Jehu's descendents, all failed to serve and worship the LORD.

Israel's last five kings (Shallum, Menahem, Pekahiah, Pekah, and Hoshea) were all wicked men who worshipped idols and lived violently. In 722 BC, Shalmaneser, king of Assyria, totally destroyed Israel. Those who were not killed were deported to Assyria. This dreadful judgment happened because Israel did not worship the LORD who had delivered them from Egypt. Over and over again, they forgot God's covenant and refused to turn from evil. All of Israel's kings, from Jeroboam I to Hoshea, were wicked men who refused to worship the LORD. In righteous anger, the LORD removed His presence from Israel. The king of Assyria brought people from other conquered nations to live in Israel, and Israel as a nation no longer existed. Now only Judah worshipped Yahweh, God of the covenant.

JUDAH REMAINS

While Joram was king in Israel, Jehoram reigned in Judah. Jehoram was evil and died after eight years as king. His son, Ahaziah, succeeded him, but Israel's king, Jehu, soon murdered him. After Jehu killed Ahaziah, Ahaziah's mother, Athaliah, made herself queen. To secure her position as ruler, she killed everyone in the royal family. (At least she thought she did. God was protecting His promise to David to have a descendent on Judah's throne. Remember, God is sovereign!) Secretly, Jehoiada, the high priest, captured baby Joash, son of Ahaziah (Athaliah's grandson) and hid him in the temple. For six years the child lived in the temple while Athaliah ruled. Then, with the help of loyal commanders, Jehoiada crowned Joash as king, and the people shouted, "Long live the king!" Joash was only seven years old. While the people were celebrating, the loyal commanders seized Athaliah and put her to death.

During his reign, Joash diligently repaired the temple, which was falling apart from neglect. The people renewed the covenant and promised to serve the Lord. While the high priest Jehoiada lived, Joash was faithful to the Lord, but Jehoiada grew old and died. Then Joash and the people abandoned the temple and worshipped Asherah poles and idols. When the priest, Zechariah, Jehoiada's son, warned Joash of his sin, Joash was furious and had Zechariah stoned to death. As a judgment, the Lord sent the Arameans to attack Judah. Joash was wounded and then killed by his own officials, who were still angry that Joash had killed Zechariah. Joash's son, Amaziah, followed him as king.

Amaziah did right in God's eyes in some ways, but not wholeheartedly. He never destroyed all the high places. After fighting against Edom, he brought back Edom's gods to Jerusalem. Conspirators chased him out of Jerusalem and killed him. At sixteen, his son, Uzziah, then became king.

At first Uzziah feared God, and God gave him military success and prosperity. However, pride led to his downfall. Arrogantly, he burned incense in the temple, something only a priest could do, and the Lord gave him leprosy. From that time, Uzziah lived alone, and his son, Jotham, ruled the nation. Jotham grew powerful, conquering the Ammonites and other enemies, and walked steadfastly in the ways of the Lord. After Jotham died, his son, Ahaz, ruled Judah. Ahaz shut the temple doors and only worshipped idols. He even sacrificed his own sons. The Lord's anger against him was very great.

Good kings and bad kings—back and forth it went. At least Judah had not totally forsaken the Lord.

Review Worksheets

A. MEMORY VERSE: "For the LORD knows the _____ of the

_____, But the way of the _____ shall _____."
(Psalm 1:6)

B. KEY FACTS: Kings and Chronicles

If the phrase describes the books of Kings, write "K" beside it. If the phrase describes the books of Chronicles, write "C" beside it.

_____ Stories about Elijah and Elisha   _____ Written by a priest

_____ History of Israel and Judah   _____ Have genealogies

_____ Theme of God's presence   _____ Written by a prophet

_____ Begin with Solomon's reign   _____ Theme of judgment

_____ Details about how the temple was built   _____ Personal stories of kings

C. STORY FACTS: Fill in the blanks.

1. Jehu killed _____ (king of Israel) and _____ (king of Judah).

2. Two wicked queens were _____ (Israel) and _____ (Judah).

3. _____ destroyed Baal worship in Israel by demolishing Baal's temple.

4. Joash was _____ years old when he became king.

5. Joash served the LORD as long as _____ lived.

6. _____ repaired the temple in Jerusalem.

7. Uzziah sinned when he _____ _____ in the temple

   because only a _____ could do that task.

8. The LORD responded to Uzziah's sin by giving him _____.

9. _____, king of _____, conquered Israel in 722 BC.

10. _____ shut the doors of the temple and worshipped only idols.

D. WHO AM I? Using the following names, fill in the blank that corresponds with the person the quote bubble describes: Uzziah, Jehoiada, Amaziah, Ahaziah, Zechariah, Athaliah, Jehu

I brought the gods of Edom to Jerusalem.

I hid baby Joash from wicked Queen Athaliah.

I was stoned because I warned Joash of his sin.

I destroyed Baal's temple but didn't serve the LORD myself.

_____ _____ _____ _____

I killed all the royal family so I could be ruler in Judah.

I sinned by offering incense in the temple. God punished me by giving me leprosy.

God punished me because I prayed to Baal-Zebub for healing instead of to God.

_____ _____ _____

E. WHY DID IT HAPPEN? In 722 BC, Israel was destroyed by Assyria. How could such a terrible thing happen?

1. The kings of Israel refused to obey God as their _____.

2. The people did not worship God as the One who had _____ them from

   _____.

3. The people forgot the _____ that God had made with them. God had

   said, "I will be _____ _____ and you will be

   _____ _____."

   so…the LORD removed His _____ from Israel.

F. FIND OUT… Read Exodus 34:10-14, NIV. How does the God of the covenant describe Himself and what He will do for Israel?

_____

_____

_____

chapter 21 Two Prophets & a Righteous King

LESSON SCOPE: 2 Kings 18–20
2 Chronicles 27–32
Isaiah 1–66, Micah 1–7

READ TO ME: 2 Chronicles 27–32

THEME: The LORD God warns of judgment and gives hope through the promise of a Messiah.

MEMORY VERSE:

"He has shown you, O man, what is good; And what does the LORD require of you But to do justly, To love mercy, And to walk humbly with your God?" (Micah 6:8)

KEY FACTS: Isaiah and the Messiah

What does Isaiah say about Jesus, the coming Messiah?

Isaiah	Scripture	Meaning
7:14	"His name [is] Immanuel."	Immanuel means "God with us."
9:6	"Unto us a child is born…His name will be called Wonderful Counselor, Mighty God, Everlasting Father, Prince of Peace."	Jesus is both God and man.
1:1-11	"Root of Jesse."	Jesus was born from David's line.
29:18	"…deaf shall hear…blind shall see."	Jesus opens ears and eyes, physically and spiritually.
40:11	"He will feed His flock like a shepherd."	Jesus is the Good Shepherd.
50:6	"I gave My back to those who struck Me."	Jesus humbly submitted to men's mistreatment of Him.
53:1-12	"He was oppressed…afflicted…they made His grave with the wicked."	Jesus suffered and died as an outlaw, taking the punishment for sin.

THINGS TO REMEMBER:

Messiah = Hebrew word meaning "the Anointed One."

MESSAGE FROM THE KING: The King says, "I sent the Messiah, just as I said I would." Every prophecy about the Messiah is fulfilled in Jesus Christ. He is your hope and your salvation.

Two Prophets & a Righteous King

"Holy, holy, holy is the Lord God Almighty." The voices of the seraphim were so thunderous that the doorposts of the temple shook, and smoke filled the temple. Overwhelmed by God's holiness and majesty, Isaiah cried out, "Woe is me! I am a sinful man!" Through this dramatic encounter, the Lord called Isaiah to be His prophet after King Uzziah died.

Isaiah had been a prophet for more than thirty years when Hezekiah succeeded his father Ahaz to Judah's throne. In contrast to his wicked father, Hezekiah trusted in the Lord. He smashed the sacred stones of idols, removed the high places, and destroyed the bronze serpent that Moses had made because people were worshipping it. He repaired the temple and consecrated all the temple furnishings to the Lord. Now people could worship at the temple. Everyone was amazed how quickly all this work was done.

However, trouble soon came to Judah. Assyria's fierce army threatened Jerusalem. Hezekiah listened to godly counsel and refused to send tribute to Assyria. (His father Ahaz had always secured Judah's safety by giving gold and silver to Assyria.). Hezekiah prepared Jerusalem for war, strengthening the walls of the city and constructing a water tunnel from the Gihon spring outside the city to the center of Jerusalem. He knew Jerusalem would need a good water supply if Assyria laid siege to the city.

All was well for a time, but soon Sennacherib, king of Assyria, threatened again. He had captured all the fortified cities of Judah so that Jerusalem sat alone, an island in Assyrian-controlled land. Once again, he demanded tribute from Hezekiah. This time, Hezekiah panicked and paid the tribute, giving Assyria all the silver from the temple and the gold from the temple doorposts. Hearing what Hezekiah had done, Isaiah confronted him. Hezekiah repented and decided that never again would he give in to Assyria's demands but instead would depend upon God's protection.

Hezekiah's tribute didn't satisfy Sennacherib. He mocked Hezekiah's courage and sent a letter to Jerusalem demanding surrender. "No god of any nation has delivered their people from my armies. Neither will your god protect you," Sennacherib boasted. "Give up and make a bargain with me."

Isaiah encouraged Hezekiah, saying, "Don't be afraid. The LORD will deliver Israel." Hezekiah took Sennacherib's threatening letter to the temple and spread it out before the LORD. "This king has insulted You, O LORD. Deliver us so all the nations will know that You alone are God."

Hezekiah then spoke to his people, saying, "Don't be afraid. There is a greater power with us. The LORD our God will fight our battles."

Without Judah shooting an arrow, the LORD gave Judah victory over the Assyrians. At night, while the people inside Jerusalem cowered in fear, the angel of the LORD moved silently amidst the Assyrian army surrounding the city. When the people awoke, they saw 185,000 dead bodies in the Assyrian camp. Defeated, Sennacherib returned to Nineveh. Years later, Sennacherib's sons murdered him while he was worshipping in the temple of his god.

After this great victory by God, grateful foreign nations sent rich gifts to Hezekiah, and he became a king of great wealth and honor.

Later that year, Hezekiah became very ill. Isaiah said to him, "Put your affairs in order, for you are going to die." Hezekiah begged God to let him live. God answered his prayer, restored him to health, and promised him fifteen more years to live. Hezekiah asked the LORD to give him a sign that this would happen, and the shadow outside his window miraculously went back ten steps.

To congratulate Hezekiah on his miraculous recovery, the king of Babylon sent envoys to Jerusalem. Hezekiah proudly showed these messengers from Babylon all the treasures of his kingdom. Upon hearing this, Isaiah was distressed. "Some day all these treasures will be taken away to Babylon, and your descendents will be their captives." Hezekiah's pride was one of several things that led to Judah's downfall.

Hezekiah repented of his pride and again became devoted to the LORD, and the LORD blessed Hezekiah. After reigning a total of twenty-nine years, Hezekiah died and his son, Manasseh, became king.

ISAIAH—PROPHET OF COMFORT

In the year that King Uzziah died, the LORD called Isaiah to be His prophet to the next three kings of Judah (Jotham, Ahaz, and Hezekiah). When the LORD asked Isaiah, "Whom should I send?" Isaiah replied, "Here I am, send me." He became the prophet of comfort.

The book of Isaiah has two parts. In chapters 1–39, Isaiah warned the people that their sin would bring judgment. Isaiah said that Judah's two main sins were its refusal to repent and its ritualistic worship that didn't come from the heart. Again and again, Isaiah uses the words "in that day" to talk about the judgment that would come.

In the second part, Isaiah gives comfort. The first words of Isaiah 40 are these: "Comfort, comfort my people" (NIV). Because of unconfessed sin, Judah would be conquered by Babylon and taken into exile. Yet there was hope because the LORD would bring His people back from captivity and send the Messiah. More than any other prophet, Isaiah prophesied what the Messiah would be like and what He would do. Even though God's people would suffer, the Messiah would bring about the Kingdom of God, a more glorious kingdom than His people had ever known.

MICAH—PROPHET OF HOPE

Early in Hezekiah's reign, Micah, the prophet of hope, prophesied that Jerusalem would be utterly destroyed. (He was the first prophet to predict Jerusalem's destruction.) As a result of Micah's words, Hezekiah began to fear God and seek His favor.

> **Jesus in the OT**
> In Matthew 2, the chief priests and teachers of the law found the answer to the wise men's question in the prophecy of Micah. The King would be born in Bethlehem.

Micah spoke out against corrupt leaders and lying prophets who rejected the LORD's authority as King and governed according to their own authority. These greedy leaders unjustly took money from the people, and proclaimed, "Peace," when there was no peace. But Micah had a message of hope! The Messiah was coming. He would be born in Bethlehem and would shepherd the people. He would bring security and peace to the land.

Micah wrote that the LORD was the light in the darkness (Micah 7:8), and the God who pardoned sin. He doesn't "stay angry forever, but delight[s] to show mercy" (Micah 7:18, NIV). Micah reminded the people that true religion is to "do justly, love mercy, and walk humbly with your God."

The book is divided into three sermons, each one beginning with the word "hear" or "listen." The LORD wants you to hear that He is the ultimate authority. He brings peace to the human heart and is the source of hope.

Review Worksheets

A. MEMORY VERSE: "He has shown you, O man, what is _____:

And what does the Lᴏʀᴅ require of you But to do _____, To love

_____, And to walk _____ with your God?" (Micah 6:8)

B. KEY FACTS: Isaiah and the Messiah

1. What does the word "Immanuel" mean? _____

2. Match the words on the left with the words on the right.

Wonderful	God
Prince of	Counselor
Everlasting	Peace
Mighty	Father

3. In what ways does Jesus open ears and eyes? _____ and _____

4. What do the words "Root of Jesse" mean?

_____

5. What does the word "Messiah" mean? _____

C. STORY FACTS: Number the story boxes in the **correct** order.

____ Hezekiah prayed for God's deliverance from the Assyrian army.	____ Hezekiah repaired the temple.	____ The angel of the Lᴏʀᴅ killed the Assyrian army.
____ Hezekiah prepared for war by building a water tunnel…and fortified the city walls.	____ Assyria captured all the cities of Judah except Jerusalem.	____ Sennacherib sent Hezekiah a threatening letter and his army surrounded the city of Jerusalem.

D. WHAT'S THE REASON? Circle the **correct** answer.

1. Hezekiah destroyed the bronze serpent because _____.

    Isaiah told him to destroy it   the people were worshipping it

2. When the shadow moved backwards, it was a sign that God would _____.

    make Hezekiah well   defeat Hezekiah's enemies

3. Hezekiah wanted deliverance from Assyria so all nations would know _____.

    the LORD was God alone   how strong Jerusalem was

4. Hezekiah told the people not to be afraid because there was _____.

    nothing to be afraid of   a greater power with them

5. In the temple, Isaiah cried out, "Woe is me," because he _____.

    had never seen seraphim before   knew he was very sinful

6. Micah wanted people to have hope because God does not _____.

    stay angry forever   punish every sin

7. Hezekiah first began to fear the LORD and seek God after _____.

    Micah prophesied   Isaiah confronted his sin

E. TWO MESSIANIC PROPHETS: Write "I" if the words describe the book of Isaiah and "M" if the words describe the book of Micah.

_____ The word "hear."   _____ Prophet of comfort.

_____ Spoke against lying prophets. _____ The words "in that day."

_____ Said, "Here I am, send me."   _____ Prophet of hope.

_____ Most Messianic prophecies.   _____ Said, "Walk humbly with God."

_____ Messiah's birth in Bethlehem. _____ First to predict Jerusalem's fall.

F. FIND OUT...Read Isaiah 6:1-8. What do seraphim look like? What do they do?

_____

_____

Chapter 22

Two Memorable Kings— Manasseh & Josiah

LESSON SCOPE: 2 Kings 21–23
2 Chronicles 33–35

READ TO ME: 2 Chronicles 33–35

THEME: The LORD God calls His unfaithful people to remember the covenant.

MEMORY VERSE:

"For assuredly, I say to you, till heaven and earth pass away, one jot or one tittle will by no means pass from the law till all is fulfilled." (Matthew 5:18)

KEY FACTS: Remember the Covenant

Let's review what Scripture says about God's covenant with His people.

Person	Content	Key Verse
Adam	Promise of a Savior to come.	"…he [Christ] will crush your head, and you [Satan] will strike his heel" (Genesis 3:15b, NIV).
Noah	Promise never to destroy the earth again with a flood.	"I establish my covenant with you: Never again will…there be a flood to destroy the earth" (Genesis 9:11, NIV).
Abraham	Promise of a son, land, and the blessing of being God's people.	"I will establish my covenant as an everlasting covenant…to be your God" (Genesis 17:7, NIV).
Moses	Promise of God's presence and giving of God's Law.	"I will take you as my own people, and I will be your God" (Exodus 6:7a, NIV).
David	Promise of an everlasting kingdom.	"Your throne will be established forever" (2 Samuel 7:16b, NIV).

THINGS TO REMEMBER:

Covenant = God's promise to be the God of His people forever.
God's covenant is **one covenant** unfolding through the years.

MESSAGE FROM THE KING:

The King says, "I will be your God, and you will be My child."

Unit IV: The Remnant Kingdom…The God Who Judges

Two Memorable Kings—Manasseh & Josiah

How would you like people to remember you? What would you like your legacy to be? (A **legacy** is something you leave behind for your descendents.) Two kings of Judah—Manasseh and Josiah—left memorable, but very different, legacies behind them.

Manasseh, son of Hezekiah and the longest reigning king, left a legacy of evil. He lead God's people astray into idolatry. The people became more wicked than the fickle Canaanites who had lived in the land centuries before them. Manasseh built altars to Baal and bowed down to the stars, worshipping God's creation, not God the Creator. Instead of seeking the LORD, he asked advice from mediums and practiced witchcraft. Like Ahaz, his grandfather, he even sacrificed his own sons on fiery altars.

The LORD God sent prophets to warn the people of their sin, but the example set by Manasseh and the hardness of their hearts led the Israelites deeper into sin and farther away from the LORD.

The prophecy against Judah was frightening: "I will bring such disaster on Jerusalem that everyone's ears will tingle. I will wipe out Jerusalem as one wipes out a dish and flips it upside down. Because of My anger against their sin, Judah will be plundered and looted by their foes."

After years and years of rejecting God's warnings, Manasseh was captured by Assyrian commanders and taken to Babylon. This distress caused Manasseh to call upon the LORD and repent of his sin. By His marvelous grace, the LORD accepted Manasseh's confession and, in time, brought Manasseh back to Jerusalem. When he returned, Manasseh rid Jerusalem of idols and foreign altars. He restored the altar of the LORD and urged all the people to serve the LORD. The influence of Manasseh's many years of evil, however, was too strong. The hearts of the Israelites were hardened against the LORD, and Manasseh's own son, Amon, ruled as an evil king. Despite Manasseh's heart change, the LORD determined that the prophecy regarding Jerusalem's destruction would not be changed.

Amon's son, Josiah, had a legacy of righteousness. At age sixteen, after reigning for eight years, Josiah turned to the LORD. He began a great reformation. All items of idol worship—Asherah poles, carved images, high places, and incense altars—were broken, crushed, or cut to pieces. He ordered that the temple be totally repaired, regardless of the expense.

One day, Hilkiah, the high priest, found the Book of the Law in the temple. When Josiah heard the words of the Law, he tore his robes, and lamented, "We haven't kept this law! Ask the LORD what we should do."

Hilkiah and men from the royal court went to Huldah, the prophetess, for counsel. She said, "Because the people have forsaken the LORD, all the curses of this book will come to pass. God will pour out His anger and bring disaster to Judah. But, because this king has been humble and seeks God from his heart, the disaster will not happen while he lives."

Josiah assembled all the people, from the greatest to the least, at the temple, and before them all, he read through the entire Book of the Covenant. Before the LORD and all the people, he renewed the covenant and promised to follow the LORD with all his heart and soul.

> **Jesus in the OT**
> Josiah had a legacy of righteousness, but it was not a perfect righteousness. Only Jesus has a legacy of perfect righteousness.

Josiah began a crusade to purge idolatry from Judah. He smashed all the high places, including the worship center at Bethel set up by Jeroboam. He did away with priests who offered sacrifices to the sun, moon, and stars, and rid the land of mediums and those who practiced witchcraft. No longer would people sacrifice their children or act immorally in God's temple.

Josiah announced to the people, "We are going to celebrate the Passover. Consecrate yourselves and prepare for the sacrifice, just as the LORD commanded through Moses." Josiah provided 30,000 sheep and goats and 3,000 cattle for the sacrifice. There was music and rejoicing. Since the days of Samuel, none of the kings had ever celebrated such a Passover.

After reigning for thirty-one years, Josiah was killed while fighting against Egypt. No king before or after Josiah followed the LORD so wholeheartedly. Yet, the people did not change from the heart. Though outwardly they worshipped the LORD, inwardly they still walked in the sinful way of Manasseh. So, the LORD said, "I will take My Presence from Judah as I did from Israel." Judgment was coming. It wouldn't be long now.

Review Worksheets

A. MEMORY VERSE: "For assuredly, I say to you, till _____ and

_____ pass away, one _____ or one _____

will by no means pass from the _____ till all is _____."
(Matthew 5:18)

B. KEY FACTS: Match the name to the covenant description.

Remember the Covenant

Adam	Promise of an everlasting kingdom
Noah	Promise of God's presence and giving of the Law
Abraham	Promise never to destroy the earth again with a flood
Moses	Promise of a Savior to come
David	Promise of a son, land, and blessing

Define covenant: _____

How many covenants did God make? _____

C. STORY FACTS: Circle the **correct** answer.

1. The longest reigning king of Judah was _____.

    Josiah   Hezekiah   Manasseh

2. After Josiah turned to the LORD, he began a reformation by _____.

    repairing the temple   writing songs of praise   crushing images

3. When Josiah heard the words from the Book of the Law, he _____.

    destroyed the book   read it to the people   lamented

4. Judgment was still coming to Judah because the people didn't _____.

    celebrate the Passover   change from the heart   offer sacrifices

5. The LORD said He'd take _____ from Judah because of their sin.

    His presence   His protection   His covenant

D. WHAT WAS THEIR LEGACY? Fill in the spaces.

1. ___ ___ ___ K ___ ___ ___
2. ___ ___ I ___
3. ___ ___ ___ ___ N ___ ___ ___
4. ___ ___ ___ G ___ ___
5. S ___ ___ ___ ___
6. ___ ___ ___ ___ ___ L
7. ___ E ___ ___ ___ ___ ___
8. ___ G ___ ___ ___
9. ___ A ___ ___ ___ ___ ___ ___ ___
10. C ___ ___ ___ ___ ___
11. ___ ___ ___ ___ ___ Y

Manasseh's Legacy:

2. Manasseh had an ____ legacy.
4. The prophecy made ears ____.
5. Manasseh worshipped the sun, moon, and ____.
7. Manasseh got advice from ____.
11. By worshipping idols, he led the people ____.

Josiah's Legacy:

1. ____ found the Book of the Law.
3. Josiah renewed the ____.
6. He destroyed the worship center at ____.
8. Josiah was killed in a battle with ____.
9. He celebrated the ____ for the first time since Samuel.
10. Huldah said the ____ in the Book of the Law would happen.

E. THE BOOK OF THE LAW

Hilkiah went to _____, the prophetess, for counsel. She said, "All the
            LAHDUH

_____ of this book will happen. _____ will come to Judah.
        RESCUS   STASIRED

Because the king is _____, the disaster won't happen while he _____."
                    BLUMEH   VILES

F. FIND OUT... Read the verses below. In the blanks write the names of the men who renewed the covenant.

Joshua 24:16-27 _____   2 Chronicles 23:15-19 _____

2 Chronicles 29:1-11 _____   2 Chronicles 34:29-34 _____

Chapter 23

GOD'S VOICES OF JUDGMENT TO THE NATIONS

LESSON SCOPE: Habakkuk 1–3
Zephaniah 1–3, Nahum 1–3
Joel 1–3, Obadiah 1

READ TO ME: Habakkuk, Nahum

THEME: The LORD God warns the nations of the judgment to come.

MEMORY VERSE:

"The LORD is slow to anger and great in power; the LORD will not leave the guilty unpunished." (Nahum 1:3a, NIV)

KEY FACTS: Getting to Know the Prophets

Prophet	Meaning	Audience	Things to Remember
Obadiah Prophet of Edom's Disaster	"Worshipper"	Edom	1. Edom betrayed Judah "in the day of their disaster." 2. God judged Edom because it gloated over Judah's destruction.
Nahum Prophet of God's Wrath	"Comforter"	Assyria	1. The LORD is jealous and takes vengeance. 2. God never changes—He always punishes the unrepentant.
Joel Prophet of God's Grace	"Jehovah is God"	Judah	1. "The day of the LORD…" 2. God restores the covenant and gives grace after His people repent. 3. The plague of locusts.
Habakkuk Prophet of Faith	"Embrace"	Judah	1. The just shall live by their faith. 2. Habakkuk's two questions: a. How long before God listens? b. Why does God use the wicked to judge His people?
Zephaniah Prophet of Total Destruction	"Jehovah hides"	Judah	1. "On that day…" 2. God's terrifying wrath is upon sinners, but His mercy is upon the repentant.

MESSAGE FROM THE KING: The King says, "Listen to my warning! Repent of your sin."

GOD's Voices of JUDgment to the Nations

"Blow the trumpet; sound the alarm. Let everyone tremble for the day of the Lord is coming!" God sent His prophets to warn Judah, Edom, and Assyria, but none of them listened, none of them repented, and all of them felt the force of God's just wrath. What did God's prophets say?

OBADIAH—THE PROPHET OF EDOM'S DISASTER

Though no one knows exactly who Obadiah was or when he lived, his grim message for Edom is very clear. The Edomites were descendents from Esau, the brother of Jacob. Esau and Jacob were born grappling with each other, and throughout their history, the Edomites and God's people feuded and battled one another. The Edomites had watched and done nothing when Judah's enemies invaded and ransacked them. Instead of helping Judah, they cheered on the attackers and made the lives of the people of Judah miserable. Obadiah's words, "in the day of their disaster," pointed out Edom's betrayal of Judah.

Obadiah predicted disaster to the people of Bozrah, the capital of Edom carved out of rocky cliffs. Those who lived "in the clefts of the rocks" were full of pride and boasted, "Who can bring us down to the ground?" God's judgment on Edom would be so severe that no one would survive.

Obadiah prophesied against Edom, but he wrote the book to Judah and has a message for you today. The prophet of Edom's disaster was declaring firmly and without any doubt that the Lord punishes those who harm His people, and He brings comfort to His people who are suffering judgment for their sins. Because of His covenant, God restores His people and utterly destroys their enemies. Obadiah's last words, "and the kingdom shall be the Lord's," remind you that God is the supreme King of the nations.

NAHUM—THE PROPHET OF GOD's WRATH

If a nation wants to survive, it must be built upon righteousness and truth. The Lord God could not permit Assyria, a nation of treachery and cruelty, to continue its evil legacy indefinitely. Jonah had preached repentance to Nineveh, and the city repented. Now a hundred years later, wickedness in Assyria was as horrific as it had been before Jonah's visit.

Unit IV: The Remnant Kingdom...The God Who Judges

Nahum's poetic prophecy has one theme: the downfall of Assyria. Nahum's first words describe the LORD as a jealous and avenging God. But isn't God a God of love? Absolutely! But a holy, loving God must be jealous when people or nations worship idols instead of worshipping Him, and He must take vengeance upon those who dishonor Him and oppress others. The LORD is slow to anger, but when He shows His wrath, the mountains shake, the hills melt, and the rocks shatter. He can't leave the guilty unpunished!

Nahum wrote to Judah about Assyria's downfall so that God's people would be comforted. Assyria had oppressed God's people for centuries, and now unrepentant Assyria would experience God's judgment. Nahum's prophecy was not a gleeful gloating over his enemy's punishment, but a righteous reaction against Assyria's disrespect of God's honor. Nahum, the prophet of God's wrath, reminded God's people that God is not patient with sin forever. The unchanging God avenges His holy name and punishes evil. The strongest enemies can't overthrow God's kingdom!

ZEPHANIAH—THE PROPHET OF TOTAL DESTRUCTION

"I will sweep away everything—men, animals, birds, and fish." Zephaniah's prophecy begins with descriptive words of God's total destruction of wicked Judah. His repeated words "on that day" gave grim pictures of what the great day of God's judgment would be like.

Zephaniah rebuked four groups of people: 1) officials who were like roaring lions, 2) rulers who were like devouring wolves, 3) prophets who were arrogant and deceitful, and 4) priests who profaned the temple. In his lament, he made four charges against God's people: 1) they didn't obey Him, 2) they didn't accept correction, 3) they didn't trust in the LORD, and 4) they didn't want to be close to the covenant God.

Zephaniah, a descendent of King Hezekiah, lived during Josiah's reign. Even though King Josiah had brought great religious reform to Judah, Zephaniah knew that the people did not serve God from their hearts. He said that God's judgment would be like a purifying fire, and from that fire a remnant would come who would trust in the name of the LORD. Zephaniah, the prophet of total destruction, ended his prophecy with the promise that the LORD would restore His people.

JOEL—THE PROPHET OF GOD'S GRACE

"A nation has invaded, powerful and unable to be numbered, with teeth like a lion." This "nation" that Joel wrote about was a swarm of locusts, millions and millions of hungry insects devouring every green plant.

Most scholars think Joel's locust swarm was an actual plague of insects that the LORD sent to Judah to bring about their repentance. Joel used the locust swarm as a picture of invading armies bringing judgment upon Judah on the "day of the LORD." Joel called the people to repentance and urged them to have broken hearts, not just torn garments, so that the gracious God might have pity and compassion on them. He promised that "everyone who calls on the name of the LORD will be saved."

Joel, the prophet of God's grace, encouraged the people with these words from the LORD: "I will repay you for the years the locusts have eaten." God's grace is so big that He gives back overwhelming blessing to His repentant people, and His people see His wonders and praise Him.

HABAKKUK—PROPHET OF FAITH

> **Jesus in the OT**
> The prophets said, "The kingdom will be the Lord's" and spoke of "the day of the Lord." Who is the Lord? Jesus Christ!

Why? Why? The prophet Habakkuk asked the LORD two "why" questions. In this conversation between Habakkuk and the LORD, Habakkuk asked, "LORD, why aren't You listening to me?" Habakkuk saw wickedness and violence everywhere in Judah, and it seemed that God was silent and uncaring. Then Habakkuk asked, "LORD, if You are righteous, why are You going to use Babylon, a cruel nation, to punish Your people?" Even though Habakkuk knew how wicked Judah was, it didn't seem right to him that ruthless Babylon should inflict such pain on God's people.

Habakkuk listened to God's answer. "I judge all nations by the same laws," the LORD answered. "Babylon will conquer Judah, but Babylon itself will one day be conquered by another nation." The LORD reminded Habakkuk that He is sovereign, absolutely righteous, and just. Habakkuk, the prophet of faith, confidently prayed, "Though the fig tree does not blossom, I will rejoice in the LORD." Habakkuk realized that "the just shall live by their faith." He learned that he could trust the LORD even in bad circumstances because the Sovereign LORD was his strength.

Review Worksheets

A. MEMORY VERSE: "The LORD is slow to _____ and great in

_____; the LORD will not leave the _____ unpunished."
(Nahum 1:3a, NIV)

B. KEY FACTS: Draw a line from the title to the name of the prophet. Then draw a line
from the meaning of the prophet's name to the prophet.

Getting To Know the Prophets

Title	Prophet	Meaning
Prophet of God's Wrath	Obadiah	"Embrace"
Prophet of Faith	Nahum	"Jehovah hides"
Prophet of Edom's Disaster	Joel	"Comforter"
Prophet of God's Grace	Habakkuk	"Jehovah is God"
Prophet of Total Destruction	Zephaniah	"Worshipper"

C. STORY FACTS: Fill in the blanks.

1. The Book of Obadiah is a prophecy against the nation of _____.

2. The theme of Nahum was the downfall of _____.

3. God judged Edom because Edom betrayed the nation of _____.

4. Nahum said that the LORD takes vengeance upon those who _____

   Him and _____ others.

5. Zephaniah was a descendent of King _____.

6. Zephaniah said God's judgment was like a _____ _____.

7. Zephaniah knew the people didn't serve God from their _____.

8. The LORD sent a plague of _____ to bring repentance to Judah.

9. In Habakkuk, the LORD said _____ would conquer Judah.

10. Habakkuk learned to trust God even in _____ _____.

D. WHO DID GOD SPEAK THROUGH? In the blanks, write the initial of the prophet.

O – Obadiah   N – Nahum   J – Joel   H – Habakkuk   Z – Zephaniah

_____ "I will sweep away everything."

_____ "I will repay you for the years the locusts have eaten."

_____ "And the kingdom shall be the LORD's."

_____ "A nation has invaded…with teeth like a lion."

_____ "The just will live by their faith."

_____ "The LORD is jealous and takes vengeance."

E. THE COVENANT AND GOD'S JUDGMENT

1. What did Nahum want to remind God's people about God?

_____

2. What charges did Zephaniah bring against God's people?

_____

_____

3. What was Zephaniah's promise to God's people? _____

4. When Joel called God's people to repentance, what did he urge them to have?

_____ _____, not just _____ _____

5. What two questions did Habakkuk ask the LORD?

1) _____

2) _____

6. What did Obadiah remind God's people? _____

F. FIND OUT… New Testament writers often quote Old Testament prophets.
   Which prophet is quoted in these New Testament verses?

Romans 10:13 _____   Romans 1:17 _____

Acts 2:16-21 _____   Galatians 3:11 _____

Chapter 24 Jeremiah Weeps & Judah Falls

LESSON SCOPE: 2 Kings 23–25
2 Chronicles 36, Jeremiah 1–52, Lamentations 1–5

READ TO ME: Jeremiah 1, 13, 36–41

THEME: The LORD God's patience and mercy do not last forever when hearts are rebellious and hard.

MEMORY VERSE:

"My people have committed two sins: They have forsaken me, the spring of living water, and have dug their own cisterns, broken cisterns that cannot hold water." (Jeremiah 2:13, NIV)

KEY FACTS: Jeremiah's Pictures

Broken Cisterns	Linen Belt	Potter's Wheel

Jeremiah 2:13 Only God can satisfy a person's spiritual thirst.	Jeremiah 13:1-11, (NIV) Trusting in idols makes people utterly useless.	Jeremiah 18 God shapes people and nations like potter's clay.
Clay Pot	**Baskets of Figs**	**Jeremiah's Field**

Jeremiah 19, (NIV) The ruin of Judah will be like a smashed clay pot.	Jeremiah 24 Good figs are exiles whom God will bring back. Bad figs are rulers whom God will destroy.	Jeremiah 32 God's people will one day buy houses and fields again in Judah.

MESSAGE FROM THE KING: The King says, "I am the only source of living water. Worship Me, and your spiritual thirst will be quenched."

Jeremiah Weeps & Judah Falls

"Jeremiah, listen to me. Before you were born, I set you apart to be My prophet," said the LORD. "Ah, Sovereign LORD, I don't know how to speak Your words. I'm only a child," lamented Jeremiah.

The LORD then gave Jeremiah two visions: 1) the branch of an almond tree to remind Jeremiah that the LORD's words would come true; and 2) a boiling pot tilted away from the north to tell Judah that judgment would come from the north. Reluctantly, Jeremiah became the LORD's prophet. For fifty years and through the reigns of five kings, Jeremiah faithfully proclaimed God's message of coming destruction, sympathy for His rebellious people, and hope of a return from exile.

From 609 BC, when King Josiah was killed in the battle with Egypt, to 586 BC when Jerusalem was totally destroyed, Judah was controlled by either Egypt or Babylon, and these nations put godless kings on the throne. Jehoahaz, Josiah's son, ruled only three months before Egypt's Pharaoh captured him, put in him chains, and carried him off to Egypt. Jehoahaz died in Egypt.

The Egyptians then put Jehoiakim, another son of Josiah, on Judah's throne. For eleven years, Jehoiakim did only evil in God's eyes. Finally, he betrayed Egypt and gave tribute money to Babylon, doing whatever Babylon told him to do. After he died, his son, Jehoiachin, was king briefly, but the Babylonians took him to Babylon and made Zedekiah, a third son of Josiah, king. Zedekiah was the last king of Judah. During Zedekiah's reign, the promised judgment upon Jerusalem finally happened.

JEREMIAH—THE PROPHET OF TEARS

During his fifty years as a prophet in Judah, Jeremiah suffered in many ways. He lived in a time of great wickedness and proclaimed a message that no one wanted to hear. He was rejected and persecuted by the kings and the people. Sometimes he wanted to run away from people. "Oh, that I had in the desert a lodging place for travelers, so that I might leave my people and go away from them" (Jeremiah 9:2, NIV). But no matter how difficult his task or how unpopular his message, he never stopped preaching God's truth, and he always had sympathy for his countrymen.

Jeremiah spoke out harshly against Judah's kings, who thought that wealth was more important than justice and mercy. He condemned the false prophets for their lies. Though he was not as harsh toward the people, Jeremiah preached that the people would go into exile because of their sin, stay in Babylon for seventy years, and then return home. No one liked what Jeremiah said. The people tried to kill him, but God protected him.

Jeremiah told his scribe, Baruch, to write God's words on a scroll and read the words at the temple. King Jehoiakim burned up the scroll and tried to arrest Jeremiah and Baruch, but the LORD kept them safe. Later, when Zedekiah was king, the king's officials got angry with Jeremiah and threw him into a deep cistern with a muddy bottom. They wanted to kill him, but they changed their minds and let Jeremiah out. During much of Zedekiah's reign, Jeremiah was imprisoned in the guard's courtyard. Despite all his troubles, Jeremiah always spoke God's truth.

> **Jesus in the OT**
>
> Jeremiah was rejected by the people and persecuted by kings. No one wanted to hear what he had to say. Like Jeremiah, people rejected what Jesus had to say, too. Both Jeremiah and Jesus cried tears of sorrow over the hardened hearts of God's people.

Jeremiah told Zedekiah to surrender to Babylon, but he refused. Eventually the Babylonian army surrounded Jerusalem and broke through the city walls. They captured Zedekiah, killed all his sons, and took him and almost all the people to Babylon. Only Jeremiah and a few people remained in Jerusalem. The Babylonians put Gedaliah in charge as governor, but a group of people assassinated Gedaliah because they believed he was a traitor. After this murder, the people in Jerusalem were terrified because they had killed the governor that Nebuchadnezzar had put over them. Against Jeremiah's urgings, these people fled to Egypt, dragging Jeremiah along with them. Years later, Jeremiah died in Egypt.

Jeremiah used many different word pictures to preach his important message of judgment. But his message also had hope. This hope had three parts: 1) the exiles would return home after seventy years, 2) the LORD would make a new covenant with His people, and 3) a Messiah would come.

While in Egypt, or shortly before, Jeremiah, the prophet of tears, wrote the book of Lamentations, a poetic description of Jerusalem burning from Babylon's torches. This man of tears loved his countrymen, his beloved Jerusalem, and, most of all, his LORD.

Review Worksheets

A. MEMORY VERSE: "My people have committed two _____: They have

_____ me, the spring of _____ _____, and

have dug their own _____, broken cisterns that cannot _____

_____." (Jeremiah 2:13, NIV)

B. KEY FACTS: Match the description to the word pictures.

Jeremiah's Pictures

_____ Broken cisterns	1. God shapes people and nations like clay.
_____ Ruined linen belt	2. Judah will be like a smashed pot.
_____ Potter's wheel	3. God's people will return and buy fields.
_____ Smashed clay pot	4. Only God satisfies spiritual thirst.
_____ Baskets of figs	5. Trusting in idols makes people useless.
_____ Field of crops	6. God will destroy wicked rulers of Judah.

C. STORY FACTS: Fill in the blanks.

1. When the LORD called Jeremiah to be a prophet, He gave him two visions:

   _____ and _____.

2. Jeremiah was a prophet for _____ years during the reign of _____ kings.

3. The last king of Judah was named _____.

4. When Jeremiah's scribe, _____, gave Jehoiakim the scroll with God's

   words, Jehoiakim _____ the scroll.

5. Two nations, _____ and _____ had control over Judah in
   the years after Josiah died.

6. Jeremiah wrote _____ to describe Jerusalem's destruction.

7. The Babylonians made _____ governor in Jerusalem.

8. Jeremiah said the exiles would return to Jerusalem after _____ years.

Unit IV: The Remnant Kingdom...The God Who Judges

D. WHAT'S WRONG WITH THIS? In the paragraph below, cross out the **wrong** words. Then write the **correct** words below, from left to right.

Before Jeremiah was grown up, the LORD set Jeremiah apart to be His prophet. Eagerly, Jeremiah became His prophet. Jeremiah lived in a time of great spiritual reform. Everyone wanted to hear Jeremiah's message. He was accepted and honored by kings and the people. Later, when Zedekiah was king, the king's officials threw Jeremiah into a deep hole. Zedekiah imprisoned Jeremiah in the guard's dungeon. After the destruction of Jerusalem, the people took Jeremiah to Babylon with them. Jeremiah often changed his message to the people. He said Assyria would conquer Jerusalem, but the exiles would return after forty years. He also said that the LORD would make a new song for His people and that some day in the future the Romans would come.

_____ _____ _____ _____

_____ _____ _____ _____

_____ _____ _____ _____

_____ _____

E. PUT THE KINGS OF JUDAH IN ORDER. Put these last five kings of Judah in chronological order.

_____ Jehoiakim _____ Zedekiah _____ Jehoahaz

_____ Josiah _____ Jehoiachin

F. FIND OUT... What does Lamentations say…

1. About God's faithfulness (3:22-23): _____

2. About calamities and good things (3:37-38): _____

3. What's the same about chapters 1, 2, 4, and 5 of Lamentations? (Hint: They all have a similar number of something.)

_____

Chapter 25 Looking Backwards...Looking Ahead

LESSON SCOPE: 2 Kings 1, 9–25, 2 Chronicles 21-36   **READ TO ME:** Psalm 68
Isaiah 1–66, Micah 1–7, Habakkuk 1–3, Zephaniah 1–3
Nahum 1–3, Joel 1–3, Obadiah 1, Jeremiah 1–52, Lamentations 1–5

Brilliant flames leapt high, turning the magnificent temple of the LORD into charred stone. Precious gems littered the streets, trampled under the feet of the battle-crazed Babylonian warriors. All around the city of Jerusalem, its mighty walls, built to protect God's people, lay in shambles. Not a home was left standing, and every building was being destroyed by fire. After six months under siege, the people were starving and despairing. Even being captured by the Babylonians seemed preferable to living in Jerusalem with no food, no houses, and no protection. With the temple gone, certainly God's presence must also be gone, the people believed.

It was sin that had brought this destruction upon Jerusalem. What was God's people's worst sin? Was it living in luxury and being greedy? Was it acting unjustly and having no mercy toward each other? Was it the lies that the false prophets told or the despicable sacrifices that the priests performed?

No, although the LORD hated all these sins, none of them was the worst. The worst sin was that the people had rejected God's covenant. The LORD had delivered them from Egypt, given them their own land, delivered them from their enemies for centuries, and blessed them in many ways. God's people had accepted all these blessings, but in return had spurned God's love by worshipping other gods and disobeying all His commands.

In Unit IV, you learned how the LORD judged first Israel and then Judah by sending vicious nations to conquer them. Many prophets tried to warn the people, but the people persisted in their rebellious ways. In Unit V, you will learn what life was like for the captives in Babylon. And, when the people returned home again after seventy years, you will also see once again that our LORD of the covenant is the God who makes promises and keeps them.

IMPORTANT THINGS TO KNOW:

Word	Meaning of the Word
Covenant	God's promise to be the God of His people forever.
Legacy	Something you leave behind for your descendants.
Messiah	Hebrew word meaning "the Anointed One."
Prophet	Person called to speak for God.
Remnant	The part left after the rest has been lost.

Review Worksheets

A. MEMORY VERSE REVIEW—WHAT DOESN'T FIT? Cross out the all the **wrong** words and write the **correct** words in the blanks. The number of blanks tells you how many words are wrong.

1. "For the LORD knows the path of the righteous, But the life of the wicked shall end." (Psalm 1:6)

   _____ _____ _____ _____

2. "For assuredly, I say to you, till day and night pass away, one word or one letter will by no means pass from the scripture till all is fulfilled." (Matthew 5:18)

   _____ _____ _____ _____ _____

3. "The LORD is quick to anger and great in justice; the LORD will not leave the wicked unpunished." (Nahum 1:3a, NIV)

   _____ _____ _____

B. MEMORY VERSE REVIEW: Answer the questions below.

1. What three things does the LORD require of you? (Micah 6:8). _____,

   _____, and _____.

2. What two sins did God's people commit? (Jeremiah 2:13, NIV).

   _____ and

   _____

C. WHAT'S THE THEME OF UNIT IV? Starting with the second letter from the far right, circle every other letter, moving from right to left. Then, beginning with the right-most circled letter, put the letters in the blanks below, starting with the far left blank.

S E E R G E D P U T J U O R H O W A D T O L G M E R H E T O

___ ___ ___   ___ ___ ___ ___ ___   ___ ___ ___ ___   ___ ___ ___ ___ ___

D. WHEN DID THE KINGS OF JUDAH REIGN? Number the kings and queens of
Judah in order from 1 to 20, starting with the king who ruled after King Solomon. Then circle all the kings who were faithful to the LORD for at least part of their reign.

_____ Asa   _____ Amaziah   _____ Josiah

_____ Zedekiah   _____ Jehoram   _____ Jehoshaphat

_____ Rehoboam   _____ Jehoiakim   _____ Jotham

_____ Abijah   _____ Ahaziah   _____ Joash

_____ Hezekiah   _____ Amon   _____ Jehoiachin

_____ Uzziah   _____ Manasseh   _____ Athaliah

_____ Ahaz   _____ Jehoahaz

E. WHAT HAPPENED NEXT? Put the story boxes in order.

_____ Athaliah tried to kill baby Joash.	_____ Rehoboam ruled Judah after Solomon died.	_____ Manasseh ruled and left a legacy of evil.
_____ Josiah read the Book of the Law to the people.	_____ Hezekiah trusted God when the Assyrians attacked.	_____ Godly King Asa removed idols and served God.
_____ Zedekiah ruled as the last king of Judah.	_____ Joash repaired the temple, and the people worshipped God.	_____ Uzziah got leprosy, and his son, Jotham, became king.

F. WHAT DO YOU REMEMBER ABOUT THE PROPHETS?

Match the prophet with the description that tells you something about him.

_____ Joel	1. Smashed pots and baskets of figs
_____ Amos	2. A large hungry fish
_____ Obadiah	3. A plague of locusts
_____ Habakkuk	4. Justice rolls on like a river
_____ Nahum	5. An unfaithful wife
_____ Jonah	6. Vision of seraphim praising God
_____ Jeremiah	7. Two difficult questions
_____ Micah	8. Judgment like a purifying fire
_____ Isaiah	9. Judgment against Edom
_____ Hosea	10. Desire to respect God's honor
_____ Zephaniah	11. The Messiah born in Bethlehem

G. WHAT IS THE DIFFERENCE BETWEEN KINGS AND CHRONICLES?

Kings	Chronicles
Written by a _____.	Written by a _____.
Theme: God's _____ and _____.	**Theme:** God's _____ and _____.
History of _____ and _____.	History of _____.
Content: Stories of _____ and _____.	**Content:** Lists of _____.

H. WHAT'S THE REASON? Circle the **correct** answer.

1. In the temple, Isaiah cried out, "Woe is me!" because he _____.

    had never seen seraphim before   knew he was very sinful

2. Judgment came to Judah because the people didn't _____.

    change from the heart   offer enough sacrifices

3. God judged Edom because it _____ when Judah was attacked.

    cheered on Judah's attackers   sent too small an army

4. The people of Judah didn't like Jeremiah because he _____.

    spoke harsh and unkind words   preached God's truth to them

5. Joel said that God sent the swarm of locusts so that the people would _____.

    remember their slavery in Egypt   repent of their sin

6. Huldah said judgment would not come during Josiah's life because _____.

    Josiah was humble and sought God   the people celebrated Passover

7. Jehoiada, the high priest, hid baby Joash in the temple because _____.

    the Assyrians were attacking   Athaliah wanted to kill him

I. WHAT DID THE PROPHETS SAY ABOUT GOD?

God judged His people because they didn't obey Him as their _____, and they
                                                          NIGK

forgot God's _____. Micah reminded the people that God does not stay
       VANECNTO

_____ forever and delights to show _____. Nahum said God
     GRANY   CYREM

was a _____ God when people worshipped idols. God is not
       LOJEASU

_____ with sin forever. Jeremiah said that God was the fountain of
    TAPINET

_____ water. Habakkuk learned that he could _____
    VIGLIN   STURT

God even in bad circumstances. Many prophets spoke about the _____
                                                          SISAMEH

who would come and bring salvation to His people.

UNIT V

The Exiled Nation...The God Who Restores

Theme: The Keeper of the Kingdom restores His people in His own time.

Oh, dear me, how sad! Judah has followed in the way of wicked Israel, and now both kingdoms have fallen into the hands of an enemy nation. Glorious Jerusalem, site of God's sacred temple and Solomon's magnificent palace, is a pile of rubble.

I, Tobias, the royal chronicler, have wept oceans of tears, and my tears have spilled, drop by drop, onto my scroll as I write with utmost accuracy the account of this tragedy. And yet, don't despair. God's story has not ended. Our God of the covenant, who makes promises and keeps them, will not forsake His people, even though they have forsaken Him.

Actually, our story in Unit V begins before the final fall of Jerusalem. Three times the Babylonians captured people from Jerusalem and carried them off to captivity in Babylon. Ezekiel and Daniel were part of the first two groups. Their mission from the LORD was to prophesy to and encourage the exiles. Daniel, captured as a young man, lived to be over 100 years old. His wisdom, leadership qualities, and ability to interpret dreams caught the attention of Nebuchadnezzar, the great Babylonian king, and Daniel's reputation and integrity earned him a position of official authority in the courts of Cyrus and Darius, Persian kings of renown.

God is so very wise. The Exile had its purpose. During those seventy long years, the LORD purged idolatry from His people and roused in them a longing for the Messiah. Although the human heart will always run after idols, the Jews as a people never again worshipped pagan idols after their return from exile. As He promised, the LORD brought the people back to their land. They had so many struggles, and their enemies made their lives very difficult, but the story of God's faithfulness is much more awesome than the story of their troubles is discouraging.

By the end of the Old Testament, God's people are once again settled in their own land. God's promises have been fulfilled, all but the most important promise: the promise of a Messiah! The Old Testament ends with hope because, someday, the King who has been keeping His kingdom safe will come in person. This King, the Messiah, is the hope for all of God's people!

PSALM 126, NIV, A Song of Ascents

1. When the LORD brought back the captives to Zion,
    we were like men who dreamed.
2. Our mouths were filled with laughter,
    our tongues with songs of joy.
    Then it was said among the nations,
    "The LORD has done great things for them."
3. The LORD has done great things for us,
    and we are filled with joy.
4. Restore our fortunes, O LORD,
    like streams in the Negev.
5. Those who sow in tears
    will reap with songs of joy.
6. He who goes out weeping,
    carrying seed to sow,
    will return with songs of joy,
    carrying sheaves with him.

Has anything ever happened to you that was so wonderful that you thought you were dreaming? It was just too good to be true! When the exiled Jews returned to Jerusalem, it felt like a dream to them.

This joyous event was so amazing that the heathen nations around them would exclaim, "Look what great things God has done for His people!" And, God's people, too, could say, "What great thing God has done for us!" They knew it was because of God's plan, not Cyrus's decree, that they could return home.

God's people prayed that the LORD would restore such plentiful prosperity to the land that it would be like the streams in the desert at flood season. The streambeds in the Negev desert are empty for much of the year. When the winter rains come, however, the dry streambeds fill up with rushing water that nourishes the arid soil and changes barren ground to pastureland. In Psalm 126, God's people were asking the LORD to bless their work and bring good things to them.

Turning ruined Jerusalem into a pleasant place to live would require sweat, toil, and tears. But one day, when the walls were rebuilt, the fields were rich with crops, and the land was filled with people, God's children again would sing praises to their God of the covenant for His blessings.

Chapter 26 God's Messenger to the Exiles

LESSON SCOPE: Ezekiel 1–48

READ TO ME: Ezekiel 1, Psalm 137

THEME: The LORD God speaks to His people in exile.

MEMORY VERSE:

"The soul who sins is the one who will die…. 'For I take no pleasure in the death of anyone,' declares the Sovereign LORD. 'Repent and live!'" (Ezekiel 18:20a, 32, NIV)

KEY FACTS: Ezekiel's Visions and Pictures

Reference	Vision or Picture	Meaning
1:1-28	Four living creatures; wheels with eyes	God is everywhere and sees everything.
1:1-28	Windstorm; fiery cloud; rainbow	Judgment is coming, but God also shows grace and mercy.
2:9–3:9	Sweet scroll eaten by Ezekiel	Ezekiel must speak the words that God gives him.
4:1-17	Ezekiel lying on his side for many days	People in Jerusalem will suffer greatly when God judges their sin.
5:1-17	Ezekiel's hair cut into three piles; small handful of hair	Only a small number of people will survive the judgment upon Jerusalem.
12:1-28	Ezekiel packing his bag and pretending to go on a long journey	The exile in Babylon will be like going on a journey and not returning for a long time.
16:1-63	The unfaithful wife	God will punish His people for their ungratefulness and unfaithfulness.
37:1-14	Dry bones come back to life	God will miraculously bring His people "back to life" as a nation.
37:15-28	Two sticks joined together as one stick	The northern and southern kingdoms will one day be united again.

MESSAGE FROM THE KING: The King says, "I will dwell in the hearts of My people."

The LORD departed from the temple in Jerusalem, but He will never depart from the hearts of those who fear Him.

God's Messenger to the Exiles

Out of the north came a mighty windstorm. It was like an immense cloud with flashing lightning ripping through it. Around the cloud was a brilliant fire, and in the fire were four strange creatures. Although these creatures looked like men, each one had four wings and four faces—the faces of a lion, an ox, a man, and an eagle. Underneath the creatures were sparkling, spinning wheels that intersected each other and were full of eyes. Over the heads of these creatures was a figure like that of a man sitting on a throne of sapphire. On top of everything was a radiant rainbow, spanning the expanse of heaven. When Ezekiel saw this vision, he fell facedown on the ground. He knew he was in the presence of the Lord's glory.

In 592 BC, after Ezekiel, a priest from Jerusalem, had been in exile for five years, God called him to be His prophet to the exiles. God's message to Ezekiel in this mysterious vision of living creatures and spinning wheels was this: "I am the Lord, the God who is present everywhere, even in Babylon, and who sees everything." The sovereign God was promising to bring judgment upon wicked Jerusalem, but in the midst of God's judgment was the rainbow of God's grace and mercy.

The Babylonians took captives from Jerusalem in three stages. In 605 BC, four years after Josiah was killed in battle with the Egyptians, Nebuchadnezzar's army captured the first group. Most of these people were of wealth and nobility. Daniel was among this group. In 598 BC, Jehoiakim rebelled against Babylon, and after Babylon besieged and conquered Jerusalem, a second group of people was captured. Ezekiel was with this second group. The final conquering of Jerusalem by Babylon was in 586 BC. This time, almost everyone in Jerusalem had either died from famine, was killed by the Babylonian army, or was taken to join the others in exile. Only a small handful of people, including Jeremiah, were left in the city.

Compared to conditions God's people had lived in previously, life in exile was not really that bad. In Babylon, the Jews built their own houses, started businesses, and worshipped the Lord the best they could without having a temple. Some Jews even took prominent positions in government. They were content—maybe too content—with their new lives. So, God's people had two very opposite problems. One problem was that they might not want to leave Babylon when the time of the exile was over. The other problem was that some people would not settle down in this foreign land and patiently wait for God's timing. They wanted to return to Jerusalem, and they wanted to do it soon!

God gave Ezekiel two messages. Before Jerusalem fell, Ezekiel insistently preached that Jerusalem would be destroyed. With their home city devastated, the Jews' hope of returning home quickly would not be realized. Yet, after Jerusalem fell, Ezekiel preached a message of hope. God was faithful to this promise and, after seventy years, the people would return and rebuild the land that the LORD had given them.

Ezekiel, the prophet of visions, saw many visions during his twenty-two years as a prophet. In another vision, Ezekiel saw pictures of crawling creatures and idols on the temple walls. In the secret chambers of the temple, the Jewish elders were doing detestable acts and offering incense to idols of animals. Beside the altar of the LORD, men were bowing down and worshipping the

> **Jesus in the OT**
> The rainbow of God's mercy covers the throne of God's judgment because Jesus the Savior paid the penalty for the sin of His people.

sun. The priests, the Jewish elders, and the ordinary people were worshipping idols and defiling the LORD's temple in many despicable ways. In a dramatic scene filled with winged cherubim and spinning wheels, the glory of the LORD departed from the temple and then from the city. This vision explained that God would judge Jerusalem because He hates sin!

In symbolic pictures, Ezekiel preached to the exiles about sin and unfaithfulness to God. Ezekiel emphasized that even though the LORD doesn't take pleasure in the death of the wicked, He holds each person responsible for his own actions. Anyone who sins and does not repent will die.

In another vision, the Spirit of the LORD took Ezekiel to a valley filled with dry bones. The LORD said, "Ezekiel, prophesy to these bones!" As Ezekiel prophesied, he heard a rattling sound. One by one, the bones came together. Then the LORD breathed life into the bones, and they became a vast army, filling the whole valley. "Just as I breathed life into these bones, I will breathe life into My people and bring them back to their land. Then you will know I am the LORD," declared the Sovereign God. Ezekiel's final vision was of a gleaming temple and city of the future, where the glory of God would live forever. In this city was divine perfection, purity of worship, and abundant blessing. The city's name was "The LORD is There," because God would dwell there with His people.

Review Worksheets

A. MEMORY VERSE: "The soul who _____ is the one who will

_____.... 'For I take no _____ in the _____

of anyone,' declares the Sovereign LORD. '_____ and _____!'"
(Ezekiel 18:20a, 32, NIV)

B. KEY FACTS: Match the word picture to its meaning.

Two sticks	Dry bones	Piles of hair	Unfaithful wife	Scroll eaten
A packed bag and a journey	Living creatures and spinning wheels		Windstorm and rainbow	Lying on his side

Ezekiel's Visions and Pictures

1. God will bring His people back to life as a nation. _____

2. God will unite the two kingdoms. _____

3. God will punish His unfaithful people. _____

4. Ezekiel must speak God's words to the people. _____

5. God is everywhere and sees everything. _____

6. The exile would last a long time. _____

7. The people in Jerusalem will suffer when judged. _____

8. God judges and shows mercy and grace. _____

9. Few people will survive the attack on Jerusalem. _____

C. STORY FACTS: Circle "T" if true and "F" if false.

1. Ezekiel was a priest before he became a prophet. T F

2. Exiles in Babylon were treated very badly by the Babylonians. T F

3. God's glory left the temple because of the people's great idolatry. T F

4. God holds each person responsible for his own sin. T F

5. The name of the city in Ezekiel's last vision was "The LORD lives." T F

6. When Ezekiel prophesied to the dry bones, they became alive. T F

D. THE STAGES OF CAPTIVITY: Fill in the blanks.

First	Second	Third
Year: _____.	Year: _____.	Year: _____.
Key people captured:	Key people captured:	Key people captured:
_____	_____.	_____
_____.		_____.
Event: Four years after	Event: After King	Event: After the final destruction of
_____	_____	
killed _____	rebelled against Babylon.	_____.
and defeated Judah.		

E. LIFE AS AN EXILE IN BABYLON: Answer the questions.

1. God's people in exile had two opposite problems. What were they?

   Some people _____

   Some people _____

2. God gave Ezekiel two messages for His people. What were they?

   Before Jerusalem's fall: _____

   After Jerusalem's fall: _____

F. FIND OUT... Read Ezekiel 1. Draw a picture below of what you think his vision looked like. Include as many details as you can.

chapter 27

Daniel & His Friends

LESSON SCOPE: Daniel 1–3   **READ TO ME:** Daniel 1–3

THEME: The LORD God cares for His people who fear Him and obey His commandments.

MEMORY VERSE:

"But the mercy of the LORD is from everlasting to everlasting On those who fear Him,… To such as keep His covenant, And to those who remember His commandments to do them." (Psalm 103:17a, 18)

KEY FACTS: The God of Miracles

God did most of His miracles during four periods in biblical history. Each time there was a reason why so many miracles happened.

Bible Books	Historical Period	Reason for Miracles
Exodus & Numbers	Days of Moses and the wilderness journey	God was establishing His nation, with which He had made a covenant.
1 & 2 Kings	Days of Elijah and Elisha	God was protecting His people from Baal worship.
Daniel	Years of exile in Babylon	God was protecting His people from the pagan influence of Babylon.
The Gospels & Acts	Days of Jesus and the early church	God was establishing His spiritual kingdom.

By miracles, God established His people and His kingdom.
By miracles, God protected His people from idolatry and pagan influences.

Miracles show God's **omnipotence** (all power) and **omniscience** (all knowledge).

MESSAGE FROM THE KING: The King says, "Fear me and be wise."

True wisdom begins with understanding what it means to fear the LORD. The LORD honors and exalts the one who shows honor to Him.

Daniel & His Friends

From outward appearances, the four young men—handsome, strong, and intelligent—looked like all the other youths in King Nebuchadnezzar's court. But one thing made these Jewish men different from all the others: They worshipped Yahweh, the God who kept His covenant with Judah.

In 605 BC, Nebuchadnezzar's army captured Daniel and his three friends (Hananiah, Mishael, and Azariah). Life in pagan Babylon brought many changes into their lives. First, they were given new names. Daniel became Belteshazzar, named after a Babylonian god, and his friends' names were changed to Shadrach, Meshach, and Abednego. They lived in royal luxury and were taught the Babylonian language and literature by the wisest teachers in the Babylonian empire. They were being trained to enter the service of the great Babylonian king, Nebuchadnezzar.

These four men determined that, even though they lived in a pagan land, they would not dishonor the LORD, the God of their ancestors. They refused to defile themselves with the royal food and wine given to them. Daniel pleaded with the court guard, "Please give us only vegetables and water for ten days. You will see that we will be as strong and healthy as the men who eat the king's fancy food." Reluctantly, the guard agreed to do this. At the end of ten days, the guard was surprised. Daniel and his friends looked stronger and healthier than the men who had eaten the king's food.

For three years, the four men studied, and God gave them wisdom and knowledge of all kinds of literature and learning. When they appeared before Nebuchadnezzar for their final test, they were ten times more knowledgeable in every subject than all the magicians and enchanters in the kingdom. Nebuchadnezzar gave them prominent positions in his government.

One night, Nebuchadnezzar had a disturbing dream. He called together all his wise men and astrologers, and demanded, "Tell me what I dreamed and what it means." Appalled, they said, "How can we interpret the dream unless you tell us first what the dream was? There is not a man on earth who can do this!" But the king didn't change his mind. If no one interpreted his dream, he intended to kill all of them, including Daniel and his friends.

God had given Daniel the ability to interpret dreams. Daniel urged his friends to pray that God would give him the answer to the king's demand. Then, after a night of seeking the LORD, Daniel received from God both the dream and the interpretation of it. That day, Daniel appeared before Nebuchadnezzar, and said, "No wise man can explain the mystery of your dream, O king, but the God in heaven who reveals mysteries has given me the answer."

Carefully, Daniel described a large statue made of gold, silver, bronze, iron, and baked clay. The statue represented great nations that would rule the world. The gold head of the statue represented Nebuchadnezzar. A rock, not made with human hands, smashed the giant statue. The meaning of the dream was that the God of heaven would set up a kingdom that would never be destroyed and that would destroy all these other great kingdoms.

> **Jesus in the OT**
> Who was that man in the furnace with Daniel's friends? It was Jesus!

Nebuchadnezzar fell on his face before Daniel and paid him honor, saying, "Surely your God is the God of gods and Lord of kings. He revealed this mystery to you." Daniel was made ruler over the province of Babylon and was put in charge of all the wise men. His friends were his assistants.

Nebuchadnezzar was an arrogant man. He built an image of gold, ninety feet high and nine feet wide, and set it up in the plain of Dura. He called all the important officials, as well as all the people, together, and said, "When the trumpet blows, bow down and worship the image."

Shadrach, Meshach, and Abednego refused to worship the image. They were determined to obey the Lord's first commandment: "Worship only the Lord." Nebuchadnezzar was furious that they did not bow down to the image. He ordered the three to be thrown into a fiery furnace, and as they were thrown in, they boldly said to the king, "Our God will rescue us, but even if He doesn't, we will not worship your image."

As Nebuchadnezzar looked, there in the middle of the furnace stood four, not three men, and the fourth man looked like an angel. The Lord was protecting the men and showing His power over Nebuchadnezzar! When the three came out of the furnace, their clothes were not burned and they didn't even smell like smoke. Nebuchadnezzar was totally baffled by this amazing event, but he praised God and promoted Shadrach, Meshach, and Abednego to higher positions of prominence.

Unit V: The Exiled Nation...The God Who Restores

Review Worksheets

A. MEMORY VERSE: "But the _____ of the LORD is from everlasting

to everlasting On those who _____ Him,…To such as keep His

_____, And to those who remember His _____ to do them."
(Psalm 103:17a,18)

B. KEY FACTS: The God of Miracles

1. Name the four historical periods in which God did many miracles:

_____   _____

_____   _____

2. God used miracles to protect His people from _____

and _____ .

3. In the days of Moses, God used miracles to establish His _____ .

In the New Testament God used miracles to establish His _____ .

4. Miracles show God's _____ (all power) and God's _____
(all knowledge).

C. STORY FACTS: Circle the **correct** answer.

1. Daniel and his friends were different from the other men because they _____.

    had a better education   worshipped the LORD

2. Daniel didn't want to eat the royal food because he didn't _____.

    want to defile himself   think the food was healthy

3. Before Daniel interpreted Nebuchadnezzar's dreams, he _____.

    asked his friends to pray   studied books about dreams

4. Nebuchadnezzar's dream meant that the LORD's kingdom would _____.

    be made of gold and silver   destroy other great kingdoms

D. WHO SAID THIS? Draw a line from the quote to who said it.

Daniel   Nebuchadnezzar   Daniel's Friends   Babylon's wise men

There is not a man on earth who can do what Nebuchadnezzar asks.

Even if God does not rescue us, we will not worship the image.

When the trumpet sounds, bow down to the image.

Please give us only vegetables and water to eat.

Surely your God is the God of gods. He has revealed this mystery to you.

The God in heaven who reveals mysteries has given me the answer.

E. NEBUCHADNEZZAR'S DREAM: Unscramble the words and write them in the blanks.

Nebuchadnezzar dreamed of a _____ made of gold, silver, _____,
USTEAT   NEBROZ

and _____ _____. The statue represented four _____.
KADBE   YCLA   TANNIOS

The _____ _____ represented Nebuchadnezzar. A rock not made
DLOG   ADEH

with human _____ smashed the statue. The meaning of the dream was that the
SHAND

God of _____ would set up a kingdom that would _____
VAHEEN   RENEV

be destroyed but would destroy other _____ kingdoms.
REGAT

F. FIND OUT... Read Genesis 41. Both Daniel and Joseph interpreted dreams for foreign kings. How are Daniel and Joseph alike? (Hint: See verses 15-16 and 39-40).

1. _____

_____

2. _____

_____

_____

Chapter 28

Daniel's Faith

LESSON SCOPE: Daniel 4–12

READ TO ME: Daniel 4–6

THEME: The LORD God answers His people when they pray to Him in faith.

MEMORY VERSE:

"But without faith it is impossible to please Him [God]." (Hebrews 11:6a)

KEY FACTS: What Faith Does

Scripture	Event	Faith means…
Daniel 1	Daniel not eating the king's food	Having courage to stand up for what's right when everyone else is doing what's wrong.
Daniel 2	Daniel interpreting Nebuchadnezzar's dream of the large statue	Praying for God's help and believing that God will answer according to His will.
Daniel 4-5	Nebuchadnezzar's dream of the large tree; the handwriting on the wall	Speaking the truth even when doing so may bring unpleasant consequences.
Daniel 6	Daniel in the lions' den	Obeying God's commands instead of man's rules.

What is faith?

Faith is believing that what God says is true and acting on this truth even before you see the results with your own eyes.

Remember…faith is a gift from God.

MESSAGE FROM THE KING: The King says, "Do you know who I am? If you're not sure who I am, how can you have faith in Me?"

Daniel's Faith

What is faith? Faith is believing certain facts to be true and then acting on those facts, even before you see the results with your own eyes. Daniel's faith in God was like this. He believed that God was sovereign and should be obeyed no matter what happened. He also knew that the LORD was good and that He would take care of His people when they trusted Him.

Daniel became an old man in exile. He served four mighty kings from three powerful nations, yet he always remained true to the LORD, because he knew that God was the supreme King of all empires.

Later in his life, King Nebuchadnezzar had another mysterious dream. This dream was about a magnificent tree with plump ripe fruit and branches that reached high into the sky. Birds made nests in its branches, and many animals found shelter under its leafy shade. Suddenly, a heavenly messenger cut down the tree, all except the stump, and scattered all the birds and animals away from the tree. The dream troubled the king, and he called on Daniel to interpret it.

At first, Daniel was puzzled by the dream, and then he was terrified. The dream was a picture of God's judgment upon Nebuchadnezzar for his pride. What would happen if Daniel told the king the true meaning of the dream? But Daniel acted in faith, and said, "You are the tree, O king. You are strong, and your greatness reaches to faraway places. But, a holy messenger will cut you down, just like this tree, and you will live like the wild animals. But the stump of the tree remains. You will get your kingdom back, but only after you acknowledge that God rules the world."

It happened just as Daniel said. A year later, Nebuchadnezzar was boasting about how great he was and God made the dream come true. Nebuchadnezzar became like an animal, eating grass and living as a wild beast in the fields. After seven years, God gave him back his sanity, and Nebuchadnezzar acknowledged that God was the exalted King of heaven.

Many years later, Belshazzar became king in Babylon. One day, he held a great banquet, and he and his guests drank wine from sacred goblets from Solomon's temple. Then, the fingers of a human hand appeared from nowhere and wrote in bold letters the words "MENE, MENE, TEKEL, UPHARSIN" on the walls of the palace. The king was so terrified that his knees knocked together, and he collapsed onto the floor.

Like Nebuchadnezzar before him, Belshazzar called upon Daniel to interpret this strange, frightening occurrence. Once again, Daniel had to relay God's message of judgment upon an arrogant, powerful king. Daniel boldly declared, "O king, you have not humbled yourself. You have defiled the Lord by drinking from the sacred goblets. Your kingdom will be taken from you and given to the Medes and the Persians." That very night, the Medes and Persians invaded the city and killed Belshazzar. Darius, the Mede, took over Belshazzar's kingdom.

Daniel had so distinguished himself as a wise man and capable administrator that Darius desired to set Daniel over the entire kingdom. The other officials hated Daniel. They wanted to find something in Daniel to make him unfit for the job, but they could find no fault in him. Finally, they devised a wicked plan. They convinced Darius to make a decree that no one could pray to any god or man except to him for the next thirty days. The punishment for breaking this decree was to be thrown into a den of lions.

When Daniel heard about this decree, he decided that he would obey God's law, not the rules of man. So, three times a day, as was his usual practice, Daniel continued to kneel down at his open window, facing Jerusalem, and pray to the Lord.

When Daniel was convicted of breaking the law, Darius regretted making this decree because he respected Daniel so much. But a law of the Medes and Persians could not be changed, not even by the king who made it. Just before Daniel was thrown into the lions' den, Darius said to Daniel, "May your God, whom you serve continually, rescue you from the lions."

For an entire night, Daniel stayed among the lions. Meanwhile, the king couldn't sleep. In the morning, the king eagerly ran to the lions' den. Daniel's voice shouted from the den, "O king, live forever! My God sent an angel to shut the lions' mouths." Daniel had no wound on him anywhere. He had trusted in the Lord, and God had protected him.

The Lord continued to prosper Daniel during the reign of Darius, king of the Medes, and Cyrus, king of Persia.

Review Worksheets

A. MEMORY VERSE: "But without _____ it is _____ to

_____ Him [God]." (Hebrews 11:6a)

B. KEY FACTS: What does faith mean?

1. Faith stands up for what's _____ when everyone else is doing what's

_____.

2. Faith prays and believes that _____ _____

_____ according to His will.

3. Faith speaks truth when speaking truth brings _____

_____.

4. Faith obeys _____ _____ instead of

_____ _____.

Faith is believing that _____.

Faith is acting on _____.

C. STORY FACTS: Unscramble the words on the right and use them to fill in the blanks.

1. What troubled Nebuchadnezzar? _____

2. What Nebuchadnezzar boasted that he was: _____

3. Number of years Nebuchadnezzar acted like an animal: _____

4. Number of days no one could pray: _____

5. Who shut the lions' mouths? _____

6. What Darius made that couldn't be changed: _____

7. What was left of the tree in the dream: _____

8. What wrote on the palace walls? _____

9. What officials could not find in Daniel: _____

VESNE

LATFU

RITTHY

SMEDRA

GIFRENS

GENLA

TEGAR

PUMST

CEDERE

D. DANIEL AND THE KINGS: Fill in the blanks.

Nebuchadnezzar	Belshazzar	Darius
King of	King of	King of
_____.	_____.	_____.
God judged him because he	God judged him because he	He made a decree that no one could
_____	_____	
_____	_____	_____
_____.	_____.	_____
		_____.
When God gave him back his sanity, he acknowledged	The very night that the handwriting appeared on the wall,	He regretted his decree and said to Daniel,
_____	_____	_____
_____	_____	_____
_____.	_____.	_____.

E. GOD'S PERFECT CARE: Cross out the **wrong** words.

1. God sent an angel to (kill the lions/shut the lions' mouths).

2. Darius wanted God to (rescue Daniel from the lions/judge him for his disobedience).

3. In the morning, Daniel had (no wound/only a scratch) from the lions.

4. The lions didn't hurt Daniel because he (was stronger than the lions/

   had faith and God protected him).

F. FIND OUT... Read Daniel 5:25-28. What is the meaning of the writing on the wall?

Mene: _____

Tekel: _____

Peres: _____

Chapter 29 The People Return—The Temple Is Rebuilt

LESSON SCOPE: Ezra 1–6, Haggai 1–2 **READ TO ME:** Ezra 3–4, 6
Zechariah 1–14

THEME: The Lord God keeps His promise and restores His people to their land.

MEMORY VERSE:

"They will call on My name, And I will answer them. I will say, 'This is My people'; And each one will say, 'The Lord is my God.'" (Zechariah 13:9b)

KEY FACTS: The People Return

Date	Event	Key People
605 BC	First group of people taken captive	Daniel
597 BC	Second group of people taken captive	Ezekiel
586 BC	Jerusalem falls to Babylon	Jeremiah
539 BC	Persia conquers Babylon	King Cyrus
538 BC	Cyrus's decree	King Cyrus
538-535 BC	First exiles return to Jerusalem	Zerubbabel, Jeshua
520-516 BC	Temple rebuilt	Haggai, Zechariah
487-465 BC	Esther saves her people	King Xerxes, Esther, Mordecai, Haman
458 BC	Ezra returns to Jerusalem	Ezra
445 BC	Nehemiah returns to Jerusalem	Nehemiah

MESSAGE FROM THE KING:

The King says, "If you love Me, be obedient, and I will bless you."

You cannot earn God's blessing by doing the right thing. But, the Lord is pleased when you obey Him, and He will bless you when you are faithful.

The People Return—The Temple Is Rebuilt

It was better than anyone could imagine! How wonderful it was! After seventy years in exile, the LORD moved the heart of Cyrus, king of Persia, to let God's people return home to Jerusalem. Cyrus decreed, "Any Jew may return to Judah. People living in the land should provide the Jews with gold, silver, livestock, and offerings."

Many Jews stayed in exile. It had become comfortable there, and they were content. But in 538 BC, under the leadership of Zerubbabel, their governor, and Jeshua, the priest, more than 40,000 Jews packed up their things and started home to Jerusalem. What a glorious thing! Who could imagine that this day would finally come? They longed to return to the land of their ancestors and to worship God as Moses's Law commanded. Along the journey, they praised the LORD who had kept His promises.

But, it was also worse than they had imagined. Jerusalem was a pile of rubble. The few people who had remained there lived in poverty, and enemies surrounded them. How sad it was!

Zerubbabel and Jeshua wouldn't let the people despair or be afraid. They urged them, "Let's rebuild the altar and offer sacrifices to our God." In the blackened ruins of the temple, they built an altar. Morning and evening they made sacrifices and celebrated their religious feasts. They began the difficult task of rebuilding the temple, and after the foundation was laid, they sang, "The LORD is good; His love endures forever." But rebuilding the temple was also sad. The older people remembered the splendor of Solomon's temple, and they knew this temple could never be that magnificent.

Three years after the Jews returned to Jerusalem, the Samaritans, enemies of the Jews, sent a letter to Artaxerxes, the new king of Persia, falsely accusing the Jews of being troublemakers. These enemies wanted the rebuilding of the temple to stop. King Artaxerxes believed the Samaritans' lies, and demanded that no more work on the temple be done. Afraid, the people stopped their work.

Fifteen years passed. People forgot about the temple. They built their houses, worked hard to survive, and tried to forget about the ugly temple ruins. Then two prophets—Haggai and Zechariah—spoke up, "How do you expect God to bless you when you refuse to rebuild the temple?"

The rebuilding began again. But, in 520 BC, enemies wrote another accusing letter, this time to the new Persian king, Darius, asking, "Did Cyrus really decree that this temple should be built in Jerusalem?" When King Darius received the letter, he researched the situation. Sure enough, deep in the archives of Babylon's treasury, Darius found Cyrus's original decree. He responded firmly, "I decree that the temple is to be built. Give the Jewish elders what expenses they need to accomplish the task. Let no man change this decree or he will be executed. Let this be done with diligence."

With great joy, the people rebuilt the temple and dedicated it to the LORD. Then they celebrated the Passover, remembering the LORD who had delivered them from Egypt and had kept all His promises.

HAGGAI—PROPHET OF ENCOURAGEMENT

Haggai was chosen by God to give one important message to God's people: "It's time to rebuild the temple." He aroused the people to action, saying, "How can God bless you when you build fancy houses for yourselves, but leave His house in ruins?"

Haggai, the prophet of encouragement, had a word of encouragement for every situation. When the people said, "It's not time," he said, "Start building right away, and the LORD will be with you." When the people complained, "This temple is not good enough," Haggai promised that the glory of this new temple would be greater than the last one. (This was because one day Jesus Christ would stand within its walls.) When the people despaired because of their poverty, Haggai declared that the LORD would bless them abundantly because of their faithfulness in building Him a house.

Haggai taught four important lessons: 1) there's a connection between being faithful to the LORD and receiving His blessings; 2) being discouraged is not a good enough reason to neglect doing what God tells you to do; 3) when a task must be done, you should do it right away; and 4) all words of encouragement or rebuke should be based upon what the LORD says. Over and over again, Haggai said the words, "This is what the LORD the Almighty says."

Haggai encouraged the people, and in four years the temple was built.

ZECHARIAH—THE PROPHET OF FUTURE GLORY

More than any other prophet, except possibly Isaiah, Zechariah prophesied about the Messiah and the glory that God has in store for His people. The book of Zechariah is the longest of the twelve minor prophets and the most difficult to understand because of the dramatic visions in the first six chapters and the three mysterious messages in the second part of the book.

Zechariah had visions about horns, dirty and clean clothes, chariots, a flying scroll, a woman in a basket, a man with a measuring line, a golden lampstand, and a man on a red horse. The visions were different pictures of how the LORD reacts when people repent of their sin.

> **Jesus in the OT**
> What is the future glory? It is a glorious day when Jesus will come and establish His Kingdom.

In this book, the LORD promised to destroy His people's enemies, take away their sin, and reign over the whole earth as King. He repeated His covenant promise to be the God of His people. The words of Zechariah, the prophet of future glory, have meaning for all of God's people—Jews and Gentiles—because they prophesy about the Messiah. He said that this Messiah, the LORD Jesus Christ, would set up His glorious kingdom and would dwell with His people forever. Zechariah spoke about two temples—the temple being rebuilt in Jerusalem and the temple in the hearts of God's people.

Review Worksheets

A. MEMORY VERSE: "They will call on My _____, And I will

_____ them. I will say, 'This is My _____'; And each one will

say, 'The _____ is my _____.'" (Zechariah 13:9b)

B. KEY FACTS: Write the name of the person that the statement describes.

The People Return

I decreed that God's people could return to Jerusalem.

I was taken into exile to Babylon in 605 BC.

I told the people to start building the temple right away.

_____

_____

_____

I was appointed governor over the people who returned to Jerusalem.

Zerubbabel and I led the first group of exiles back to Jerusalem.

I prophesied about the future glory of the temple.

_____

_____

_____

C. STORY FACTS: Fill in the blanks.

1. God moved the heart of _____ to let His people return home.

2. God's people were in exile for _____ years.

3. _____ and _____ led the first group back to Jerusalem.

4. The prophets _____ and _____ encouraged
   the people to rebuild the temple even when it was hard to do so.

5. For _____ years the people forgot about the temple and did nothing.

6. The older people were sad because they remembered the splendor of

   _____ _____.

7. Zechariah's visions were about God's reaction when people _____.

8. Haggai taught that there is a connection between being _____ and

   receiving God's _____.

Unit V: The Exiled Nation...The God Who Restores

D. TWO LETTERS FROM THE ENEMIES OF GOD'S PEOPLE:

First Letter (535 BC)

To: _____

The people in Jerusalem are

_____ .

Make them stop

_____ .

The king's response:

_____

_____ .

Second Letter (520 BC)

To: _____

Please answer our question:

Did Cyrus really _____

_____

_____ ?

The king's response:

_____

_____

_____ .

E. HAGGAI OR ZECHARIAH:

Put "H" if the sentence describes Haggai and "Z" if it describes Zechariah.

_____ The longest of the minor prophets.

_____ Connected the people's faithfulness to God's blessing.

_____ Said the words, "This is what the LORD says" over and over again.

_____ Saw visions of a flying scroll, a man on a red horse, and other strange things.

_____ Prophesied about the Messiah and future glory for God's people.

F. FIND OUT...

Read Psalm 126. How did the people feel when they returned to Jerusalem from exile?

_____

_____

_____

chapter 30

The Story of Esther

LESSON SCOPE: Esther 1–10   **READ TO ME:** Esther 1–10

THEME: The LORD God protects His people from the schemes of wicked men.

MEMORY VERSE:

"Who can speak and have it happen if the Lord has not decreed it? Is it not from the mouth of the Most High that both calamities and good things come?" (Lamentations 3:37-38, NIV)

KEY FACTS: Drama in Exile

When wicked men schemed to kill God's people, God protected them with an amazing plan.

Characters:	King Xerxes: King of Persia
	Esther: Jewish woman who became queen
	Haman: Persian official who tried to kill the Jews
	Mordecai: Esther's cousin
The Scene:	Palace of King Xerxes in the city of Susa in Persia
The Plot:	Haman plotted the destruction of the Jews, and the LORD saved His people through a strange set of events.
Esther's Role:	Esther risked her life to save her people, trusting that whether she lived or died, the LORD would honor her faithfulness.
God's Message:	God saved His people from destruction, according to the covenant He made with them, even though many of them were not faithful to Him.

THINGS TO REMEMBER:

Providence of God = God's holy, wise, and powerful preserving and governing of everything in His creation.

MESSAGE FROM THE KING: The King says, "My faithfulness to you does not depend upon your faithfulness to Me."

The Story of Esther

Danger and suspense, a plot with unexpected twists and turns, a surprise ending—these are what make Esther's story exciting. And, even though God is not mentioned by name in the story, it is obvious that He directed every scene of this intriguing drama.

The story begins at a lavish banquet in the grand palace of King Xerxes, the mighty king of Persia. (Persia had conquered Babylon, and the Jewish exiles were now living under Xerxes's rule.) For seven days, the king partied with his guests, eating, drinking, and acting rowdy. On the seventh day, when he was drunk, King Xerxes demanded that his wife, Queen Vashti, come and show her beauty to his guests.

Queen Vashti appropriately refused the king's request, and the king was furious. He was also embarrassed that his wife would not obey him. At the advice of his wise men, the king decreed that Vashti would no longer be queen. Afterwards, King Xerxes regretted his rash decision, but he couldn't change it. He began a search for a new queen. Women came from all over the kingdom, but no one pleased the king enough to be the queen.

Living in the king's fortified palace was a Jewish man named Mordecai. With him was his cousin named Hadassah (her Persian name was Esther) whom he had raised from a child. She was young and beautiful, and everyone who knew her loved her. Esther caught the eye of one of the king's officials, and after a time of preparation, Esther was taken before the king. Immediately, the king was attracted to her, more than to any other woman, and Esther, a Jewish girl, became the queen of Persia.

One day, while busy at his official business at the palace, Mordecai heard about a plot to kill the king. Quickly, he told Queen Esther about the conspiracy, and the two conspiring officials were caught and hanged.

After this, King Xerxes honored one of his royal officials, Haman, making him the highest of all the king's nobles. After that, Haman, an arrogant man, required that everyone kneel down and pay honor to him. All palace officials—except Mordecai—did as Haman asked. As a faithful worshipper of Yahweh, Mordecai refused to kneel down to any man.

Haman was so angry with Mordecai that he told the king that all Jews were dangerous people. The king believed this lie, and decreed that on a certain day all Jews, young and old, should be killed. When Mordecai heard of the decree, he persuaded Esther to help. He said to Esther, "Who knows whether you have become queen for such a time as this?"

Esther's task was risky. If she approached the king and he didn't hold out his scepter to her, she would be killed. She said, "I will go to the king, and if I perish, I perish." Bravely, she put on her royal robes and entered the king's inner chamber. Amazingly, he put out his scepter and welcomed her. Then she made a strange request, "Please, I want you and Haman to come to dinner with me." The king agreed.

Meanwhile, two other events happened. First, Haman built a gallows seventy-five feet high upon which to hang Mordecai. At the same time, the king learned that Mordecai had saved his life from the conspirators and decided to honor him. The next day, King Xerxes asked Haman, "What should be done to honor a man that the king delights in?" Haman, thinking the king wanted to honor him, described an elaborate celebration. "Good," said the king. "Go at once and do as you described for Mordecai."

What a surprise for Haman! He had to lead Mordecai through the city, proclaiming, "This is the man the king delights to honor!" But the situation got even worse for Haman. Esther had two special dinners for King Xerxes and Haman. At the second dinner, she told the king that she was Jewish and that Haman, the Jews' enemy, had plotted her people's destruction. In a rage, the king shouted, "Hang Haman on the gallows built for Mordecai!"

Haman was killed, but what about the decree? No decree written by a Persian king and sealed with his ring could ever be changed, even by the king. So, the king made a second decree: "Jews in every city can protect themselves and kill those who try to kill them." Just like the first decree, this decree went throughout all the land by couriers riding on royal horses.

God protected His people, even though many had not been faithful to Him. On the appointed day, the Jews defended themselves from all those who tried to kill them. Esther and Mordecai told the people to have a great feast, and from that time onward, this feast, called Purim, was celebrated every year to remember God's deliverance of the Jews from their enemies.

Review Worksheets

A. MEMORY VERSE: "Who can _____ and have it _____

if the Lord has not _____ it? Is it not from the mouth of the Most High that

both _____ and _____ _____ _____ come?"
(Lamentations 3:37-38, NIV)

B. KEY FACTS: Put the story boxes in order.

Drama in Exile

____ Haman was hanged on the gallows he made for Mordecai.	____ At a special dinner, Esther told King Xerxes about Haman's plot.	____ Haman persuaded King Xerxes to decree that the Jews should be killed.
____ King Xerxes chose Esther to be his new queen.	____ Mordecai saved the king's life by uncovering a conspiracy against him.	____ King Xerxes's second decree allowed the Jews to defend themselves.

C. STORY FACTS: Circle the **correct** answer.

1. King Xerxes wanted to honor Mordecai because he _____.

   had saved the king's life   was a competent official

2. Haman wanted to kill Mordecai because he wouldn't _____.

   kneel down to him   conspire against the king

3. The king made a second decree so that the Jews could _____.

   hang Haman on the gallows   defend themselves

4. Even though His people weren't faithful, God _____.

   saved them from destruction   gave them many blessings

D. WHAT DO YOU REMEMBER?

Across

4. The king made a _____ to kill the Jews.

5. Queen _____ was King Xerxes's first wife.

7. The king held out his ____ to Esther.

11. Haman wanted everyone to kneel down to him and pay _____ to him.

Down

1. The _____ decree of King Xerxes said the Jews could defend themselves.

2. _____ was a feast to celebrate God's deliverance.

3. The king's banquet lasted _____ days.

4. Esther invited the king to two _____.

6. _____ wanted to kill Mordecai.

8. The king regretted his decision but couldn't _____ it.

9. King Xerxes was king of _____.

10. _____ was a Jewish girl who became queen of Persia.

E. ESTHER'S RISKY JOB:
Going to the king was risky. What did Esther say before she visited the king? Starting with the first letter on the left, cross out every other letter and then put the remaining letters on the spaces below to find out.

F I S F R I M P I E T R U I L S A H T I H P C E V R W I F S O H

_____ ____ ____ _____ , ____ _____

F. FIND OUT...
Read Psalm 135:6, Psalm 145:17, and Proverbs 15:3. What do these verses say about God's providence (his care and governing of all the earth)?

Psalm 135:6 _____

Psalm 145:17, NIV _____

Proverbs 15:3 _____

Chapter 31 — The Story of Ezra & Nehemiah

LESSON SCOPE: Ezra 7–10
Nehemiah 1–13, Malachi 1–4

READ TO ME: Ezra 7–8
Nehemiah 1–2, 4–6, 8–9

THEME: The LORD God helps His people, who trust in Him.

MEMORY VERSE:

"You have kept your promise because you are righteous." (Nehemiah 9:8b, NIV)

KEY FACTS: Messages to God's People

Scripture	Event	God's Message
Ezra 1–6	God's people rebuilt the temple in Jerusalem.	God's desire: "I want My people to meet together and worship me."
Esther 1–10	God saved His people from being destroyed by Cyrus's decree.	God's promise: "I am the supreme King, and I will protect My people."
Ezra 7–10	God's people repented of marrying foreign wives and of being unfaithful to the LORD.	God's warning: "My people must be separate from everything that might make them unfaithful to Me."
Nehemiah 1–6	Nehemiah rebuilt Jerusalem's walls in spite of obstacles and troubles.	God's encouragement: "When My people trust Me, I help them do difficult things."
Nehemiah 7–13	Ezra read God's Word to the people, and they confessed their sins and renewed the covenant.	God's command: "Listen to My Word and confess your sin because I am your God."
Malachi 1–4	Malachi's task was to prepare God's people for the coming Messiah.	God's conclusion: "Because you are My people, and I love you, I am sending the Messiah. Be watchful and wait for His coming."

MESSAGE FROM THE KING: The King says, "I am your God and you are My people. I will always keep My promises to you."

The Story of Ezra & Nehemiah

As Erza looked at the people camped beside the canal, he realized something was wrong. That's it! There were no Levites in the assembly. How could God's people go to Jerusalem and worship the LORD if no Levites went with them? God spoke to Sherebiah, a capable Levite, and he, his sons, and his brothers as well as a number of other men agreed to go with the Jews from Babylon to Jerusalem.

It was a long and dangerous journey. "I am ashamed to ask the king for soldiers and horsemen to protect us," Ezra said to himself, "because I told the king that God's gracious hand was with us." So they traveled the whole way without military protection. The LORD was with them, and everyone arrived safely in Jerusalem.

Once in Jerusalem, Ezra became distressed. The remnant in Jerusalem had married sons and daughters of the pagan people around them. Even the leaders had been unfaithful to the LORD in their marriages. Ezra prayed, "O my God, I am so ashamed. Your people are all guilty and cannot stand in Your presence. The guilt of our sin has reached to the heavens. We have filled the land with impurity. But You, O LORD, are righteous and gracious." The people heard Ezra's prayer, and, with great sorrow and weeping, they confessed their sin. They separated themselves from the foreigners and made an oath to serve the LORD.

Meanwhile, Nehemiah, a cupbearer in King Artaxerxes's court, heard about Jerusalem's broken walls and burned gates, and he wept. He prayed, "O God who keeps the covenant, listen to my prayer and give me success by giving me the favor of the king." Nehemiah wanted permission from King Artaxerxes to go to Jerusalem and help rebuild Jerusalem's walls.

The king saw Nehemiah's sad face, and asked, "What do you want?" Quickly, Nehemiah prayed, then said, "If it pleases you, let me go to Jerusalem so I can rebuild the walls." The king agreed, and Nehemiah left.

Immediately upon his arrival in Jerusalem, Nehemiah set about repairing the city walls. It wasn't easy! There were so many troubles and obstacles. Three men (Sanballat, Tobiah, and Geshem) shouted out, "What are you feeble men doing? Your wall is so weak that if a fox walked on it, it would fall down!" In spite of constant ridicule, the people labored with all their strength. The task was so great that they often got discouraged, but eventually, the wall was halfway built.

However, the trouble wasn't over yet. Enemies threatened the Jews. Nehemiah prayed to the LORD, then posted guards around the city. The builders had to hold a sword in one hand and carry stones in the other. But God frustrated the scheming plots of the enemies, and the work on the wall continued.

Then the people complained, "We need to stop building the wall so we can harvest our crops. We must earn money to protect our fields and houses." Some Jewish landowners were burdening the people with unjust mortgages. Angry, Nehemiah reproached these unjust men. "What you are doing is not just! This must stop! You must fear the LORD and be fair." Amazingly, these landowners stopped charging the people unfair mortgages and gave back what they had taken unjustly.

Now the building project was going well, but Sanballat and his friends were not done causing trouble. Once again, they tried to frighten Nehemiah, saying, "Come down and talk with us." Nehemiah stubbornly replied, "I am doing a great work. I can't stop what I'm doing to talk with you." After Nehemiah refused four times, Sanballat sent a letter to him, accusing him of trying to be king in Jerusalem and conspiring against the Persian king. Nehemiah's response was to pray, saying, "LORD, strengthen my hands." The LORD answered Nehemiah's prayer. No obstacle was too big and no enemy too frightening to prevent Nehemiah and his workers from completing the repair of the city walls.

Finally the project was done. Strong walls surrounded the city and protected the Jews from their enemies. It was time to renew the covenant. Ezra, the priest, stood before the people and read the Book of the Law. When the people heard God's Word, they wept, because they were aware of their sin. Nehemiah encouraged the people, "Do not weep. Do not grieve, for the joy of the LORD is your strength." The people confessed their sin and worshipped the LORD.

In front of all the people, the Levites prayed, "Blessed be Your glorious name, O LORD. You alone are the LORD. You made the heavens and gave life to everything. You made promises to Abraham, and You have kept Your promises because You are righteous."

MALACHI—PROPHET OF PREPARATION

By the time Malachi wrote his short book, the LORD had spoken many times to His people. He had made promises and kept them. He had warned of judgment and reassured His people of His everlasting love. Over and over again, He had repeated the covenant promise: "I will be your God, and you will be My people." What was left to say?

Malachi's task was to prepare God's people for the coming Messiah. His message of preparation had three parts. First, the LORD reminded His people that He loved them ("I have loved Jacob, but Esau I have hated"). Both the Jews (the descendents of Jacob) and the Edomites (the descendents of Esau) had been defeated by enemies. After seventy years in exile, the LORD showed His love to the Jews by allowing them to return to their land and become a nation again. By contrast, after its fall, Edom was never again a nation.

> **Jesus in the OT**
> The LORD said, "Look for My messenger. He will announce the Messiah."

Second, God reminded His people that He is always holy and hates sin. Because God does not change, preparing for the Messiah meant repentance. God's people were sinning in their worship by bringing crippled or diseased animals for the sacrifices and by robbing God of tithes and offerings. They were also sinning by being unfaithful in their marriages and divorcing each other. The LORD does not bless His people when they stubbornly sin against Him and each other. But when His people obey Him, His blessings pour forth like a flooding river.

Third, the LORD told His people to look for His messenger, the prophet Elijah, who would precede the Messiah and announce the wonderful day of the LORD's coming.

The words of Malachi, the prophet of preparation, did not change everyone who heard them, only those who feared the LORD. What did the LORD Almighty say about those who fear Him? The covenant LORD promised, "They will be mine, on the day when I make up my treasured possession."

Review Worksheets

A. MEMORY VERSE: "You have kept your _____ because you are

_____." (Nehemiah 9:8b, NIV)

B. KEY FACTS:

God's Messages to His People

Draw a line from the message God gave His people to the book in which the message is found.

| "I am the supreme King, and I protect My people." | **Ezra** | "Listen to My Word and confess your sin because I am your God." |

| "When My people trust Me, I help them do difficult things." | **Esther** | |

| "I want My people to meet together and worship Me." | **Nehemiah** | "My people must be separate from everything that might make them unfaithful to Me." |

C. STORY FACTS: Circle the **correct** answer.

1. Levites went with Ezra to Jerusalem so that the people could _____.

     worship God   have skilled workers

2. The Jews had a safe journey to Jerusalem because _____.

     they had military protection   the LORD was with them

3. The first thing Nehemiah did when the king saw his sad face was ____.

     ask to go to Jerusalem   pray to the LORD

4. When the people repented of their sin, Nehemiah told them _____.

     to weep and grieve   that God's joy was their strength

D. NEHEMIAH'S TROUBLES: While building the city wall, Nehemiah had many troubles. Put the events in order.

_____ The people wanted to stop building the wall to harvest their crops.

_____ Sanballat and his friends ridiculed Nehemiah and the workers.

_____ Four times Sanballat asked Nehemiah to stop working and talk with him, and each time Nehemiah refused.

_____ Nehemiah gave the workers swords to hold while they worked.

_____ Sanballat accused Nehemiah of conspiring against the Persian king.

_____ Enemies threatened to attack the Jews working on the wall.

_____ The people completed the wall and renewed the covenant.

E. MALACHI'S MESSAGE OF PREPARATION: Fill in the blanks.

Message of Love

God showed His love to Judah because after seventy years the Jews could

1._____

_____.

2._____

_____.

Message of Repentance

God's people sinned in their

_____

and in their

_____

God never changes. He is always

_____ and

_____ sin.

Message of the Messiah

God said, "Look for My

_____."

The messenger will announce

_____

_____

_____.

F. FIND OUT... Nehemiah was a man of prayer and action. Read the verses below to find out what his prayer request was or what action he took after he prayed.

Nehemiah 2:4-5 (Action) _____

Nehemiah 4:7-9 (Action) _____

Nehemiah 6:8-9 (Request) _____

Chapter 32 Looking Backwards...Looking Ahead

LESSON SCOPE: Ezekiel 1–48, Daniel 1–12   **READ TO ME:** Isaiah 40
Ezra 1–10, Nehemiah 1–13, Esther 1–10
Haggai 1–2, Zechariah 1–14, Malachi 1–4

The Old Testament is over, and it's not exactly a happily-ever-after ending. There's no glorious kingdom with a rich and famous king. There's no mighty army or magnificent palace with a gold and ivory throne. There's not even a vast company of people who worship God with all their hearts.

Arising from the ruins of conquered Jerusalem is a poverty-stricken city populated by a remnant of God's people—people who are supposed to fear God but who continue to sin against Him. What happened to the LORD's promise to make a great nation from the descendents of Abraham? How can this sorry bunch of refugees bring blessing to the whole world?

The failures of God's people in the Old Testament show one thing—there has to be a new and better way. God has not failed. He is still the covenant LORD who says to His people, "I am your God, and you are My people." He is still the supreme King who keeps His kingdom secure. He is still the God who makes promises and keeps them. But something needs to change. For the next 400 years, the prophets will be silenced. Then the LORD will make a new covenant. A baby will be born in Bethlehem—a baby who is a King and Savior.

The story is not over. The LORD has gathered together the exiles in Jerusalem, but there are still others who must be gathered into His kingdom. So be patient. Be alert because the King Himself is coming!

"The Sovereign LORD declares—he who gathers the exiles of Israel:
'I will gather still others to them besides those already gathered.'"(Isaiah 56:8, NIV)

IMPORTANT THINGS TO KNOW:

Word	Meaning of the Word
Faith	Believing that what God says is true and acting on this truth even before you see the results with your own eyes; a gift from God.
Providence of God	God's holy, wise, and powerful preserving and governing of everything in His creation.

Review Worksheets

A. MEMORY VERSE REVIEW—UNSCRAMBLE THE VERSES: Put the words in the boxes in the **correct** order for these memory verse phrases.

Ezekiel 18:20a, NIV: _____

_____

soul die one The who the will is sins who

Nehemiah 9:8b, NIV: _____

_____

your righteous have are kept promise you You because

Hebrews 11:6a: _____

_____

without please faith to But impossible is Him it

B. MEMORY VERSE REVIEW—FILL IN THE BLANKS: Answer these questions.

1. What two things come from God's mouth? _____ and

    _____ _____ (Lamentations 3:37-38, NIV)

2. Upon whom does God show His everlasting mercy? To "those who

    _____ Him,...[and] To such as keep His _____, And...

    remember His _____ to do them." (Psalm 103:17a, 18)

3. What will God say to those who call on Him? (Zechariah 13:9b)

    _____

C. WHAT IS THE THEME OF UNIT V? Decode the message to find out. (Clue: Write down the letter that occurs in the alphabet after each letter written. For example, if the letter in the message is "S," write the letter "T" in the blank.)

S G D   F N C   V G N   Q D R S N Q D R

___ ___ ___   ___ ___ ___   ___ ___ ___   ___ ___ ___ ___ ___ ___ ___

D. WHO WERE THE PROPHETS OF THE EXILE? Identify which prophet the words describe by using the prophet's first initial.

E – Ezekiel   D – Daniel   H – Haggai   Z – Zechariah   M – Malachi

_____ Declared Elijah as God's messenger

_____ "It's time to rebuild the temple"

_____ Handwriting on the wall

_____ Prophet of preparation

_____ "I, the Lord, do not change"

_____ Prophet of encouragement

_____ Dramatic visions about repentance

_____ Prophet of God's sovereignty

_____ Prophet of future glory

_____ Last prophet

___ Vision of dry bones

_____ Prophet to exiles

_____ Two temples

_____ Interpreted king's dream

_____ Eating vegetables

_____ "Don't rob God"

_____ Prophet of visions

_____ Lion's den

E. WHAT DO YOU REMEMBER ABOUT THESE KINGS?

Unscramble the king's name and then draw a line from the king's name to the words that describe the king.

SADIUR   _____   His army was defeated by Egypt

HOSIJA   _____   Married the Jewish girl named Esther

REXXES   _____   Threw Daniel into a lions' den

SUCRY   _____   Decreed that the exiles could go home

F. WHAT HAPPENED NEXT? Starting at the star, draw a line connecting the events in chronological order, ending at the X.

Daniel is taken into exile.	Cyrus makes a decree and the first exiles return to Jerusalem.	Jeshua and Zerubbabel return to Jerusalem with the people.	The people finish the walls of Jerusalem.
Ezekiel is taken into exile.	Jerusalem is conquered by Babylon.	Haggai said, "It's time to build the temple."	Malachi prophesies that the Messiah will come.
The people finish rebuilding the temple.	Esther saves her people from Xerxes's decree of death.		Ezra and Nehemiah return to Jerusalem.

G. WHAT IS FAITH? What is God's providence?

1. Faith has two parts: believing _____

acting on _____

How did these people show their faith in the LORD?

_____ Daniel   1. Didn't bow down to the image

_____ Esther   2. Continued to pray to God every day

_____ Nehemiah   3. Invited King Xerxes to dinner

_____ Daniel's friends   4. Built the wall in spite of many troubles

2. God's providence is God's _____, _____, and

_____ preserving and governing of _____ in His creation.

H. WHAT'S THE REASON? Circle the **correct** answer.

1. Daniel and his friends didn't eat the king's food because they didn't _____.

        want to defile themselves   like the taste of foreign food

2. Daniel asked his friends to pray that God would give him _____.

        the dream's interpretation   power over all the wise men

3. Many Jews stayed in exile in Babylon because they were _____.

        afraid to make the long journey   too content to leave Babylon

4. Haman wanted to kill Mordecai because Mordecai _____.

        had saved the king's life   wouldn't bow down to him

5. Ezra was ashamed of the people in Jerusalem because they were _____.

        unfaithful in their marriages   complaining all the time

6. Nehemiah had a sad face when he went before the king because _____.

        Jerusalem had broken walls   the exiles had gone home

I. WHAT HAS HAPPENED AND WHAT IS TO COME?

What Has Happened	What Is To Come
God made a _____, saying, "I will be your God, and you will be My people." God was always _____ to keep His covenant, but His people were _____. Even when His people sinned, God was the Keeper of His _____.	Through the prophets, God promised that a _____ would come. God would send His _____, Elijah, to announce the wonderful day of the _____'s coming. God would make a _____ _____. Be alert because the _____ Himself is coming!

APPENDIX A

Memory Verse Summary

PSALM 23, A Psalm of David

1. The LORD is my shepherd;
   I shall not want.
2. He makes me to lie down in green pastures;
   He leads me beside the still waters.
3. He restores my soul;
   He leads me in the paths of righteousness
   For His name's sake.
4. Yea, though I walk through the valley of the shadow of death,
   I will fear no evil;
   For You are with me;
   Your rod and Your staff, they comfort me.
5. You prepare a table before me in the presence of my enemies;
   You anoint my head with oil;
   My cup runs over.
6. Surely goodness and mercy shall follow me
   All the days of my life;
   And I will dwell in the house of the LORD
   Forever.

Chapter 1: The Call of Samuel

"In those days there was no king in Israel; everyone did what was right in his own eyes." (Judges 21:25)

Chapter 2: Samuel—The Last Judge

"Remember the former things of old, For I am God, and there is no other; I am God, and there is none like Me." (Isaiah 46:9)

Chapter 3: Saul—The First King

"Behold, to obey is better than sacrifice, And to heed than the fat of rams."
(1 Samuel 15:22b)

Chapter 4: David Anointed as King

"For the LORD does not see as man sees; for man looks at the outward appearance, but the LORD looks at the heart." (1 Samuel 16:7b)

Chapter 5: David in Saul's Court

"In God I trust; I will not be afraid. What can mortal man do to me?" (Psalm 56:4b, NIV)

Chapter 6: David—The Fugitive

"For the word of the LORD is right, And all His work is done in truth. He loves righteousness and justice; The earth is full of the goodness of the LORD." (Psalm 33:4-5)

Unit II: The Glorious Kingdom...The God Who Blesses

PSALM 51:1-6, A Psalm of David

1. Have mercy upon me, O God,
   According to Your lovingkindness;
   According to the multitude of Your tender mercies,
   Blot out my transgressions.
2. Wash me thoroughly from my iniquity,
   And cleanse me from my sin.
3. For I acknowledge my transgressions,
   And my sin is always before me.
4. Against You, You only, have I sinned,
   And done this evil in Your sight—
   That You may be found just when You speak,
   And blameless when You judge.
5. Behold, I was brought forth in iniquity,
   And in sin my mother conceived me.
6. Behold, You desire truth in the inward parts,
   And in the hidden part You will make me to know wisdom.

Chapter 8: The Covenant with David

"I have made a covenant with My chosen, I have sworn to My servant David: 'Your seed I will establish forever, And build up your throne to all generations.'" (Psalm 89:3-4)

Chapter 9: David's Kindness & David's Sin

"Blessed is he whose transgression is forgiven, Whose sin is covered." (Psalm 32:1)

Chapter 10: Troubles in the Kingdom

"But you, O Lord, are a shield for me, My glory and the One who lifts up my head… I lay down and slept; I awoke, for the Lord sustained me." (Psalm 3:3, 5)

Chapter 11: The Wisdom of Solomon

"The fear of the Lord is the beginning of wisdom, And the knowledge of the Holy One is understanding." (Proverbs 9:10)

Chapter 12: The Reign of Solomon

"Praise be to the Lord who has given rest to his people Israel just as he promised. Not one word has failed of all the good promises he gave through his servant Moses." (1 Kings 8:56, NIV)

Unit III: The Divided Kingdom…The God Who Reigns

PSALM 121, A Song of Ascents

1. I will lift up my eyes to the hills—
    From whence comes my help?
2. My help comes from the Lord,
    Who made heaven and earth.
3. He will not allow your foot to be moved;
    He who keeps you will not slumber.
4. Behold, He who keeps Israel
    Shall neither slumber nor sleep.
5. The Lord is your keeper;
    The Lord is your shade at your right hand.
6. The sun shall not strike you by day,
    Nor the moon by night.
7. The Lord shall preserve you from all evil;
    He shall preserve your soul.
8. The Lord shall preserve your going out and your coming in
    From this time forth, and even forevermore.

Chapter 14: A Nation Divided

"[They] exchanged the truth of God for the lie, and worshiped and served the creature rather than the Creator, who is blessed forever. Amen." (Romans 1:25)

Chapter 15: Elijah—God's Voice of Judgment to a Wicked King

"The steps of a good man are ordered by the LORD, And He delights in his way. Though he fall, he shall not be utterly cast down; For the LORD upholds him with His hand." (Psalm 37:23-24)

Chapter 16: Ahab & Jehoshaphat—Two Very Different Kings

"Many are the plans in a man's heart, but it is the LORD's purpose that prevails." (Proverbs 19:21, NIV)

Chapter 17: Elisha—God's Voice to Rulers & Ordinary People

"[The Most High] does according to His will in the army of heaven And among the inhabitants of the earth. No one can restrain His hand Or say to Him, 'What have you done?'" (Daniel 4:35b)

Chapter 18: Three Prophets of Judgment

"Those who cling to worthless idols forfeit the grace that could be theirs." (Jonah 2:8, NIV)

Unit IV: The Remnant Kingdom...The God Who Judges

PSALM 99:1-5, 8-9, NIV

1. The LORD reigns,
      let the nations tremble;
      he sits enthroned between the cherubim,
      let the earth shake.

2. Great is the LORD in Zion;
      he is exalted over all the nations.

3. Let them praise your great and awesome name—
      he is holy.

4. The King is mighty, he loves justice—
      you have established equity,
      in Jacob you have done
      what is just and right.

5. Exalt the LORD our God
      and worship at his footstool;
      he is holy.

      * * * * *

8. O Lord our God,
   you answered them;
   you were to Israel a forgiving God,
   though you punished their misdeeds.

9. Exalt the Lord our God
   and worship at his holy mountain,
   for the Lord our God is holy.

Chapter 20: Israel Falls & Judah Remains

"For the Lord knows the way of the righteous, But the way of the ungodly shall perish." (Psalm 1:6)

Chapter 21: Two Prophets & a Righteous King

"He has shown you, O man, what is good; And what does the Lord require of you But to do justly, To love mercy, And to walk humbly with your God?" (Micah 6:8)

Chapter 22: Two Memorable Kings—Manasseh & Josiah

"For assuredly, I say to you, till heaven and earth pass away, one jot or one tittle will by no means pass from the law till all is fulfilled." (Matthew 5:18)

Chapter 23: God's Voices of Judgment to the Nations

"The Lord is slow to anger and great in power; the Lord will not leave the guilty unpunished." (Nahum 1:3a, NIV)

Chapter 24: Jeremiah Weeps & Judah Falls

"My people have committed two sins: They have forsaken me, the spring of living water, and have dug their own cisterns, broken cisterns that cannot hold water." (Jeremiah 2:13, NIV)

Unit V: The Exiled Nation...The God Who Restores

PSALM 126, NIV, A Song of Ascents

1. When the Lord brought back the captives to Zion,
   we were like men who dreamed.

2. Our mouths were filled with laughter,
   our tongues with songs of joy.
   Then it was said among the nations,
   "The Lord has done great things for them."

3. The LORD has done great things for us,
   and we are filled with joy.

4. Restore our fortunes, O LORD,
   like streams in the Negev.

5. Those who sow in tears
   will reap with songs of joy.

6. He who goes out weeping,
   carrying seed to sow,
   will return with songs of joy,
   carrying sheaves with him.

Chapter 26: God's Messenger to the Exiles

"The soul who sins is the one who will die…. 'For I take no pleasure in the death of anyone,' declares the Sovereign LORD. 'Repent and live!'" (Ezekiel 18:20a, 32, NIV)

Chapter 27: Daniel & His Friends

"But the mercy of the LORD is from everlasting to everlasting On those who fear Him, …to such as keep His covenant, And to those who remember His commandments to do them." (Psalm 103:17a, 18)

Chapter 28: Daniel's Faith

"But without faith it is impossible to please Him [God]." (Hebrews 11:6a)

Chapter 29: The People Return—The Temple Is Rebuilt

"They will call on My name, And I will answer them. I will say, 'This is My people'; And each one will say, 'The LORD is my God.'" (Zechariah 13:9b)

Chapter 30: The Story of Esther

"Who can speak and have it happen if the Lord has not decreed it? Is it not from the mouth of the Most High that both calamities and good things come?" (Lamentations 3:37-38, NIV)

Chapter 31: The Story of Ezra & Nehemiah

"You have kept your promise because you are righteous." (Nehemiah 9:8b, NIV)

APPENDIX B
Pictures of Jesus Christ in the Old Testament

Jesus Christ is not mentioned by name in the Old Testament. Yet, in many ways—sometimes in comparison and sometimes by contrast—you can see glimpses of Jesus in the Old Testament biblical story. In the Old Testament, you read about prophets, priests, and kings. Sometimes a person was both a prophet and a priest, such as Samuel. Sometimes a person was a king who tried to act like a priest. Saul did this when he offered a sacrifice instead of waiting for Samuel to come and make the sacrifice to the LORD. The LORD judged Saul severely for his rash action.

Some prophets, priests, and kings were godly and worshipped the LORD. Many, however, were not godly and angered the LORD by speaking lies, sacrificing to other gods, and ruling as though they were the supreme king instead of acknowledging that God is the King.

Jesus Christ is unique because He is the only Person who holds (or ever has held) all three roles of prophet, priest, and king. As you read stories of the Old Testament prophets, priests, and kings, you will see pictures of Jesus, the perfect Prophet, Priest, and King who fulfilled all His roles perfectly and without sin.

In this book, you will see text "bubbles" that give you biblical truths about who Jesus is and what He has done for you as your Savior and King. Be alert. Maybe you can find even more pictures of Jesus than are mentioned in this text.

Chapter 1: The Call of Samuel

A prophet is a person called to speak God's words. How is Samuel, the prophet, like Jesus Christ, the Prophet?

A prophet is a person chosen by God and equipped by God's Spirit to speak truth to God's people. Often, speaking God's truth involves pointing out sin and calling God's people to repentance. As a child, Samuel had the difficult and unpleasant task of giving God's message of judgment to Eli. Jesus Christ is the divine Prophet. In the Gospels, Jesus spoke God's truth to people, pointing out their sin and calling them to repentance.

Chapter 2: Samuel—The Last Judge

What does a priest do? A priest makes sacrifices for sin. Samuel, as priest, offered a sacrifice for the people's sin, and the LORD forgave them. What does Jesus' sacrifice on the cross do for you?

As priest, Samuel assembled the people at Mizpah so they could confess their sins and make a sacrifice to the LORD. The LORD knew that the people had repentant hearts, so He accepted Samuel's offering. The LORD not only forgave their sin, but He protected them from their enemies. (The Philistines had tried to take advantage of this great gathering and attacked Israel during the sacrificial ceremony.) Jesus is the great High Priest. He not only prays for you when you sin, but He is the sacrifice for sin as well. When you confess your sin, Jesus' sacrifice on the cross gives you forgiveness and deliverance from your greatest enemy—sin!

Chapter 3: Saul—The First King

Saul thought that because he was king he could do whatever he wanted. He forgot that God is the great King above all kings. In the New Testament, we learn that Jesus is the King of kings.

Saul usurped God's authority as supreme King when he disobeyed God and did as he pleased. By punishing Saul for his disobedience, the LORD was telling Saul and all the people that He was and always will be the supreme King. Jesus Christ is the King of kings and LORD of lords. All kings and peoples from every nation must obey Him, and if they choose to disobey, they will have to give account of their actions when they stand before the LORD.

Chapter 4: David Anointed as King

How is David, the shepherd, like the Lord Jesus? How is Jesus, the Good Shepherd, greater than David?

In Psalm 23, David used his experiences as a shepherd to write a beautiful picture of the Lord Jesus. As the Great Shepherd, Jesus tenderly guides and cares for His people. John 10 describes Jesus as the Good Shepherd who protects His sheep even to the point of dying for them. What else can you learn from Psalm 23 and John 10 about how much Jesus loves you?

David was anointed king, but it wasn't time for him to rule yet. How is this like the Lord Jesus' life?

God had anointed David as king, but before he took over the throne, David had to suffer many hard things and learn what it meant to trust the LORD His God. Jesus has always been the King of all kings, but He laid aside His kingly glory to wander on the earth, suffer, and die. He was obedient to God the Father, even when obedience meant dying on the cross. Jesus was humiliated before He was exalted.

Chapter 6: David—The Fugitive

Rejected, homeless, hated by authorities—there are so many ways in which David's life as a fugitive was like Jesus' life.

Both David and Jesus were rejected by the people that God had anointed them to rule over. They were wanderers, having no permanent place to live. (Jesus said, "Foxes have holes and birds of the air have nests, but the Son of Man has no place to lay His head" [Matthew 8:20, NIV]). Both David and Jesus were hated by wicked kings and those in authority. In many ways, the life of David gives you pictures of the life of Jesus.

Chapter 8: The Covenant with David

Jesus Christ is the fulfillment of God's covenant promises to David. He is the Son of David who rules forever and whose kingdom will never fail.

The covenant promises that the LORD made to David have been fulfilled in two ways. In the short-term of history, Solomon was David's son who ruled after him and built a temple for the LORD. But the greater fulfillment of the covenant is through Jesus Christ. Jesus is the Messiah born from David's line—a king who reigns forever in heaven on the throne at God's right hand. Jesus is building a temple much greater than Solomon's temple. Jesus' temple is a spiritual temple being built of "living stones," who are people from every nation who trust Jesus as Savior and Lord (see 1 Peter 2:4-5).

Chapter 9: David's Kindness & David's Sin

What did Mephibosheth do to merit kindness from King David? Absolutely nothing. What do you do to merit salvation from Jesus? Absolutely nothing. It's all by grace.

Mephibosheth did nothing to deserve David's kindness. It was by grace that he enjoyed the blessings of David's household. In the same way, you do nothing to deserve God's kindness and forgiveness. Although what you do can please or displease God, nothing you do can ever earn His favor, even if you live in a God-pleasing way. This is because our obedience to God is always imperfect, due to our sinful nature. Even our best behavior cannot be worthy of God, whose love for us is perfect, constant, and eternal, which is why we must always approach Him in humility and gratitude. You are forgiven of your sin and become a child in God's family because of Jesus' gift of grace. That's what grace is all about—unmerited, unearned favor and blessing from a gracious God!

Chapter 10: Troubles in the Kingdom

David was a good king, but his son, Absalom, plotted against him and the people turned against David. Jesus Christ is the perfect King, yet people refused to allow Him to rule over them.

David was not a perfect king. He sinned in many ways. Yet he was a good king and a man who had a heart to follow the LORD. Many times during David's reign, people rejected him.

From the short reign of Ishbosheth to the rebellions of Absalom and Sheba, David felt the sting of his people turning against him. In a like manner, the people that the LORD has created continue to reject His rule in their lives. Even Christians often refuse to acknowledge the rightful Lordship of Jesus Christ in their lives.

Chapter 11: The Wisdom of Solomon

Was Solomon really the wisest man of all? In Colossians 2:2-3, the Apostle Paul said that all the treasures of wisdom and knowledge are found in Jesus Christ.

Solomon was the wisest man living during the days of his life. His wisdom was a gift from God, and wise men from all over the world came to learn from him. In Colossians 2:2-3, the Apostle Paul said that all wisdom and knowledge are in Jesus Christ. No person who has ever lived or will ever be born has greater wisdom than Jesus, because Jesus is God Himself.

Chapter 12: The Reign of Solomon

"I will establish your throne forever." These were God's words to Solomon. Who would be on Solomon's throne forever? Jesus Christ!

The LORD renewed the covenant with Solomon, and promised, "I will establish your royal throne...forever" (1 Kings 9:5, NIV). How could Solomon's throne last forever? That's a long time! Solomon's throne could be eternal because Jesus Christ, the Son of David, would reign forever as King of kings and Lord of lords.

Chapter 14: A Nation Divided

Rehoboam promised to put heavy burdens on the people. In contrast, King Jesus' "burdens" are not hard to carry. In fact, Jesus said, "My yoke is easy, and My burden is light."

Jesus rules as a wise king who looks after the well-being of His people. He is a strong, powerful ruler, but He never uses His power to oppress His subjects. In Matthew 11:28-29, Jesus says that he will not impose heavy burdens upon people. He says, "My yoke is easy and My burden is light" (Matthew 11:30). How different King Jesus is from King Rehoboam, who vowed to make the burdens of his people even heavier than his father, Solomon, had!

The king was the representative of the covenant between God and the people. Isn't it sad that most of the kings forgot the covenant and led their people far from the Lord? Jesus, the King, is the representative of the covenant with you. Following Him brings you closer to your heavenly Father.

The LORD used Israel's monarchy to fulfill His covenant promises. As political head of the nation, the king represented his people in a special way. His obedience led to blessing for the nation, and his sin brought judgment. He was responsible to obey and enforce the law of God, and his obedience or disobedience set the pattern for how the entire nation would go. The role of king did not eliminate the need for prophets and priests, because the prophets spoke God's counsel and rebuke to the king, and the priests offered sacrifices for the sins of the king and his people. In contrast to the wicked kings of Israel and Judah, Jesus is the perfect king. He represents His people before Almighty God, and He is the mediator who takes the prayers of His people before God's throne (see 1 Timothy 2:5-6). When you follow Jesus, God blesses you.

Chapter 15: Elijah—God's Voice of Judgment to a Wicked King

Even when Elijah was discouraged and ready to die, the Lord was with him, speaking in a gentle, encouraging voice. Jesus, your Lord, is always with you. He promises, "I will never leave you nor forsake you."

In Hebrews 13:5, God promises, "Never will I leave you; never will I forsake you" (NIV). God's presence is always with His people because He promises to be with them. God's presence was with Elijah at the most discouraging moment in his life. Elijah was all alone, hiding for his life, feeling worthless and afraid. The Lord was gently and lovingly giving Elijah encouragement, telling him that he was not alone and that God still had work for him to do. The Lord's words gave Elijah strength, just like Jesus' words can give you strength when you are discouraged.

Chapter 16: Ahab & Jehoshaphat—Two Very Different Kings

When Ahab refused to kill Ben-Hadad, he was not a faithful king. He wasn't defending the honor of the Lord and wasn't protecting his people from enemies who wanted to destroy them. Jesus, as King, always honors God the Father and protects His people from those who would destroy them.

The kings of Israel and Judah were supposed to rule in such a way that they would point God's people to Jesus, the supreme King. However, all the kings of Israel were ungodly, so their reigns were a stark contrast to the way Jesus rules as King. As leader of Israel, Ahab's job was to protect the people from their enemies and to defend the honor of the Lord before pagan rulers. When Ahab refused to kill Ben-Hadad, he failed to do both these things. By contrast, King Jesus always brings honor to God the Father, and always protects and defends His people from whatever forces threaten to destroy them.

Chapter 17: Elisha—God's Voice to Rulers & Ordinary People

Elijah introduced the ministry of Elisha as John the Baptist introduced the ministry of Jesus. In what other ways was Elijah like John the Baptist and Elisha like Jesus?

Elijah was a voice of judgment in the land of Israel. He wandered throughout the land dressed in a garment of animal hair (see 2 Kings 1:8), and in a direct, often confrontational manner, he called the people of Israel, particularly King Ahab, to repentance. The prophet Malachi prophesied about God's coming messenger, the one who would announce the Messiah (see Malachi 3:1). Malachi's prophecy was fulfilled by John the Baptist. As God's messenger, John the Baptist wore clothing made from camel's hair and preached in the same forthright style as Elijah. He spoke about the need for repentance and declared judgment on those who refused to repent, saying, "Repent, for the kingdom of heaven is near" (Matthew 3:2, NIV). On the other hand, Elisha's ministry was similar to Jesus' ministry. Both Elisha and Jesus performed many miracles of mercy and compassion. Also, they both wandered throughout the land, getting involved in people's lives and turning hearts back to the LORD.

Chapter 18: Three Prophets of Judgment

Hosea loved a woman who was unfaithful to him. The Lord Jesus loved you and died for you when you were unfaithful to Him.

The LORD told Hosea to marry a woman who would be unfaithful to Him. This was a strange command, but the LORD wanted Hosea's sad marriage to be a vivid picture of the LORD's love for His people through His faithfulness to His covenant with them. Just like Gomer was unfaithful to Hosea, not once but several times, so God's people were repeatedly unfaithful to Him. God's love for His people did not depend upon their faithfulness, but upon His faithfulness. And, just as Hosea had a broken heart when Gomer was unfaithful to him, so the Lord Jesus has a broken heart when we worship idols. Even though our love for God may at times be as wispy as the morning mist, God never stops loving us.

Chapter 20: Israel Falls & Judah Remains

The Keeper of the Kingdom protected the royal line from which Jesus, the Messiah, would come.

Wicked Queen Athaliah was tricky. She thought she had successfully secured her kingdom by killing everyone in the royal family. But she had forgotten that Judah was not her kingdom. It was God's kingdom! Through the secretive actions of Jehoiada, the LORD preserved Joash's life, the only person left from the royal line of David. The LORD had promised that David's kingly line would last forever, and Joash was the one through whom Jesus the Messiah would come.

Chapter 21: Two Prophets & a Righteous King

In Matthew 2, the chief priests and teachers of the law found the answer to the wise men's question in the prophecy of Micah. The King would be born in Bethlehem.

Micah 5:2 is one of the best-known fulfilled prophecies of the Old Testament. When the wise men led by the brilliant star came to Jerusalem looking for the new king, the learned Jewish scholars found the answer to the wise men's question in the book of Micah. The prophecy said that the King of the Jews would be born in Bethlehem. The books of Micah and Isaiah give many prophecies about the Messiah, and every one of them came true exactly as it was written.

Chapter 22: Two Memorable Kings—Manasseh & Josiah

Josiah had a legacy of righteousness, but it was not a perfect righteousness. Only Jesus has a legacy of perfect righteousness.

Josiah was a godly king and left behind him a legacy of righteousness. His heart for God delayed the judgment that would eventually come upon Judah. Jesus, also, left behind a legacy of righteousness, but his legacy was different from Josiah's in two ways. First, Jesus' righteousness is perfect. He never sinned either in His actions or in His heart. Second, He gives His righteousness to every person who turns away from his sin and toward Him in sincere repentance. When you repent, God takes away your sin and gives you Jesus' righteousness.

Chapter 23: God's Voices of Judgment to the Nations

The prophets said, "The kingdom will be the Lord's," and spoke of "the day of the Lord." Who is the Lord? Jesus Christ!

See Obadiah 1:15, 21; Joel 2:1, 11, 31; 3:14; and Zephaniah 1:14. When the prophets said, "The kingdom will be the Lord's," they were speaking about Jesus, the King who would come to earth some day. When the prophets warned about the "day of the Lord," they were reminding people that the Messiah who saves would also be the judge who judges all men justly according to their deeds. Those who trust Him can rest secure under His sovereign rule, but those who harden their hearts against Him should fear Him as a God of righteous anger.

Chapter 24: Jeremiah Weeps & Judah Falls

Jeremiah was rejected by the people and persecuted by kings. No one wanted to hear what he had to say. Like Jeremiah, people rejected what Jesus had to say, too. Both Jeremiah and Jesus cried tears of sorrow over the hardened hearts of God's people.

God's message of repentance has never been a message that people want to hear. Jeremiah said hard words to the people in Jerusalem, and then they did terrible things to him because they did not want to hear about their sin. But Jeremiah's tears were not just because the people treated him badly. Jeremiah cried because he had compassion on God's people. Likewise, Jesus' words were not accepted, and the stubbornness of people's hearts made Jesus weep over Jerusalem's sins (Luke 19:41-44).

Chapter 26: God's Messenger to the Exiles

The rainbow of God's mercy covers the throne of God's judgment because Jesus the Savior paid the penalty for the sin of His people.

The rainbow around God's throne reminded Ezekiel that God would show mercy to His sinful people by providing a Savior. Without the death of Jesus Christ, there could be no permanent sacrifice for sin, but through Jesus' death, God could make a way for forgiveness and grace.

Chapter 27: Daniel & His Friends

Who was that man in the furnace with Daniel's friends? It was Jesus!

The Lord protected Shadrach, Meshach, and Abednego in an amazing way! When Nebuchadnezzar looked into the furnace, he saw four, not three, men. The fourth man was Jesus Himself. This is called a "theophany." (A theophany is an appearance of Jesus during Old Testament times, before He was born in Bethlehem.) There are several occasions when Jesus appeared to people in the Old Testament (for example, He appeared to Abraham [Genesis 18] and Joshua [Joshua 5:13-15]).

Chapter 29: The People Return—The Temple Is Rebuilt

What is the future glory? It is a glorious day when Jesus will come and establish His Kingdom.

Zechariah's visions spoke of two "days of the Lord" and two temples. The first day of the Lord was when Jesus came to earth to live and die as a man and as your God and Savior. The second day of the Lord will happen when Jesus comes again to judge and rule the earth as King of kings and Lord of lords. The first temple was the temple in Jerusalem built by the returning exiles. The second temple is found in the bodies of believers. The Holy Spirit dwells within all God's people, who are part of the spiritual temple God is building for His eternal Kingdom.

Chapter 31: The Story of Ezra & Nehemiah

The Lord said, "Look for My messenger. He will announce the Messiah."

The Lord ends the Old Testament story by saying, "Look for My messenger. He will announce the Messiah." God has kept His Kingdom safe. He has protected the remnant through the trials of judgment and exile. He will continue to guard His people while, at the same time, He prepares the world for the coming of the King. Jesus Christ is coming! Watch for Him!

HOW to USe the Psalms

Through centuries of recorded history, has God ever changed? Absolutely not! God never changes. ("I the LORD do not change" [Malachi 3:6, NIV]).

Through the ages of time, has mankind changed? Yes. In a short span of time, the languages, geographical boundaries, religions, and political systems of mankind have changed, and nations and cultures have disappeared forever. Yet at the same time, the hard things that happen to people (sickness, death, poverty, broken friendships, etc.) and the way people think and feel about these circumstances don't change. The LORD gave you the book of Psalms, God's "Book of Praises," written 3,000 years ago, so that you can find songs to sing in every situation.

When you read the psalms, ask yourself several questions. These questions will help you understand each psalm better and will help you find encouragement from its words.

Question #1: Who sang this psalm at the time it was written?

Some psalms were written for God's people to sing together in the temple while they worshipped or on their pilgrimages as they walked. Other psalms were written as personal songs of prayer or praise. Knowing who sang the psalm helps you to understand the reason why the psalmist wrote the psalm and how it can encourage you.

Question #2: What is the purpose of this psalm?

Men wrote psalms for many reasons, including praising God, confessing sin, giving thanks, remembering God's faithfulness, and crying out for God's help. For every life situation, the LORD has provided a divinely written song to help you praise Him and feel His comfort. (Chapter 4 describes the different types of psalms.)

Question #3: What does this psalm teach you about yourself?

Just like David, you get angry when friends betray you (see Psalm 55:12-14). Just like Asaph, you're confused when everything goes well for wicked people but goes wrong for you (see Psalm 73). Sometimes it seems that you pray and pray, and God doesn't hear you (see Psalm 13). The psalmists have put into words what you are often thinking and feeling, but can't find the words to say, and then they point you to the LORD, who shows you the world from His point of view.

Question #4: What does this psalm teach you about God?

The LORD is the Shepherd who tenderly cares for His people (see Psalm 23), yet He sends a storm of fiery coals upon violent men who hurt others (see Psalm 11:6). The LORD hears and answers prayer (see Psalm 34:4), but sometimes it seems as though He is silent (see Psalm 88:13-14). Each psalm lets you see another part of what God is like, and putting all the pieces together gives you a big picture of all the traits that make God who He is.

The book of Psalms is a hymnbook, giving you beautiful songs of worship. Today, some churches sing only songs from the book of Psalms in their worship services. Through the years, some psalms, like Psalm 23, have been put to music using many different tunes. Maybe you can make up your own musical tune for a favorite psalm.

The book of Psalms is a prayer book. Praying the words of the psalms as though they are your own thoughts and words can be a powerful way to talk to the LORD when you just don't know what to say.

Through the book of Psalms you can ask the LORD the questions that bother you. "Why, O LORD,...do you hide yourself in times of trouble?" (Psalm 10:1, NIV). "Has the LORD's love vanished forever? Has God forgotten to be merciful?" (see Psalm 77:7-9). The psalmist asked these questions, just as the LORD wants us to ask questions when we are doubting or afraid.

Most important, you must remember that the book of Psalms is poetry that expresses the deepest thoughts and emotions of the human soul. Isn't it amazing that the LORD included in His Holy Scriptures these precious poems to remind you how much our God of the covenant loves you?

HOW to UnDerstanD the ProverBs

"Trust in the LORD with all your heart, And lean not on your own understanding" (Proverbs 3:5).

It's not education and it's not experience that makes a person wise. It's only when knowledge and experience are linked with fearing God that a person becomes truly wise.

The book of Proverbs is a collection of wise sayings written for the purpose of attaining wisdom, developing discipline and self-control, and doing what is morally right and just (Proverbs 1:1-6).

The first nine chapters of Proverbs describe in poetic pictures the conflict between Lady Wisdom and Woman Folly. Woman Folly is "loud;...undisciplined and without knowledge" (Proverbs 9:13, NIV), while Lady Wisdom "dwell[s] together with prudence" and "possess[es] knowledge and discretion" (Proverbs 8:12, NIV). Following in the footsteps of Lady Wisdom brings life and happiness, while the path of Woman Folly only leads to destruction, unhappiness, and eventually death.

The book of Proverbs has something to say about anger, friendship, wealth, poverty, the wise use of words, justice, hard work, and many other topics. All through the book, you read about the contrast between wisdom and folly, good and evil, and self-control and bad judgment. Though the proverbs are generally simple, "tell it like it is" life truths wrapped in picturesque language, they are not always easy to understand. Several important principles must be remembered when trying to understand the book of Proverbs.

Principle #1: The sayings in Proverbs are principles, not promises. In other words, Proverbs tells you that, generally speaking, certain actions bring specific results. For example, Proverbs 10:27 says that a person who fears God will live a long time. ("The fear of the LORD adds length to life, but the years of the wicked are cut short," NIV.) But some godly people die young and some wicked people seem to live forever. So, God is not promising that every godly person will live a long time or that every wicked person will die young. God is, however, making a strong connection between being obedient to God and living a long, complete life.

Principle #2: All proverbs can be misunderstood, so you must read them carefully. Because of our sinful hearts, we can make a proverb mean just about whatever we want it to mean, often distorting its real meaning. One biblical proverb can't contradict another one, however, so all Scripture must be understood in the context of all other Scripture.

Principle #3: The sayings in the book of Proverbs can sound as though the writer is saying two opposite things at the same time. Because all Scripture is inspired by God, all Scripture is true. Therefore, when trying to understand the meaning of contradictory proverbs, you must assume both proverbs are true and then try to understand what each proverb means in its own context. (Proverbs 26:4-5 is an example of two proverbs that appear to contradict each other.)

Principle #4: The book of Proverbs teaches you that consequences follow actions. When you do the right thing, generally speaking, good things happen. When you do the wrong thing, generally speaking, misfortune and bad consequences follow. Most of the time, bad consequences are the result of poor decisions or disobedience, not the deliberate punishment from an "angry" God.

Principle #5: The book of Proverbs makes comparisons between two disagreeable things. ("Better to live in a desert than with a quarrelsome and ill-tempered wife" [Proverbs 21:19, NIV]). These "better" proverbs have an uncomfortable feel, taking something that most reasonable people would think is unpleasant and comparing it with an even more disagreeable thing so that the first thing actually becomes something you would choose. These strange comparisons give little windows into the mind of God, whose thoughts are so very different from our thoughts.

So, a wise person fears God, makes good choices, and acts rightly. Do you want to be wise? Try this. Since Proverbs has thirty-one chapters, you can read one chapter on each day of the month. Without even trying too hard, you will remember these sayings, and then, by practicing them, you can become a wise person.

Kings & Prophets

	JUDAH			ISRAEL	
Kings	**Prophets**	**Date**	**Prophets**	**Kings**
Rehoboam		930 BC	Ahijah	Jeroboam
Abijah		913 BC		
ASA	Azariah	910 BC		
	Hanani	909 BC		Nadab
		908 BC	Jehu	Baasha
		885 BC		Elah, Zimri, Tibni
		880 BC		Omri
		874 BC	Elijah	Ahab
JEHOSHAPHAT		869 BC	Micaiah	
		853 BC	Elisha	Ahaziah
	Jahaziel	852 BC		Joram (a.k.a. Jehoram)
Jehoram	Obadiah (Edom)	848 BC		
Ahaziah		841 BC		Jehu
Queen Athaliah				
JOASH (a.k.a Jehoash)	Joel*	835 BC		
		814 BC		Jehoahaz
AMAZIAH		798 BC		Jehoash
		782 BC		Jeroboam II
UZZIAH (a.k.a. Azariah)		767 BC		
		760 BC	Amos Hosea (760–725)	
		753 BC		Zechariah
		752 BC	Jonah (Assyria)	Shallum Menahem
		742 BC		Pekahiah

| JUDAH | | | ISRAEL | |
Kings	Prophets	Date	Prophets	Kings
JOTHAM	Isaiah (740–687)	740 BC		Pekah
Ahaz		731 BC		Hoshea
HEZEKIAH		727 BC		
		722 BC		**Israel's Fall**
	Micah	701 BC		
Manasseh		687 BC		
Amon	Nahum (Assyria)	642 BC		
JOSIAH	Zephaniah (630–620)	640 BC		
	Jeremiah (627–586)	627 BC		
Jehoahaz Jehoiakim	Habakkuk (610–600) Daniel (605–536)	609 BC		
Jehoiachin		598 BC		
Zedekiah		597 BC		
Judah's Fall	Ezekiel (593–571)	**586 BC**		
Post-Exilic Prophets	Haggai Zechariah	520 BC		
	Malachi	433 BC		

NOTE: The kings whose names are in capitalized italics were kings who served the LORD for at least part of their reign. None of Israel's kings did right.

NOTE: All dates are approximate. Different dating timelines are used by various biblical scholars. Dates for this timeline are taken from *Old Testament Survey* by Paul R. House.

*Biblical scholars are uncertain as to exactly when Joel was prophesying. Some sources cite the 800s BC and others the 300s BC.

APPENDIX F
Reigns of the Kings of Israel & Judah

KINGS OF ISRAEL

King	Father	Years Reigned	Death
Jeroboam	Nebat	22	Natural death
Nadab	Jeroboam	2	Killed by Baasha
Baasha	Ahijah	24	Natural death
Elah	Baasha	2	Killed by Zimri
Zimri	unknown	7 days	Died at Tirzah
Tibni	Ginath	1	Unknown
Omri	unknown	12	Natural death
Ahab	Omri	22	Killed in battle
Ahaziah	Ahab	2	Accident; died from injuries
Joram	Ahab	12	Killed by Jehu
Jehu	Jehoshaphat (son of Nimshi)	28	Natural death
Jehoahaz	Jehu	17	Natural death
Jehoash	Jehoahaz	16	Natural death
Jeroboam II	Jehoash	41	Natural death
Zechariah	Jeroboam II	6 months	Killed by Shallum
Shallum	Jabesh	1 month	Killed by Menahem
Menahem	Gadi	10	Natural death
Pekahiah	Menahem	2	Killed by Pekah
Pekah	Remaliah	20	Killed by Hoshea
Hoshea	Elah	9	Captured by Assyria

KINGS OF JUDAH

King	Father	Years Reigned / Age When Reign Began	Death
Rehoboam	Solomon	17 yrs/age 41	Natural death
Abijah	Rehoboam	3 yrs	Natural death
ASA	Abijah	41 yrs	Natural death
JEHOSHAPHAT	Asa	25 yrs	Natural death
Jehoram	Jehoshaphat	8 yrs/age 32	Natural death
Ahaziah	Jehoram	1 yr/age 22	Killed by Jehu
Athaliah	Omri (grandfather)*	6 yrs	Killed by Jehoiada's action
JOASH	Ahaziah	40 yrs/age 7	Murdered by his officials
AMAZIAH	Joash	29 yrs/age 25	Killed by conspirators
UZZIAH	Amaziah	52 yrs/age 16	Died of leprosy
JOTHAM	Uzziah	16 yrs	Natural death
Ahaz	Jotham	16 yrs/age 20	Natural death
HEZEKIAH	Ahaz	29 yrs/age 25	Natural death
Manasseh	Hezekiah	55 yrs/age 12	Natural death
Amon	Manasseh	2 yrs/age 22	Assassinated by his officials
JOSIAH	Amon	31 yrs/age 8	Killed in battle against Egypt
Jehoahaz	Josiah	3 mths/age 23	Captured and died in Egypt
Jehoiakim	Josiah	11 yrs/age 25	Natural death
Jehoiachin	Jehoiakim	3 mths/age 18	Taken to Babylon
Zedekiah	Josiah	11 yrs/age 21	Taken captive to Babylon and died

NOTE: The kings whose names are in capitalized italics were kings who served the LORD for at least part of their reign. Many of these kings began their rule well, but turned away from the LORD before they died.

*It is unclear as to who Athaliah's father was. Some sources suggest that it was Ahab, but Scripture is unclear on this point.

Intertestamental History

A nd then, God was silent. No booming voices of judgment from wild-eyed Elijahs or soulful pleadings from Jeremiahs. No dramatic displays of fire from heaven or unexplainable healings. The Jews, having returned from exile, lived in Palestine for 400 years as one empire after another rose to power and then collapsed. Yet, while God was silent, He was not sleeping. God was changing and maneuvering governments, religious practices, languages, and literature so that at just the right time, when the King Himself would come to earth, the earth would be ready for Him!

History

In the years from Malachi to Matthew, five different empires ruled Palestine. The Persians, whose rule began under Cyrus in 536 BC, governed the Jews for 200 years. Persian rule was tolerant, and the Jews were able to practice their religion. During this time, the Samaritans erected a separate temple in Samaria. (The Samaritans were an interracial mixture of remnant Israelites and people from conquered Assyrian cities.) Building this temple brought about a total separation between the Jews of Judea and the Samaritans of Samaria, and explains why they hated each other so much. (John 4 tells you about this ongoing hatred between the Jews and the Samaritans.)

In 332 BC, Alexander the Great marched southward to Jerusalem, and Judea became part of the Greek empire. Though Alexander treated the Jews well, another danger threatened God's people. The Greeks were determined to unite the world with one language and culture, a process called "Hellenization." This process had damaging effects on Jewish worship, but it set into place certain things that prepared the world for the King's coming.

When Alexander died at a young age, chaos erupted in the empire. With no strong leader to guide the empire, it split into four parts under four generals. After fierce fighting, Judea came under the control of Ptolemy, who ruled his part of the empire from Egypt. (The Ptolemies were a dynasty of Greeks, each named Ptolemy, who ruled Egypt and the surrounding territories.) Under the first three Ptolemies, the Jews had kind treatment, and they prospered, growing in population and wealth. Later Ptolomies didn't treat the Jews well. Then Palestine became a battleground between the Ptolemies of Egypt and the Seleucid empire of Syria. In 204 BC, all of Palestine, including Judea, Samaria, and Galilee came under Syrian rule.

The Syrian rulers were harsh toward the Jews, but the most infamous of all the Syrians was Antiochus Epiphanes. This tyrant used the Jews' rebellious attitude toward Syria as a reason to plunder Jerusalem and defile the temple. In 170 BC, after massacring thousands of people and selling women and children as slaves, he desecrated the temple by offering a pig on the altar as a sacrifice. He also erected a statue of the Greek god Zeus in the middle of the temple. His intention was to destroy the Jewish religion.

An old priest named Mattathias, a father of five sons, began the next "empire" in Judea, called the Maccabean Period. After killing a messenger of Antiochus Epiphanes, Mattathias led a revolt against the Syrian oppressors. His rebel army grew in number and fought against traitorous Jews and hated Syrians. His passion was to restore true religion to the Jews. After his death, his son, Judas Maccabeus, the best known of the Maccabean leaders, became military commander. He was a fierce fighter who employed guerilla army tactics to fight the Syrians.

Judas Maccabeus was killed in battle, but his brothers, first Jonathan and then Simon, continued the revolt, a twenty-four year struggle that resulted in independence for the Jews that lasted until the Romans conquered Palestine in 63 BC. Between the time of Simon's death and the Roman conquest, several Maccabean descendents ruled Judea, beginning with Simon's son, John Hyrcanus. These rulers are called the Hasmonean dynasty.

The Hasmonean rule started well, with prosperity and peace in the land, but with John Hyrcanus's death, strife and civil war erupted. The rulers adopted Hellenistic ways of thinking, and Mattathias's passion for pure religion was rejected for a mixture of Greek thought and Jewish religion.

In 63 BC, Pompey conquered Jerusalem after a three-month siege. Because this Roman general massacred the priests and raided the Most Holy Place of the temple, the Jews hated the Romans. This hatred remained unchanged and was the basis for the hatred between the Jews and the Romans during the time of Jesus' life.

Language, Literature, and Religion

The religious and cultural impact that these 400 years had upon the world made it possible for Jesus Christ to be born "when the fullness of the time had come" (Galatians 4:4).

The conquering of the known world by the Greeks changed history permanently. The Greek language soon became the one language that united people. In Alexandria, during the reign of the Ptolemies, a group of scholars gathered together, and in a short time they translated the Jewish Scripture into Greek. This book is called the Septuagint, meaning "seventy." (Legend says that seventy-two men completed the entire translation in seventy-two days.)

This meant that as the Jews became Hellenized and could no longer speak Hebrew, and as the gospel later spread to Gentiles in the Roman world, God's Word was still accessible to many people.

During this time, the books of the Apocrypha were written. This collection of fifteen books provides historical and cultural information about life during the silent years. Though some Bibles today include these books, the Church does not consider them to be divinely inspired Scripture.

God used the Romans to prepare the world for Christ's coming. The Romans united the known world in a more complete way than even the Greeks had. They built a system of roads, some of which can still be walked on today. Once Rome conquered the nations, the Pax Romana (meaning "the peace of Rome") settled over the empire. This one-government system, and the ability to travel between distant parts of the empire, made it possible to spread the gospel message to many countries during the first century AD.

A very significant change happened in the Jewish nation after the Exile. From the time of their wilderness journey to the destruction of Jerusalem, God's people repeatedly turned from the LORD and worshipped the gods of other nations. However, after returning from Babylon, the Jews never again worshipped Baal, Asherah, Molech or other pagan gods. Though they were not always faithful to the LORD, and did not always worship Him appropriately, they always claimed that Yahweh was their God.

In the Jewish community, two major religious institutions came about during this time. The synagogue that didn't exist before the Exile and was an established part of Jewish society in the New Testament had its origins in Babylon. Separated from the temple and surrounded by pagan idolatry, the Jews in Babylon didn't want to forget the religion of their ancestors. They met in groups to study the Torah (the five books of Moses). By the time they went back to Jerusalem, they regularly studied and discussed the Scriptures and made this habit part of their new life. They called these meeting places "synagogues." During the time of Jesus' life, synagogues were found in cities throughout Judea and Galilee.

Another religious institution that began in the silent years of the Exile was the formation of new religious and social groups (scribes, Pharisees, and Sadducees) that, along with the chief priests, controlled Jewish life. The scribes were a group of professionals who were experts in interpreting and applying the Old Testament Law. Arising out of the synagogue movement, their function was different from that of the priests who offered sacrifices in the temple. The passion of the scribes was instilling the idea of the Law's holiness into the people's minds and protecting Judaism from outside influences or internal heresy that would defile God's Law and lead His people astray.

The Pharisees and Sadducees were different from the scribes and priests because they were distinguished by their religious views, not their religious function. A man could be a scribe or a priest or actually do both jobs. As a scribe or priest a man could have the religious views either of a Pharisee or Sadducee (although there is no known record that any scribe was a Sadducee) or be independent from either religious viewpoint.

The Pharisees and Sadducees had different religious views and opposed each other on everything. The word "Pharisees" means "Separatists." They believed in strict obedience to the written law given by the LORD and to the oral law and traditions that they created to help them to keep God's Law "perfectly." They concentrated on behaving correctly, but didn't always keep the Law in their hearts. Sadducees for the most part belonged to wealthy priestly families and were more of a social group than a religious one. They were more interested in political power than in the hope of a coming Messiah or in keeping God's Law. They were religious skeptics and didn't believe in the universal resurrection.

Four hundred years of preparation—a Greek-speaking world, the Pax Romana throughout the known world, and an established Jewish religious system were all part of God's way of getting the world ready because the King Himself was coming!

Glossary

Abednego (n.): Babylonian name of Azariah, who was with Daniel in exile in Babylon

Abiathar (n.): Son of Ahimelech, a priest at Nob; the only priest who escaped slaughter at Nob; banished after he supported Adonijah's attempt to be king

Abijah (n.): Wicked king of Judah; son of Rehoboam

Abishai (n.): One of David's men; went with David to cave and stole Saul's spear and water jug

Abinadab (n.): Man at whose house the ark of the covenant stayed for twenty years

Abner (n.): Commander of Saul's army; made Ishbosheth king in Israel after Saul died; killed Asahel, Joab's brother

Absalom (n.): Son of David; led a conspiracy against David; killed Amnon; killed by Joab

Adonijah (n.): Son of David who tried to become the king who succeeded David

Agag (n.): King of the Amalekites whose life Saul spared

Agur (n.): One of the writers of Proverbs

Ahab (n.): Wicked king of Israel; son of King Omri; husband of Queen Jezebel; enemy of Elijah

Ahaz (n.): Son of Jotham and father of Hezekiah who became king of Judah; known for his great idolatry

Ahaziah (n.): Ahab's son who became king of Israel after Ahab died; brother of Queen Athaliah; worshipped Baal-Zebub instead of the LORD

Ahaziah (n.): Jehoram's son who became king of Judah after Jehoram died; son of Queen Athaliah

Ahijah (n.): Prophet who prophesied that Jeroboam would be king of ten tribes of Israel

Ahimelech (n.): Priest at Nob who gave David and his men consecrated bread to eat

Ahio (n.): Son of Abinadab who guided the ark from Abinadab's house; brother of Uzzah

Amalekites (n.): Descendents of Amalek, the grandson of Esau; enemy of Israel

Amasa (n.): Commander of Absalom's army; killed by Joab

Amaziah (n.): Son of Joash who became king of Judah; brought Edom's gods to Jerusalem

Amnon (n.): Son of David who sinned against his half sister Tamar and was killed by Absalom

Ammonites (n.): Descendents of Ben-Ammi, son of Lot and his second daughter; enemy of Israel

Amos (n.): Herdsman and tree farmer from Tekoa in Judah called to be a prophet of God to Israel; prophet of justice; name means "bearer of burdens"

Anoint (v.): Chosen by God and equipped by God's Spirit to serve the LORD in a particular job (priest, prophet, king, etc.)

Ark of the Covenant (n.): Box that contained the Ten Commandments and reminded Israel that God was with them; located in the Holy of Holies in the tabernacle

Aram (n.): Nation north of Israel that often fought against Israel; Ben-Hadad was a king of Aram (Syria)

Artaxerxes (n.): King of Persia during the days of Zerubbabel and Jeshua

Asa (n.): Godly king in Judah; son of wicked king Abijah

Asahel (n.): Brother of Joab who was killed by Abner

Asaph (n.): Writer of some of the book of Psalms

Ashdod (n.): City in Philistia where Dagon's temple was located; God sent a plague of tumors and rats to this city

Asherah (n.): Name of a Canaanite goddess

Ashtoreth (n.): Name of a goddess of the Sidonians in Phoenicia

Athaliah (n.): Queen who killed the royal family and then ruled in Judah; sister of Ahaziah (king of Israel) and mother of Ahaziah (king of Judah)

Azariah (n.): Prophet of God in Judah to King Asa

Azariah (n.): Son of Amaziah who became king of Judah; commonly called Uzziah

Azariah (n.): Hebrew name of one of Daniel's three friends who was with Daniel in exile in Babylon

– B –

Baal (n.): Canaanite god

Baal-Zebub (n.): Philistine idol to which Ahaziah (Israel) prayed; means "lord of the flies"

Baasha (n.): Wicked king in Israel; killed Nadab, Jeroboam's son, and all Jeroboam's family

Babylon (n.): Nation that conquered Judah in 586 BC and took God's people as captives

Baruch (n.): Jeremiah's scribe who wrote the scroll sent to Jehoiakim

Bathsheba (n.): Wife of Uriah; woman whom David loved as only a husband should love

Belteshazzar (n.): The Babylonian name of Daniel, who was taken into exile in Babylon

Belshazzar (n.): King of Babylon during Daniel's life; king who saw the handwriting on the palace walls and was then killed by Darius, king of the Medes

Ben-Hadad I (n.): King of Aram in Damascus who made a treaty with King Asa in Judah

Ben-Hadad II (n.): King of Aram who attacked Israel during the time of Elisha

Benjaminite (n.): Person from the tribe of Benjamin

Bethel (n.): One of two cities where Jeroboam set up a worship center with a golden calf

Bethlehem (n.): City where David was born; city in which the Messiah was to be born

Blessed (adj.): Contented because God is pleased with you

Boaz (n.): Name of northern pillar of Solomon's temple; means "in Him is strength"

Bozrah (n.): Capital of Edom carved out of rocky cliffs

– C –

Chemosh (n.): Name of the chief god of the Moabites

Continuing (adj.): Type of Hebrew poetry in which the second line adds meaning to or continues the thought of the first line

Contrasted (adj.): Type of Hebrew poetry in which the second line has an opposite meaning to the first line

Covenant (n.): God's promise to be the God of His people forever

Cyrus (n.): King of Persia who was king when Daniel lived in exile; king who decreed that Jews could go back to their land

– D –

Dagon (n.): One of the primary gods of the Philistines; his temple was located at Ashdod

Dan (n.): One of two cities where Jeroboam set up a worship center with a golden calf

Daniel (n.): One of God's people who was captured and taken to Babylon, where he became prominent in the courts of Nebuchadnezzar, Cyrus, and Darius; prophet of God's sovereignty

Darius (n.): King of the Medes who killed Belshazzar and took over his kingdom; king who made the decree that resulted in Daniel being thrown into the lions' den

Darius (n.): One of the kings of Persia during the days in which the Jews had returned to Jerusalem

David (n.): Israel's second king; writer of many of the Psalms; the Lord called David, "a man after [My] own heart"

Desert of Ziph (n.): Desert where David and his men hid in caves

Doeg (n.): The Edomite who killed the eighty-five priests at Nob

Dothan (n.): City where the Aramean army was struck with blindness by Elisha

Dura (n.): Plain where Nebuchadnezzar set up the large image that he commanded to be worshipped

– E –

Ebenezer (n.): Memorial stone set up by Samuel after Israel's victory over the Philistines; means "thus far has the LORD helped us"

Ecclesiastes (n.): Book in the Old Testament written by The Preacher that teaches how to find purpose in the fear of God, not earthly pleasures

Edomites (n.): Descendents of Esau; enemy of Israel

Ekron (n.): City in Philistia where God sent a plague of tumors and rats because the Philistines had captured the ark of the covenant

Elah (n.): Wicked king in Israel

Eleazar (n.): Man who guarded the ark of the covenant while it stayed in his father Abinadab's house

Eliab (n.): Oldest son of Jesse; the brother of King David

Elijah (n.): Prophet of God who spoke judgment to Ahab and challenged the prophets of Baal

Elisha (n.): Prophet of God who succeeded Elijah

Elkanah (n.): The husband of Hannah and the father of Samuel

Eli (n.): Priest in Israel with whom Samuel lived

Elohim (n.): Hebrew name for God that means might, strength, and majesty; the name that reminds us that God is the creator of all things

Endor (n.): Town where medium who called up Samuel for Saul lived

Esther (n.): Jewish woman who became the wife of King Xerxes, king of Persia, and who saved her people from destruction

Ezekiel (n.): Prophet of visions; prophet of God to the exiles in Babylon

Ezra (n.): Jewish priest who led the people from exile in Babylon back to Jerusalem

– F –

Faith (n.): Believing what God says is true and acting on this truth even before you see the results with your own eyes; a gift from God

Fear God (v. + n.): Be in awe of God so that you respect and obey Him

– G –

Gath (n.): City in Philistia where God sent a plague of tumors and rats because the Philistines had captured the ark of the covenant

Gedaliah (n.): Man appointed governor over Jerusalem by Babylon after the destruction of the city

Geshur (n.): Country that Absalom fled to after killing Amnon

Geshem (n.): One of the three men who gave Nehemiah problems as he was rebuilding the walls of Jerusalem

Gibeon (n.): City where the tabernacle was located during the reigns of David and Solomon until the temple was built

Goliath (n.): Giant whom David killed

Gomer (n.): Unfaithful wife of the prophet Hosea

– H –

Habakkuk (n.): Prophet to Judah who asked the LORD two questions; prophet of faith

Haggai (n.): Prophet who encouraged the returned exiles in Jerusalem to rebuild the temple; prophet of encouragement

Hallelujah Psalm (n.): Psalm that gives praise to God (Psalms 146–150)

Haman (n.): Official in King Xerxes's court who plotted to have all the Jews killed

Hannah (n.): The mother of Samuel; dedicated Samuel to the Lord after He answered her prayer for a child

Hanani (n.): Seer who rebuked Asa for making a treaty with Ben-Hadad

Hananiah (n.): Hebrew name of one of Daniel's friends who was with Daniel in exile in Babylon

Hazael (n.): King of Aram anointed by Elijah; killed Ben-Hadad II

Hebron (n.): City in Judah where David was anointed king after Saul died

Hilkiah (n.): High priest during Josiah's reign; found the Book of the Law in the temple

Hiram (n.): King of Tyre who gave Solomon cedar wood for the temple

Historical Psalm (n.): Psalm that reminds Israel of who God is and what He has done (Psalms 105–106)

Holy (adj.): Means "set apart by God" or "living in a way that pleases God"

Hophni (n.): One of Eli's wicked sons

Hosea (n.): Prophet of God to the nation of Israel; prophet of the broken heart; name means "salvation"; married Gomer, an unfaithful woman because God told him to marry her; his marriage was a picture of Israel's unfaithfulness to the Lord

Hoshea (n.): Son of Elah who was the last king of Israel before Assyria conquered Israel

Huldah (n.): Prophetess during the reign of Josiah; she said Judah would suffer all the curses in the Book of the Law

Huram (n.): Skilled craftsman from Tyre hired by Solomon to make the two bronze pillars for the temple

– I –

Ichabod (n.): Name of Phinehas's wife's son; means "the glory [of the Lord] has departed from Israel"

Idol (n.): Anything we trust in rather than God; any desire or fear that controls our behavior

Immanuel (n.): Name of Jesus Christ, the Messiah; means "God with us"

Ishbosheth (n.): King over eleven tribes in Israel after Saul died

Isaiah (n.): Prophet of comfort; prophesied to kings of Judah (Jotham, Ahaz, and Hezekiah)

Israel (n.): Name for God's people, with whom He made a covenant; also, name for the northern kingdom after the nation of Israel split in two (ten tribes)

– J –

Jabesh Gilead (n.): Israelite city besieged by the Ammonites

Jachin (n.): Southern pillar of Solomon's temple; means "He establishes"

Jahaziel (n.): Prophet of Israel who told Jehoshaphat that God would deliver Israel from the Moabites and Ammonites

Jehoahaz (n.): Son of Jehu who became king of Israel

Jehoahaz (n.): Son of Josiah who became king of Judah for three months

Jehoash (n.): Son of Jehoahaz who became king of Israel

Jehoiachin (n.): Son of Jehoiakim who became king of Judah for three months

Jehoiada (n.): High priest who hid baby Joash from wicked Athaliah

Jehoiakim (n.): Son of Josiah who became king of Judah

Jehoram (n.): King of Judah who became king after his father Jehoshaphat; also called Joram

Jehoshaphat (n.): Godly king of Judah who ruled when Ahab was king of Israel

Jehovah (n.): The name of God as used in the covenant; written as "Lord" in the English Bible; same as the word "Yahweh"

Jehu (n.): Prophet of God who warned Baasha, king of Israel, of his wickedness and blessed Jehoshaphat, king of Judah

Jehu (n.): Man who became king of Israel after killing Joram (Israel) and Ahaziah (Judah); also killed Jezebel and all Ahab's family

Jeremiah (n.): Prophet to Judah during the last five kings; prophet of tears

Jeroboam (n.): First king of Israel after the kingdom split in two

Jeroboam II (n.): Son of Jehoash who became king in Israel

Jerusalem (n.): Jebusite city captured by David and made the capital of Israel; capital of the southern kingdom of Judah after the nation of Israel split in two

Jeshua (n.): Priest who led the first group of exiles back home to Jerusalem (some versions of the Bible call him Joshua)

Jesse (n.): Son of Obed and father of King David (Obed was the son of Ruth)

Jezebel (n.): Wicked queen in Israel; wife of King Ahab; enemy of Elijah

Joab (n.): Commander of David's army; killed Abner (commander king of Saul's army), Absalom, and Amasa

Joash (n.): Son of Ahaziah (Judah) who became king of Judah at age seven; hid by the high priest Jehoiada to protect him from wicked Athaliah

Joel (n.): Prophet to Judah; spoke about the plague of locusts; prophet of God's grace

Jonah (n.): Prophet of God to the city of Nineveh; prophet of salvation

Jonathan (n.): King Saul's son, who made a covenant of friendship with David

Joram (n.): Son of Ahab who became king of Israel after his brother Ahaziah died (also called Jehoram)

Joshua (n.): Man chosen by God to lead the Israelites into the Promised Land and conquer it

Josiah (n.): King of Judah who read the Book of the Law at the temple and began great religious reform; considered the godliest of Judah's kings

Jotham (n.): Son of Uzziah who became king of Judah after Uzziah got leprosy

Judah (n.): Name of the southern kingdom after the nation of Israel split in two (two tribes)

Judge (n.): Person chosen by God to be a deliverer, peacemaker, and civil leader in Israel

Judgment Psalm (n.): Psalm that asks God to judge the wicked (Psalms 35, 52, 55, 109)

– K –

Keilah (n.): Town David saved from the Philistines; Keilah's inhabitants were not friendly toward David

Kerith Ravine (n.): Place where the ravens fed Elijah

– L –

Lamentations (n.): Book written by Jeremiah describing the destruction of Jerusalem

Legacy (n.): Something you leave behind for your descendents

Lemuel (n.): One of the writers of Proverbs

Levites (n.): Tribe of Israel responsible for transporting the ark and fulfilling the priestly functions in worship

Lyre (n.): Small stringed musical instrument that David played

– M –

Malachi (n.): The prophet who wrote the last book of the Old Testament; prophet of preparation

Manasseh (n.): Son of Hezekiah who was the longest reigning king of Judah; considered one of Judah's most wicked kings

Medium (n.): Person who talks to the spirits of people who have died

Menahem (n.): Wicked king of Israel who reigned after Shallum

Meshach (n.): Babylonian name of Mishael, who was with Daniel in exile in Babylon

Mephibosheth (n.): Son of Jonathan and grandson of Saul that David showed kindness

Messiah (n.): Hebrew word meaning "the Anointed One"; the prophets spoke of the Messiah as the one who was to come to deliver God's people; He was to have a kingly and a priestly role; Jesus Christ fulfilled all the prophecies of the Messiah

Messianic Psalm (n.): Psalm that talks about the Messiah who will come (Psalms 2, 22, 45, 72)

Micaiah (n.): Prophet in Israel during the reign of King Ahab

Micah (n.): Prophet of hope; prophesied in Judah during the reign of Hezekiah

Michal (n.): Daughter of King Saul and first wife of David

Mishael (n.): Hebrew name of one of Daniel's friends who was with Daniel in exile in Babylon

Mizpah (n.): City where Samuel called the people to repentance; location of the Ebenezer stone; city where Saul was anointed as king

Moabites (n.): Descendents of Moab, son of Lot and his first daughter; enemy of Israel

Molech (n.): Name of the chief god of the Ammonites

Mordecai (n.): Jewish man living in court of King Xerxes; cousin of Esther

Moses (n.): Man chosen by God to lead the Israelites out of Egypt and to the Promised Land

Mt. Carmel (n.): Mountain where Elijah challenged the prophets of Baal

Mt. Horeb (n.): Mountain where the LORD spoke to Elijah in a gentle whisper; also called the "mountain of God"

– N –

Naaman (n.): Commander of Ben-Hadad's army; Elisha healed him from leprosy

Naboth (n.): Man whose vineyard King Ahab coveted and then stole; Jezebel falsely accused him of blasphemy, and he was therefore stoned to death

Nadab (n.): Wicked king in Israel; Jeroboam's son

Nahum (n.): Prophet who prophesied destruction to Assyria; prophet of God's wrath

Nathan (n.): Prophet who spoke God's words to David

Nazirite (n.): Person set apart for God; he could not drink wine, cut his hair, or touch a dead body

Nebuchadnezzar (n.): King of Babylon who conquered Judah

Nehemiah (n.): Jewish man who was cupbearer to King Artaxerxes and went to Jerusalem to rebuild the city walls

Nineveh (n.): Capital of Assyria; city that repented after Jonah warned it of God's judgment

Nob (n.): Town where the tabernacle was located during Saul's reign; town where Doeg the Edomite killed eighty-five priests

– O –

Obadiah (n.): Prophet who prophesied disaster to Edom; prophet of Edom's disaster

Obed-Edom (n.): Man in whose house David kept the ark after Uzzah died

Omnipotence (n.): Having all power

Omniscience (n.): Having all knowledge

Omri (n.): Wicked king in Israel; father of King Ahab

– P –

Passover Psalm (n.): Psalm sung during the Passover meal (Psalms 113–118)

Pekah (n.): Wicked king of Israel who followed Pekahiah

Pekahiah (n.): Wicked king of Israel who reigned after Menahem

Peninnah (n.): Elkanah's second wife, who teased Hannah about her barrenness

Persia (n.): Nation who conquered Babylon

Phinehas (n.): One of Eli's wicked sons

Philistines (n.): People from the Aegean Sea and Captor (Crete) who settled in Canaan; enemy of Israel

Pilgrim Psalm (n.): Psalm sung by the Israelites on their journeys to Jerusalem to worship (Psalms 120–134)

Priest (n.): Man in charge of offering sacrifices and offerings in the tabernacle

Prophet (n.): Person called to speak for God

Proverbs (n.): Book in the Old Testament that contains wise sayings and teaches wisdom through the fear of the LORD and godly choices

Providence of God (n.): God's holy, wise, and powerful preserving and governing of everything in His creation

Psalms (n.): Book in the Old Testament that contains Hebrew poetry for the worship and praise of God; also called the "Book of Praises"

Purim (n.): Feast celebrated by the Jews to remember their deliverance from the decree of King Xerxes to kill them

– Q –

Queen of Sheba (n.): Queen who heard of Solomon's wisdom and wealth and therefore came to visit him

– R –

Rehoboam (n.): Solomon's son who became the first king in the southern kingdom of Judah

Remnant (n.): The part left after the rest has been lost

Repeated (adj.): Type of Hebrew poetry in which the second line has a similar meaning to the first line

Repentance Psalm (n.): Psalm expressing sorrow for sin and asking for God's forgiveness (Psalms 6, 32, 51, 130)

–S –

Samaria (n.): Capital of the northern kingdom (Israel); city where Ahab built the temple to Baal

Samaritans (n.): People who lived in Samaria, the land that once belonged to Israel's ten tribes; they were enemies of the Jews who returned from exile

Samuel (n.): The last of the judges and the first of the great Old Testament prophets; means "heard of God"

Sanballat (n.): One of the three men who caused Nehemiah problems when Nehemiah was rebuilding the walls of Jerusalem

Saul (n.): Israel's first king; he was eventually rejected by God because of his disobedience

Sennacherib (n.): King of Assyria who captured Samaria and threatened Judah during the reign of Hezekiah

Shadrach (n.): Babylonian name of Hananiah, who was with Daniel in exile in Babylon

Sherebiah (n.): The Levite who went to Jerusalem with Ezra

Shalmaneser (n.): King of Assyria who conquered Israel in 722 BC

Shallum (n.): Wicked king of Israel who reigned one month

Shechem (n.): First capital of the northern kingdom of Israel

Sheba (n.): Man who led a revolt against David when he was king

Shiloh (n.): The place where the tabernacle was located during the days of Eli and Samuel

Shunammite woman (n.): Woman whose son was raised from the dead by Elisha

Solomon (n.): Second son of David and Bathsheba; king of Israel after David; means "peace"

Song of Songs (n.): Book in the Old Testament written by Solomon that celebrates the gift of God's love

Sons of Korah (n.): Writers of some of the book of Psalms

Sovereign (adj.): Possesses supreme power; controls all things

– T –

Tamar (n.): Sister of Absalom who was sinned against by her half brother Amnon

Tarshish (n.): City to which Jonah tried to flee when he was running away from God

Tekoa (n.): Hometown village of the prophet Amos

Thanksgiving Psalm (n.): Psalm thanking God for His mercy and answers to prayer (Psalms 18, 66, 107, 138)

Theophany (n.): An appearance of Jesus during Old Testament times, before He was born in Bethlehem

Tibni (n.): Wicked king of Israel who vied with Omri for the throne and lost

Tobiah (n.): One of the three men who caused problems for Nehemiah when he was rebuilding the walls of Jerusalem

Transgression (n.): The breaking of one of God's laws

– U –

Uriah (n.): Husband of Bathsheba killed in the battle with the Ammonites

Uzzah (n.): Son of Abinadab who guided the move of the ark from Abinadab's house; killed when he touched the ark to steady it

Uzziah (n.): Son of Amaziah who became king of Judah; also called Azariah; got leprosy after he offered incense in the temple

– V –

Valley of Elah (n.): Valley where David killed Goliath

Vashti (n.): Queen of the Persian king Xerxes

– W –

Wisdom Psalm (n.): Psalm giving wise counsel to the godly and warning the ungodly (Psalms 1, 37, 49)

– X –

Xerxes (n.): Persian king who married the Jewish woman Esther

– Y –

Yahweh (n.): Hebrew word for the God who established a covenant with His people, Israel; same meaning as the word "Jehovah"

– Z –

Zadok (n.): Priest during the reign of David and Solomon; anointed Solomon to be king

Zarephath (n.): City where the widow lived who cared for Elijah

Zechariah (n.): Son of Jeroboam II; became king of Israel

Zechariah (n.): Son of the high priest Jehoiada; killed by Joash when he warned Joash of his sin

Zechariah (n.): Prophet who prophesied to the people in Jerusalem who had returned from exile; prophet of future glory

Zedekiah (n.): Son of Josiah who became king after Jehoiachin was removed by the Babylonians

Zephaniah (n.): Prophet to Judah during reign of Josiah; prophet of total destruction

Zerubbabel (n.): Governor and leader of the first group of Jews who returned to Jerusalem after the exile

Ziba (n.): Servant in Saul's household who told David about Mephibosheth

Zimri (n.): Wicked king in Israel who reigned for seven days; killed King Elah of Israel

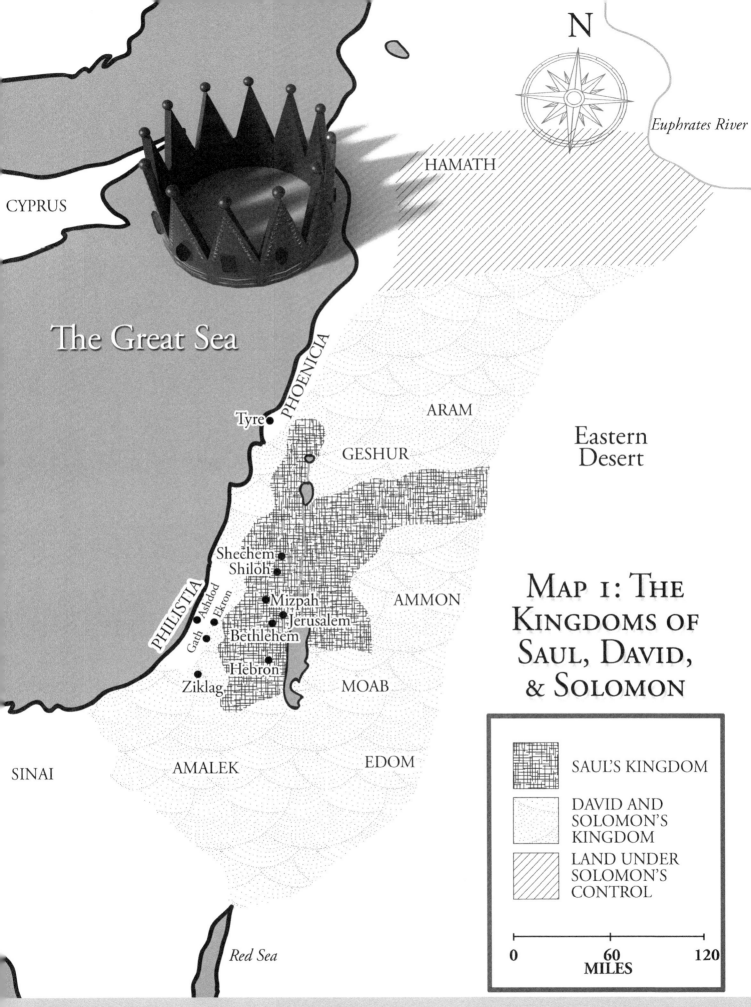

N

Euphrates River

CYPRUS

HAMATH

The Great Sea

PHOENICIA

ARAM

Eastern
Desert

Tyre

GESHUR

Shechem
Shiloh

PHILISTIA
Ashdod
Gath Ekron

Mizpah

Jerusalem

Bethlehem

Hebron

Ziklag

AMMON

MOAB

SINAI

AMALEK

EDOM

MAP 1: THE
KINGDOMS OF
SAUL, DAVID,
& SOLOMON

SAUL'S KINGDOM

DAVID AND
SOLOMON'S
KINGDOM

LAND UNDER
SOLOMON'S
CONTROL

0   60   120
MILES

Red Sea

MAP II: ISRAEL AND ITS NEIGHBORS

| 0 | 10 | 20 | 30 | 40 | 50 miles |

NOTE: Dan and Manasseh each had two portions of land (see Joshua 17:7-18, 19:40-48).

Red Sea

Mediterranean Sea

Desert of Zin

Simeon

Judah

Dan

Benjamin

Ephraim

Manasseh

Issachar

Zebulun

Naphtali

Asher

Dan

Dead Sea

Reuben

Gad

Manasseh

Midian

Edom

Moab

N

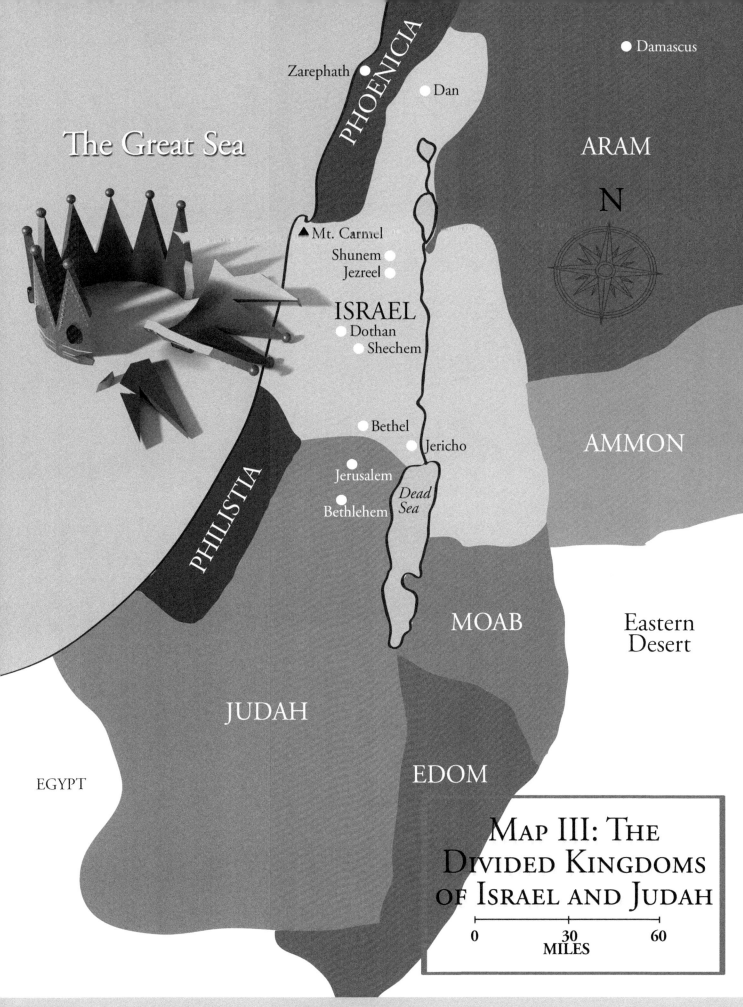

The Great Sea

PHOENICIA

Zarephath

Dan

Damascus

ARAM

N

▲ Mt. Carmel

Shunem

Jezreel

ISRAEL

Dothan

Shechem

PHILISTIA

Bethel

Jericho

AMMON

Jerusalem

Dead
Sea

Bethlehem

MOAB

Eastern
Desert

JUDAH

EDOM

EGYPT

Map III: The
Divided Kingdoms
of Israel and Judah

0   30   60
MILES

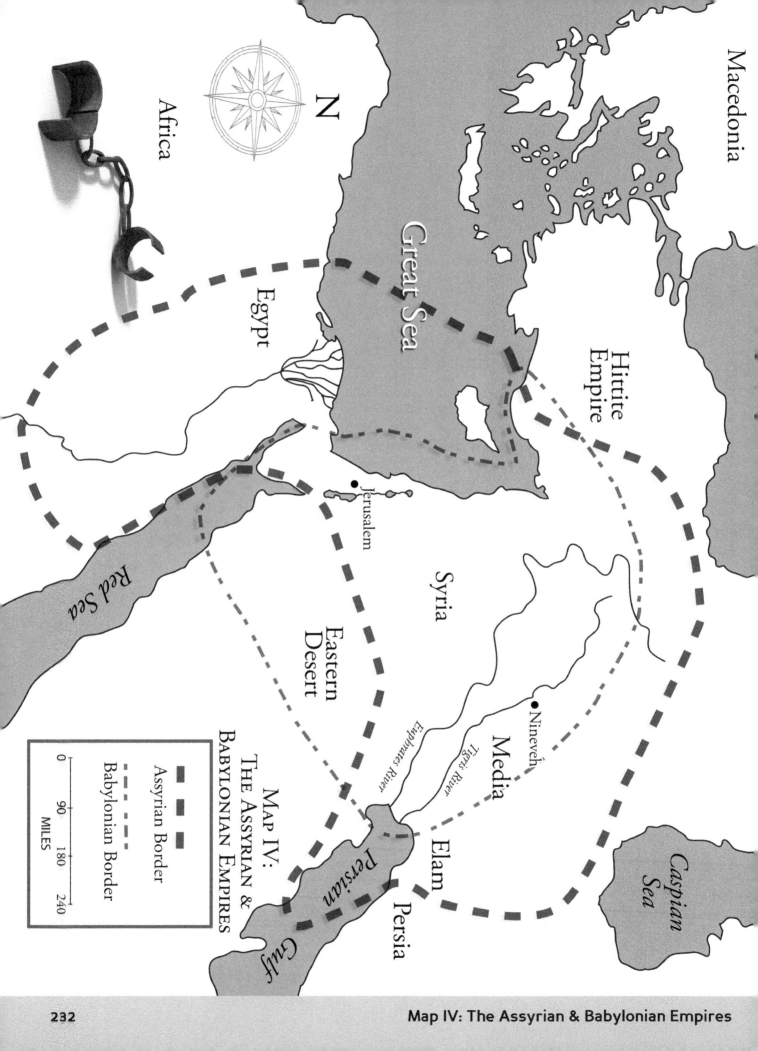

Macedonia

Africa

N

Great Sea

Hittite
Empire

Egypt

Jerusalem

Syria

Red Sea

Eastern
Desert

Euphrates River

Tigris River

Nineveh

Media

Elam

Caspian
Sea

Persian

Persia

Gulf

MAP IV:
THE ASSYRIAN &
BABYLONIAN EMPIRES

Assyrian Border

Babylonian Border

0   90   180   240
MILES

chapter 1 Quiz

A. MEMORY VERSE:

"In those days there was no _____ in Israel; everyone did what was

_____ in his own _____." (Judges 21:25)

B. KEY FACTS: Circle "T" if the sentence is true and "F" if the sentence is false.

1. Samuel was a judge all the days of his life.   T   F

2. In his job as judge, Samuel offered sacrifices in the tabernacle.   T   F

3. Samuel judged Israel for only a few years.   T   F

4. Samuel was set apart to be a Nazirite before he was born.   T   F

5. Everyone in Israel knew that Samuel was called to be a prophet.   T   F

C. STORY FACTS: Cross out the word(s) that is/are not correct.

1. God's promise to be the God of His people is His (covenant/blessing).

2. The tabernacle was located in the city of (Shechem/Shiloh).

3. The LORD's message to Eli was a message of (blessing/judgment).

4. The word "anoint" means (chosen to serve/make sacrifices to) God.

D. WHO AM I? Use the names below to fill in the blanks.

       Hannah   Eli   Samuel   Phinehas   The LORD

1. I was the priest at the tabernacle in Shiloh.   _____

2. I called Samuel four times in one night.   _____

3. I prayed that the LORD would give me a son.   _____

4. Before I was born, I was set apart to serve the LORD.   _____

5. I was a wicked priest who sinned against God.   _____

Across

3. A person called to speak for God is a _____.

5. Eli _____ God's judgement on his family.

8. Who called Samuel one night when he was in bed?

9. A person set apart to serve God is a _____.

10. Hannah prayed that God would give her a _____.

Down

1. A man who offered sacrifices is a _____.

2. God's promise to be the God of His people forever is His _____.

4. A deliverer, peacemaker, and civil leader is a _____.

6. Judges 21:25 says that "everyone did what was right in his own _____."

7. Elkanah's family worshipped at the tabernacle at _____.

Chapter 2 Quiz

A. MEMORY VERSE: "Remember the _____ _____

of old, For I am God, and there is no _____; I am God, and there is

_____ like Me." (Isaiah 46:9)

B. KEY FACTS: Number these events from 1 to 5 in the correct order.

The Ark of the Covenant's Journey

_____ The ark was at Abinadab's house for 20 years.

_____ The priests took the ark to the battlefield.

_____ The ark sat in the tabernacle at Shiloh.

_____ God sent rats and tumors to the people at Ekron and Gath.

_____ The Lord destroyed the idol Dagon at Ashdod.

C. STORY FACTS: Fill in the blanks.

1. Eli fell backwards and died when he heard that the _____ had been captured by the Philistines.

2. Phinehas' wife named her son _____, meaning "the _____ [of the Lord] has departed."

3. The Lord wanted Israel to know that He _____ those who obeyed Him and brought _____ to those who disobeyed Him.

4. The Lord sent a plague of _____ and _____ to the Philistines in Ashdad, Gath, and Ekron.

5. Samuel called the memorial stone _____.

6. _____ was the chief god of the Philistines.

7. When Samuel assembled the Israelites at Mizpah, they did two things:

   a. _____ their sin.

   b. _____ to the Lord.

8. The Philistines sent Israel a _____ _____ of gold tumors.

Across

1. Samuel assembled the people at _____.

4. Samuel ruled over Israel as a _____.

6. The Philistines sent a _____ offering of five gold tumors and five gold rats.

7. Where did the Israelites take the ark to give them good fortune?

9. Where did the ark stay for twenty years?

10. In Isaiah 46:9 God says "I am God, and there is _____ like me."

Down

2. The Israelites moved the ark from Shiloh to the battlefield because they thought it would protect them from the _____?

3. What name means "the glory of the LORD has departed"?

5. What name means "thus far has the LORD helped us"?

8. Where was Dagon's temple located?

chapter 3 Quiz

A. MEMORY VERSE: "Behold, to _____ is better than sacrifice,

And to _____ than the fat of rams." (1 Samuel 15:22b)

B. KEY FACTS: Draw a line from the nation to the phrase that describes it.

Israel's Neighbors

Amalek	Ehud defeated King Eglon from this nation.
Ammon	This nation captured the ark.
Edom	Agag was this nation's king.
Moab	Esau was the founder of this nation.
Philistia	Defeating them led to accepting Saul as king

C. STORY FACTS: Cross out the **wrong** answer.

1. The LORD said that the people were rejecting (Samuel/the LORD).

2. Saul was looking for his father's (donkeys/sheep).

3. Samuel's sons were (wicked/righteous) men.

4. Samuel was (pleased/sad) that the Israelites wanted a king.

5. Saul was (eager/reluctant) to become Israel's first king.

6. After the battle with the Ammonites, the people had (doubts/no doubts) that Saul should be king.

7. Saul could not make a sacrifice because he was not a (priest/prophet).

8. Because Saul disobeyed, God said He would take away Saul's (army/kingdom).

9. Samuel said that (obedience/sacrifice) was the better way to please God.

10. The LORD was (pleased/grieved) that He had made Saul king in Israel.

Across

2. Who was the king of Moab?

4. Who was the king of the Amalekites?

5. What was Saul looking for when Samuel anointed him?

6. The Israelites demanded to have a _____.

7. In John 14:15 Jesus says "If you love Me, you will keep My _____."

8. Saul was anointed _____ times.

Down

1. Saul was not allowed to make sacrifices because he was not a _____.

2. Esau was the founder of _____.

3. What does the LORD say is better than sacrifice?

4. What was the nation that Jephthah fought and defeated?

Chapter 4 Quiz

A. MEMORY VERSE: "For the LORD does not see as _____ sees;

for man looks at the _____ _____, but the LORD looks at

the _____." (1 Samuel 16:7b)

B. KEY FACTS: Draw a line from the type of psalm to the words that best describe its purpose.

Types of Psalms

Repentance Psalm	Gives good advice
Hallelujah Psalm	Sung on a journey
Pilgrim Psalm	Confesses sin
Judgment Psalm	Praises God
Wisdom Psalm	Requests justice

C. STORY FACTS: Circle "T" for true or "F" for false.

1. Samuel was happy that the LORD rejected Saul as king.   T F

2. David's family lived in the city of Jerusalem.   T F

3. Psalm 119 is the longest psalm in the Bible.   T F

4. The LORD chose David even though he was Jesse's youngest son.   T F

5. While watching the sheep, David killed a lion and a wolf.   T F

D. WHAT DO YOU REMEMBER? Circle the **correct** answer.

1. God's plan _____.

    is always good   depends upon our choices

2. A distressing spirit came upon Saul because _____.

    he worried too much   the LORD had left him

3. In God's time, David would one day rule over Israel because _____.

    he was handsome and strong   he had a godly heart

4. David would be a good king for Israel because _____.

    he served God as his King   he was a brave man

Across

3. What type of psalm is sung on journeys to Jerusalem?
6. What type of psalm gives wise counsel
8. What type of psalm talks about the Messiah?
9. What type of psalm thanks God for His mercy?
10. What type of psalm gives praise to God?

Down

1. What is the Hebrew title for Psalms?
2. What type of psalm reminds Israel of what God did?
4. What type of psalm expresses sorrow over sin?
5. What type of psalm asks God to judge the wicked?
7. What type of psalm is sung during the Passover meal?

Chapter 5 Quiz

A. MEMORY VERSE: "In God I _____; I will not be _____.

What can mortal _____ do to me?" (Psalm 56:4b, NIV)

B. KEY FACTS: Put an "X" in front of the sentences that are true.

_____ David trusted the LORD by faith.

_____ When facing Goliath, David put his confidence in his slingshot skills.

_____ David was successful because the LORD gave him success.

_____ Saul sent David to battle so people would sing David's praises.

_____ Saul threw spears at David because he was jealous of David.

_____ David played music for Saul even after Saul tried to kill him.

_____ When David went to battle, God gave him victory over his enemies.

_____ Jonathan refused to help David escape from Saul's anger.

C. STORY FACTS: Circle the **correct** answer.

1. David wanted to accept Goliath's challenge because Goliath _____.

   had insulted King Saul   had defied Israel's God

2. David was confident when he faced Goliath one-on-one because _____.

   the LORD was with him   he had good slingshot skills

3. Saul was jealous of David because _____.

   all the people praised David   David played the lyre well

4. Saul was afraid of David because _____.

   the people praised David   the LORD was with David

5. The message of Jonathan's three arrows was _____.

   Saul didn't want to kill David   Saul did want to kill David

Across

4. Psalm 56:4b says "What can _____ man do to me?"

7. What did David's wife put in the bed to trick Saul's soldiers?

8. Jonathan was Saul's _____.

9. David put his trust in the _____.

10. What did Saul throw at David?

Down

1. The women's praise of David made Saul _____.

2. Who did David kill with one stone?

3. Saul's intention was to _____ David.

5. Who was David's wife?

6. How many arrows did Jonathan shoot to warn David?

Chapter 6 Quiz

A. MEMORY VERSES: "For the word of the LORD is _____, And

all His work is done in _____. He loves _____ and

_____; The earth is full of the _____ of the LORD." (Psalm 33:4-5)

B. KEY FACTS: Match the word on the left with its meaning on the right.

_____ Fortress   1. God gives you strength.

_____ King   2. God cares for you perfectly.

_____ Light   3. God never changes.

_____ Rock   4. God is a strong, safe place to hide.

_____ Shepherd   5. God is in charge of the whole world.

_____ Shield   6. God defends you from your enemies.

_____ Strength   7. God shows you the right thing to do.

C. STORY FACTS: Cross out the **wrong** word and put the **correct** word in the blank at the end of the sentence.

1. Abiathar killed the eighty-five priests at Nob. _____

2. At Gath the Philistines thought David was silly. _____

3. David secretly took Saul's spear and shield. _____

4. When David was in hiding, the tabernacle was located at Shiloh. _____

5. Ahimelech gave David consecrated meat to eat. _____

6. Ahimelech also gave David Goliath's helmet. _____

7. Saul went to a prophet to get advice before the battle. _____

D. WHAT'S THE POINT? Complete these sentences.

David knew that the LORD's plan was _____ and _____.

He had to _____ patiently for the LORD's will to happen.

Across

2. David depicts God as _____ because He shows His people the right thing to do.

4. David did not kill Saul because Saul was God's _____.

7. When you feel weak and helpless, God is your _____.

9. Ahimelech gave David consecrated bread from the _____.

10. In what hills did David and his men hide?

Down

1. Saul visited a _____ to get advice.

3. Psalm 33:5 says "The earth is full of the _____ of the Lᴏʀᴅ."

5. Psalm 33:4 says "For the word of the Lord is _____."

6. God is like a _____ because He protects His people from their enemies.

8. Where did David pretend to be insane?

Chapter 7 Quiz

A. MEMORY VERSE: Cross out the **wrong** word.

1. "To obey is better than (worship/sacrifice)." (1 Samuel 15:22b)

2. "The earth is full of the (goodness/lovingkindness) of the LORD." (Psalm 33:5)

3. "In those days there was no (king/judge) in Israel." (Judges 21:25)

4. "In God I (trust/hope); I will not be (sad/afraid)." (Psalm 56:4b, NIV)

5. "The LORD looks at the (heart/outward appearance)." (1 Samuel 16:7b)

B. STORY FACTS: Circle "T" for true and "F" for false.

1. The LORD was faithful to David because he never sinned.   T   F

2. Israel wanted a king so it could be like other nations.   T   F

3. The covenant is God's promise to be the God of His people.   T   F

4. A judgment psalm asks God for forgiveness of sin.   T   F

5. Pilgrim psalms were sung at the Passover meal.   T   F

6. The LORD rejected Saul because Saul didn't obey God as King.   T   F

7. David killed Goliath with Saul's sword.   T   F

8. David refused to kill Saul because he was God's anointed king.   T   F

C. WHICH OF THESE GO TOGETHER? Match the things on the right with the correct description on the left.

_____ Samuel	1. A Philistine god
_____ Saul	2. Means "thus far has the LORD helped us"
_____ Jonathan	3. Priest at the tabernacle in Shiloh
_____ Ebenezer	4. David's loyal friend
_____ Ichabod	5. Last judge of Israel
_____ Eli	6. Means "the glory [of the LORD] has departed from Israel"
_____ Dagon	7. First king of Israel

Across

2. Who was the last judge in Israel?

4. Who was a loyal friend of David?

6. In what town were eighty-five priests killed?

8. 1 Samuel 16:7b says that "Man looks at the _____ _____, but the LORD looks at the heart."

9. How many feet tall was the giant Goliath?

10. According to Psalm 33:4-5, the LORD loves _____ and justice.

Down

1. If the second line in a Hebrew poem has a similar meaning to the first line, then it is part of what category?

3. God's promise to be the God of His people forever is His _____.

5. Who was the king that Saul didn't kill?

7. If something is "set apart by God" then it is _____.

Chapter 8 Quiz

A. MEMORY VERSE: "I have made a covenant with My _____, I have

sworn to My _____ David: 'Your _____ I will establish

_____, And build up your _____ to all generations.'"
(Psalm 89:3-4)

B. KEY FACTS: Fill in the blanks below.

1. What four things about the covenant with David were like the covenant with Abraham?

_____ _____ _____ _____

2. God promised David that his son would build the _____.

3. The _____ would be born from David's line.

4. God said that David's kingdom would endure _____.

5. The everlasting kingdom is the _____.

C. STORY FACTS: Circle the **correct** answer.

1. David was anointed king of Judah in the city of _____.

    Jerusalem   Hebron   Shiloh

2. Joab killed Abner because Abner killed _____.

    Asahel   Ishbosheth   Uzzah

3. The LORD told Nathan that _____ would build the temple.

    David   David's son   Obed-Edom

4. Uzzah was killed when the ark was moved because _____.

    people were dancing   Uzzah laughed   Uzzah touched it

D. WHAT'S THE POINT? Complete these sentences.

The covenant with David promised David a _____ name, and a

_____ that would last forever. God also promised that the

_____ would come from David's line.

Across

3. The LORD promised that David's son would build God a _____.

6. The everlasting kingdom is the kingdom of _____.

8. Who was the prophet that told David not to build a temple?

9. Who touched the ark and died?

10. What city did David make his capital?

Down

1. In what city was David first crowned king?

2. In Psalm 89:4 the LORD says to David that He will "build up your throne to all _____."

4. The LORD promised that the _____ would be born from David's line.

5. David eventually became king of _____.

7. Who was Saul's commander?

Chapter 9 Quiz

A. MEMORY VERSE: "Blessed is he whose _____ is forgiven, Whose _____ is covered." (Psalm 32:1)

B. KEY FACTS: Fill in the blanks.

When David sinned…

1. He stayed home while his army went to _____.

2. He loved another man's _____.

3. He _____ Uriah and then _____ Bathsheba.

When God showed His grace to David…

1. God sent _____ to confront David.

2. David _____, and God _____ him.

3. Even though he was forgiven, David had to bear consequences from his _____.

C. STORY FACTS: Match the word on the left with its description on the right.

_____ Mephibosheth   1. Husband of Bathsheba killed in battle

_____ Ziba   2. Prophet who confronted David

_____ Joab   3. Woman whom David loved too much

_____ Nathan   4. Servant of Saul's household

_____ Bathsheba   5. Son of Jonathan

_____ Uriah   6. Commander of David's army

D. WHAT'S TRUE AND WHAT'S NOT? Circle "T" for true, and "F" for false.

1. David showed kindness instead of revenge to Mephibosheth.   T   F

2. By his own words, David condemned himself for his sin.   T   F

3. The Lord opened David's eyes to his sin.   T   F

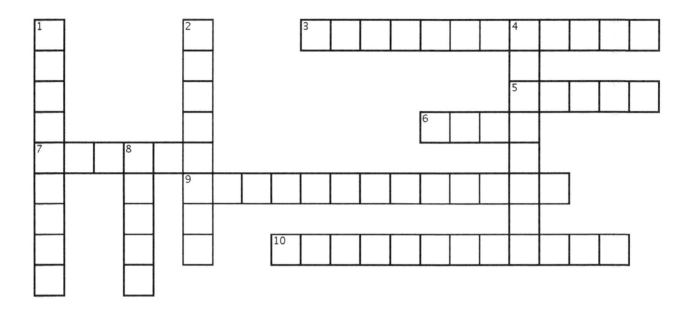

Across

3. David showed kindness to _____ because of his friendship with Jonathan.
5. When _____ refused to go home to be with his wife, David plotted to have him killed.
6. Who was David's chief commander?
7. God sent _____ to confront David with his sin.
9. Psalm 31:1 says "Blessed is he whose _____ is forgiven"
10. David had to bear the _____ of his sin, and his son died.

Down

1. In the spring, David should have led his army against the _____.
2. David _____ after he heard Nathan's story about the rich man.
4. David had a _____ heart and refused to repent for a long time.
8. David was a man after God's _____.

Chapter 10 Quiz

A. MEMORY VERSE: "But You, O Lord, are a _____ for me,

My _____ and the One who lifts up my _____.... I

_____ _____ and _____; I _____,

for the Lord sustained me." (Psalm 3:3, 5)

B. KEY FACTS: Number (1-7) the events in the **correct** order.

_____ Absalom killed Amnon when Amnon was not punished for his sin.

_____ Sheba revolted against David, and eleven tribes rejected David.

_____ Absalom plotted to take the kingdom from his father, David.

_____ David ordered a census to count the number of fighting men.

_____ Joab killed Amasa and then pursued Sheba to kill him.

_____ Joab killed Absalom in battle.

_____ Amnon sinned against his half sister Tamar.

C. STORY FACTS: Circle the **correct** answer.

1. David had troubles in his family and in his kingdom because _____.

   God was angry with him   his sin had consequences

2. When Amnon sinned against Tamar, David _____.

   did nothing   punished him severely

3. David made Amasa commander of his army because _____.

   Joab was not loyal to him   he wanted to win back Israel

4. When David took a census of fighting men, he was trusting in _____.

   the Lord's strength   the strength of his army

5. David was a king who pleased the Lord because he _____.

   showed kindness to people   remembered God was King

Across

1. "But You, O Lord, are a _____ for me..." (Psalm 3:3)

5. David pleased God because he remembered that the LORD was the real _____ of Israel.

6. When David took a census, he was trusting in the strength of his army instead of in the _____.

7. Who was the son of David and Bathsheba?

9. "I lay down and slept; I awoke for the LORD _____ me." (Psalm 3:5)

Down

1. After David sinned and ordered the census, he chose three days of _____ as a consequence.

2. How many tribes followed Sheba?

3. David worshipped God by building an _____.

4. Who was the commander that replaced Joab?

8. Who killed Absalom?

Chapter 11 Quiz

A. MEMORY VERSE: "The _____ of the LORD is the beginning of

_____, And the knowledge of the _____

_____ is _____ _____." (Proverbs 9:10)

B. KEY FACTS: Cross out the **wrong** word(s) in each sentence and write the **correct** word(s) in the blank beside it.

1. Psalms is the book that teaches us how to be wise.   _____

2. The Preacher tells us to find purpose in fame and possessions. _____

3. Most of the book of Proverbs was written by David.   _____

4. Song of Songs tells you to celebrate God's gift of wisdom.   _____

5. Job teaches you how to trust God in times of happiness.   _____

C. STORY FACTS: Circle "T" if the sentence is true and "F" is the sentence is false.

1. Nathan and Zadok anointed Solomon as king.   T   F

2. To fear God means God's children should be terrified of God.   T   F

3. Job never asked God why he was suffering.   T   F

4. The woman willing to give up the child was the real mother.   T   F

5. When God came to Solomon in a dream, Solomon asked for joy.   T   F

6. The Old Testament has five books of poetry.   T   F

7. Solomon was wiser than the greatest wise men of Egypt.   T   F

D. WHO AM I? Match the person with the description.

_____ Solomon   1. Solomon's mother

_____ Adonijah   2. David's son who became king

_____ Agur   3. Priest who anointed Solomon

_____ Zadok   4. David's son who schemed to be king

_____ Bathsheba   5. Man who wrote a few Proverbs

Across

4. "And the knowledge of the Holy One is _____." (Psalm 9:10)

7. Wisdom begins with _____ God.

8. What Old Testament book is about finding purpose in the fear of God?

9. Proverbs 31 descibes the _____ woman.

10. Who wrote Song of Songs?

Down

1. Job never _____ God.

2. What Old Testament book is about being wise and making good choices?

3. Job's friends said he was suffering because he was _____.

5. David, the Sons of Korah, and _____ wrote Psalms.

6. "The fear of the LORD is the beginning of _____." (Psalm 9:10)

Chapter 12 Quiz

A. MEMORY VERSE: "Praise be to the LORD, who has given _____

to his people Israel just as he _____. Not _____

_____ has failed of all the _____ _____

he gave through his servant _____." (1 Kings 8:56, NIV)

B. KEY FACTS: Circle the **correct** answer.

1. God wanted Solomon to have an _____ heart before Him.

      upright   honest   fearful

2. God said he would establish Solomon's _____ forever if he obeyed God.

      wisdom   temple   throne

3. If Solomon worshipped idols, then the LORD would reject _____.

      Solomon's family   the consecrated temple   the Israelites

4. If Solomon turned from the LORD, then other nations would _____ Israel.

      laugh at   give gifts to   attack

C. STORY FACTS: Fill in the blanks.

1. David couldn't build the temple because he had been a _____.

2. Hiram, king of Tyre, gave Solomon _____ for the temple.

3. Building the temple took _____ years.

4. The queen of _____ heard of Solomon's fame and visited him.

5. Ahijah told Jeroboam that someday he would rule _____ tribes.

D. HOW DID SOLOMON SIN? Write a sentence about one way that Solomon sinned against the LORD.

_____

_____

Across

1. The names of the two temple _____ were Boaz and Jachin.

5. The LORD was angry with Solomon because he forgot the _____.

8. How many years did it take to build the palace?

9. Hiram of _____ gave Solomon cedars of Lebanon for the temple.

Down

1. "Praise be to the LORD, who has given rest to his people Israel just as he _____." (1 Kings 8:56)

2. How many years did it take to build the temple?

3. One way Solomon sinned against the LORD was by marrying _____ wives.

4. God's covenant with Solomon required Solomon to have an _____ heart and obey God.

6. The prophet _____ told Jeroboam he would rule ten tribes.

7. The Queen of _____ heard of Solomon's fame and visited him.

Chapter 13 Quiz

A. MEMORY VERSE: Use the words in the box to answer the questions below. Use the words only once.

Holy One   My chosen   The LORD   His people   Servant David

1. To whom did the LORD swear, "I will establish your seed." _____

2. The knowledge of whom gives understanding? _____

3. To whom did the LORD make a covenant? _____

4. To whom did the LORD give rest? _____

5. Who is the One that sustains me when I lay down and sleep? _____

B. STORY FACTS: Fill in the blanks with the correct answers.

1. Because David was a warrior, he couldn't build the _____.

2. Uzzah was killed when he touched the ark because the ark was _____.

3. _____ means being contented because God is pleased with you.

4. _____ God means respecting and being in awe of God.

5. When God appeared to Solomon in a dream, Solomon asked for _____.

6. Satan wanted Job to _____ God, but Job never did.

7. Solomon loved his many wives and began to worship _____.

C. WHICH OF THESE GO TOGETHER? Match these things.

_____ Joab   1. Prophet who spoke to David

_____ Ishbosheth   2. Author of Ecclesiastes

_____ Absalom   3. Saul's son who was king briefly

_____ Molech   4. Commander of David's army

_____ Nathan   5. David's rebellious son

_____ The Preacher   6. God of the Ammonites

ACross

3. What word means "contented because God is pleased with you"?

5. What instrument did David play?

6. God promised to make David's _____ great.

10. God blesses us by giving _____ for sins.

Down

1. Who built the temple?

2. Transgression is the _____ of one of God's laws.

4. After God asked Job question upon question, Job was overwhelmed by God's _____.

7. How many books of poetry are in the Old Testament?

8. Solomon was the wisest of all men because he asked God for _____.

9. Song of Songs celebrates God's gift of _____.

Chapter 14 Quiz

A. MEMORY VERSE: "[They] exchanged the _____ of God for the

_____, and _____ and _____ the creature

rather than the _____, who is blessed _____. Amen."
(Romans 1:25)

B. KEY FACTS: Match the words with their descriptions.

_____ King Rehoboam   1. Prophet in Israel

_____ Ahijah   2. Solomon's son who became king

_____ Bethel   3. First capital of Israel

_____ King Asa   4. King who made golden calves

_____ King Jeroboam   5. A worship center in Israel

_____ Shechem   6. Capital of Judah

_____ Jerusalem   7. A godly king of Judah

C. STORY FACTS: Circle "T" for true and "F" for false.

1. After Rehoboam became king, the people's lives were easier.   T   F

2 Jeroboam wanted his people to worship in Jerusalem.   T   F

3. Ahijah had prophesied that Jeroboam would be king in Israel.   T   F

4. Asa's heart was committed to worshipping the LORD.   T   F

5. Israel's neighbors thought Omri was an impressive king.   T   F

6. Rehoboam listened to the advice of the older, wise men.   T   F

7. Jeroboam was more evil than all who had lived before him.   T   F

D. WHY WAS ASA A GODLY KING?

Write one thing that Asa did that pleased the LORD:

_____

Across

1. Jeroboam sent his _____ to Ahijah to ask for his son's healing.

6. "They exchanged the truth of God for the lie, and _____ and served the creature rather than the Creator..." (Romans 1:25)

8. What was the name of Jeroboam's son who ruled after him?

10. Who was Solomon's son?

Down

2. Because Asa was committed to them LORD, he smashed _____ altars and removed idols.

3. Rehoboam took the advice of the _____ men.

4. Ahab was a king of _____.

5. When Rehoboam became king, the people got upset about the _____ _____ and harsh labor.

7. Who plotted against and killed Jeroboam's family?

9. Jehoshaphat was a king of _____.

Chapter 15 Quiz

A. MEMORY VERSE: "The steps of a _____ _____

are ordered by the _____, And He _____ in his way.

Though he _____, he shall not be utterly _____

_____; For the LORD upholds him with His _____."
(Psalm 37:23-24)

B. KEY FACTS: Answer the questions below.

1. What did God stop in Israel for several years? _____ and _____

2. Who did Elijah bring back to life? _____ _____

3. What did God provide for the widow to eat? _____ and _____

4. What was the name of Ahab's wicked wife? _____

5. How did the LORD speak to encourage Elijah? _____

C. STORY FACTS: Match the words/numbers with their description.

_____ Rain

_____ Flour and oil

_____ 450

_____ Mt. Carmel

_____ Three

_____ Mt. Horeb

_____ Jezebel

_____ Widow's son

_____ Widow from Zarephath

_____ Bread and meat

_____ Fire

1. What fell down on Elijah's sacrifice

2. Person Elijah brought back to life

3. Times water was poured on sacrifice

4. Where the LORD encouraged Elijah

5. What the ravens brought Elijah to eat

6. Person who wanted to kill Elijah

7. Number of prophets of Baal

8. What didn't fall in Israel for several years

9. Where Elijah challenged Baal's prophets

10. Person who provided food for Elijah

11. What God provided for the widow

D. WHY WAS AHAB A WICKED KING?

Write one way that Ahab sinned against the LORD.

_____

ACross

1. What did Elijah have poured on his sacrifice three times?

4. The Lord sent _____ to bring food to Elijah.

5. Who was the wife of Ahab?

8. "Though he fall, he shall not be utterly _____ _____..." (Psalm 37:24)

9. "The steps of a _____ man are ordered by the Lord..." (Psalm 37:23)

Down

1. God spoke to Elijah in a _____.

2. Abah was more wicked than Jeroboam because he built a temple for _____.

3. Elijah said, "Shout louder. Maybe your god is _____."

6. Elijah promised the widow would always have _____ and oil to make bread.

7. When Elijah spoke the words from God, the _____ and dew stopped for several years.

Chapter 16 Quiz

A. MEMORY VERSE: "Many are the _____ in a man's

_____, but it is the LORD's _____ that prevails."
(Proverbs 19:21, NIV)

B. KEY FACTS: Circle "T" for true and "F" for false.

1. Jehoshaphat turned his people back to the LORD.   T   F

2. Ahab put the prophet Jehu in prison.   T   F

3. Ahab followed in the ways of King Jeroboam.   T   F

4. Jehoshaphat was always in battle with neighboring nations.   T   F

5. The nation of Aram attacked Judah several times.   T   F

6. Jehoshaphat prayed before he went to battle with his enemies.   T   F

7. Ahab built a temple to worship the Canaanite god, Baal.   T   F

C. STORY FACTS: Circle the **correct** answer.

1. The prophet said that Ahab would die because he _____.

    refused to kill Ben-Hadad   took Naboth's vineyard

2. When he wanted to go to war with Aram, Ahab listened to _____.

    400 prophets   the prophet Micaiah

3. Jezebel's false witnesses accused Naboth of _____.

    stealing from the king   blaspheming God

4. Ahab was killed on the battlefield by _____.

    the king of Aram's sword   a random arrow

5. Before the battle, the prophet Jahaziel told Jehoshaphat that _____.

    God would deliver Judah   he would die in battle

D. WHAT'S THE POINT? From the battle of Jehoshaphat and Ahab against the king of
Aram, what do you learn about God?

God's plan _____

Across

1. Who owned the vineyard that Ahab wanted?
3. "Many are the _____ in a man's heart, but it is the Lord's purpose that prevails." (Proverbs 19:21)
4. When Ahab worshipped Baal, he was rejecting God's _____.
6. The prophet Jahaziel told Jehoshaphat not to be _____.
8. King Jehoshaphat served the _____ and walked in the ways of David.
9. Jehoshaphat told his judges to fear the Lord and judge _____.
10. A person becomes a prophet when the Lord sends, _____, and speaks to them (see Jeremiah 14:14, NIV).

Down

2. Ahab disobeyed God when he refused to kill _____.
5. If a prophet says to _____ idols, he is not from God.
7. When Judah arrived at the battlefield, they saw only _____ bodies.

chapter 17 Quiz

A. MEMORY VERSE: "[The Most High] does according to His will in the

_____ of _____ And among the _____

of the _____ _____. No one can restrain His _____ Or say to Him,

'_____?'" (Daniel 4:35b)

B. KEY FACTS: God is sovereign over everything. Draw a line from the category on the left to the event on the right.

Category	Event
God is sovereign over…	**By God's power Elisha was able to…**
Nature	Fill jars with oil
Ordinary People	Bring the dead to life
Life and Death	Divide the Jordan River
Disease	Know when the siege would end
Enemies and Nations	Prophesy who will be king
Disaster/Good Fortune	Heal from leprosy
Rulers	Know enemy battle plans

C. STORY FACTS: Cross out the **wrong** answer.

1. Elijah went to heaven in a (chariot/whirlwind).

2. Elisha received a double portion of Elijah's (spirit/boldness).

3. Elisha put (oil/salt) in the bad spring water to make it healthy.

4. Elisha was not afraid because (God's heavenly host/Israel's army) was protecting the city of Dothan.

5. God's sovereignty means that God (knows/controls) everything.

D. WHAT'S THE POINT OF ELISHA'S MINISTRY?

God is _____.

Across

1. God made the Shunammite woman's _____ come back to life.

3. Elijah and _____ both went to heaven without dying first.

6. God has all power. That means he is _____.

7. God told _____ about Aram's war plans.

8. God knows all things. That means he is _____.

9. God healed _____ of leprosy

Down

1. God controls all things. That means he is _____.

2. Elisha was not afraid because God's _____ were protecting the city.

4. What item did Elisha use to divide the Jordan River?

5. Elisha received a double portion of Elijah's _____.

Chapter 18 Quiz

A. MEMORY VERSE: "Those who cling to _____ _____

forfeit the _____ that could be theirs." (Jonah 2:8, NIV)

B. KEY FACTS: Circle "T" for true and "F" for false.

1. A true prophet is always called by God.   T   F
2. One test of a prophet is that his words must come true.   T   F
3. All the prophets wrote books in the Old Testament.   T   F
4. A prophet doesn't talk about sin, only about God's love.   T   F
5. A prophet reminds people that repentance brings mercy.   T   F
6. A true prophet spoke only to people in Israel and Judah.   T   F

C. STORY FACTS: In the blanks, write the name of the prophet who fits the description (Amos, Hosea, Jonah).

1. I was a herdsman and farmer in a wilderness village.   _____

2. I didn't want to be God's prophet and ran away.   _____

3. I spoke about fire to remind people that sin was terrible.   _____

4. I had a broken heart over Israel's unfaithfulness.   _____

5. I learned that God gives salvation to whom He chooses.   _____

6. I had children named "not loved" and "not my people."   _____

7. My name means "bearer of burdens."   _____

8. I urged Israel to return to the LORD because He loved them.   _____

9. I said the words, "Let justice roll like a river."   _____

10. I was angry when the people I talked to repented.   _____

D. WHAT'S THE REASON? What is the meaning of Amos's words "for three sins and even for four sins?"

God had been _____ with Israel's sin for a _____.

Across

4. Inside the great fish, Jonah _____ of his sin.
5. When Amos said, "For three sins, and even for four," he meant that God had been _____.
6. A prophet must be _____ by God.
9. The religious Israelites to whom Hosea spoke worshipped golden _____.
10. Four themes of prophets are: sin, punishment, repentance, and _____.

Down

1. Who did Hosea marry?
2. The test of the true prophet is that his words must be true and _____ with God's law.
3. "Those who cling to _____ idols forfeit the grace that could be theirs." (Jonah 2:8)
7. Being a prophet meant that most people _____ you.
8. Who came from the village of Tekoa in Judah and went to preach to the people in Israel?

Chapter 19 Quiz

A. MEMORY VERSES: Cross out the **wrong** word and write the **correct** word in the blank.

1. "[They] exchanged the purposes of God for the lie." _____

2. "The ways of a good man are ordered by the LORD." _____

3. "Many are the plans in a man's mind." _____

4. "No one can restrain His power." _____

5. "Those who cling to worthless idols forfeit the mercy that could be theirs." _____

B. STORY FACTS: Cross out the **wrong** word.

1. God spoke to Elijah through (an earthquake/a gentle whisper).

2. The kingdom split in two when (Rehoboam/Jeroboam) became king.

3. Hosea's marriage to Gomer was a picture of God's (love/power).

4. Jonah didn't want the Ninevites to (kill him/repent of their sin).

5. All of the first eight kings of Israel worshipped (idols/the LORD).

6. The (kings/prophets) were called by God to speak God's words.

7. (Elijah/Elisha) told Naaman to wash in the river to be healed.

8. The prophets told the people that repentance brings (mercy/judgment).

C. WHICH OF THESE GO TOGETHER? Match these things.

_____ Jonah	1. King of Aram who fought against Israel
_____ Ben-Hadad	2. King of Israel who made golden calves
_____ Ahab	3. Prophet of salvation
_____ Elijah	4. King who disguised himself in battle
_____ Amos	5. Prophet who loved an unfaithful woman
_____ Jehoshaphat	6. Prophet who challenged prophets of Baal
_____ Hosea	7. Prophet of justice
_____ Jeroboam	8. King of Judah who turned people back to God

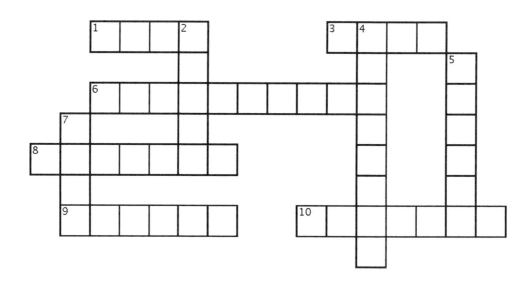

Across

1. Abijah was a _____.

3. Which prophet was born in Judah but prophesied in Israel?

6. Hosea's marriage to Gomer was a picture of God's love toward His _____ people.

8. Micaiah was a _____.

9. The king of Israel know all about Ben-Hadad's battle plans because God revealed them to _____.

10. The people rebelled against Rehoboam because he wouldn't make their _____ lighter.

Down

2. An idolater forfeits _____ from God.

4. Naaman was a _____ officer.

5. Naaman didn't want to wash in the _____ River because he thought it was a ridiculous idea.

7. Elijah challenged the prophets of Baal because he wanted people to know that Israel's God was the _____ God.

Chapter 20 Quiz

A. MEMORY VERSE: "For the LORD knows the _____ of the

_____, But the way of the _____ shall _____."
(Psalm 1:6)

B. KEY FACTS: Draw a line from the phrase to the proper box.

History of both Israel and Judah

Written by a priest

Stories of Elijah and Elisha

Have genealogies

Theme of judgment

Written by a priest

Theme of God's presence

KINGS

CHRONICLES

C. STORY FACTS: Circle the **correct** answer.

1. _____ hid baby Joash from wicked Queen Athaliah.

    Jeroboam   Jehoiada   Jehu

2. _____ of the kings of Israel were wicked kings.

    Most   Some   All

3. Uzziah sinned against the LORD when he _____ in the temple.

    offered incense   destroyed the altar   killed priests

4. _____ was stoned when he warned Joash of his sin.

    Jehoiada   Zechariah   Amaziah

5. In 722 BC, Israel was conquered by the nation of _____.

    Assyria   Babylon   Egypt

D. WHAT'S THE REASON?

Israel was destroyed because the kings didn't obey God as their _____

and the people forgot God's _____.

Across

2. The stories about Elijah and Elisha are in the books of _____.

5. Who brought the gods of Edom to Jerusalem?

7. Who was stoned because he warned Joash of his sin?

8. How old was Joash when he became king?

9. Two wicked queens were Jezebel and _____.

Down

1. "For the LORD knows the way of the _____, But the way of the ungodly shall perish." (Psalm 1:6)

3. Jehu killed _____, king of Israel, and Ahaziah, king of Judah.

4. Uzziah _____ when he burned incense in the temple because only a priest could do that.

5. Shalmaneser, king of _____, conquered Israel in 722 BC.

6. The books of Chronicles was written by a _____.

Chapter 21 Quiz

A. MEMORY VERSE: "He has shown you, O man, what is _____;

And what does the LORD require of you But to do _____, To love

_____, And to walk _____ with your God?" (Micah 6:8)

B. KEY FACTS: Cross out the **wrong** word.

1. The word "Messiah" means the (Anointed One/redeemer).

2. The Messiah will be called (Mighty God/Everlasting Savior).

3. Micah says that the Messiah would be born in (Jerusalem/Bethlehem).

4. The "Root of Jesse" means Jesus would be born of (Abraham/David).

5. The name Immanuel means ("God with us"/"loved of God").

6. Isaiah said the Messiah would open (eyes and ears/mouths and hearts).

C. STORY FACTS: Number the events from 1-7 in chronological order.

_____ Envoys from Babylon visited King Hezekiah.

_____ Hezekiah removed the high places and repaired the temple.

_____ The angel of the LORD killed 185,000 Assyrian soldiers.

_____ Hezekiah fortified Jerusalem and constructed a water tunnel.

_____ Assyria conquered all Judah's cities but Jerusalem.

_____ Hezekiah became ill, but the LORD healed him.

_____ The Assyrian army surrounded the city of Jerusalem.

D. WHO ARE THE PROPHETS?

Isaiah – Prophet of _____: When God asked, "Who should I send?" Isaiah

said, "_____ _____ _____, _____ _____."

Micah – Prophet of _____: Micah knew that God does not stay

_____ forever and delights to show _____."

Across

1. Jesus opens ears and eyes both physically and _____.

3. The word _____ means "The Anointed One."

8. Assyria captured all the cities of Judah except _____.

10. Hezekiah first began to fear the LORD and seek God after Micah _____.

Down

2. The word _____ means "God with us."

4. Hezekiah destroyed the bronze serpent because the people were _____ it.

5. "And what does the LORD require of you But to do justly, To love _____, And to walk humbly with your God?" (Micah 6:8)

6. _____ prayed for God's deliverance from the Assyrian army.

7. When the shadow moved _____, it was a sign that God would make Hezekiah well.

9. "He has shown you, O man, what is _____..." (Micah 6:8)

Chapter 22 Quiz

A. MEMORY VERSE: "For assuredly, I say to you, till _____ and

_____ pass away, one _____ or one _____

will by no means pass from the _____ till all is _____."
(Matthew 5:18)

B. KEY FACTS: Match the name with the description.

_____ **Adam**   1. Promise of God's presence/giving of the Law

_____ **Noah**   2. Promise of an everlasting kingdom

_____ **Abraham**   3. Promise of a coming Savior

_____ **Moses**   4. Promise never to flood the earth again

_____ **David**   5. Promise of a son, land, and blessing

"Covenant" means, God's _____ to be the God of His people _____.

C. STORY FACTS: Circle "T" if true and "F" if false.

1. Manasseh had the longest reign of all Judah's kings.   T   F

2. Manasseh served the LORD wholeheartedly all his life.   T   F

3. When Manasseh returned from Babylon, he served the LORD.   T   F

4. When Hilkiah found the Book of the Law, Josiah lamented.   T   F

5. Because Josiah served the LORD, God decided not to judge Judah.   T   F

6. Josiah read the Book of the Covenant to all the people.   T   F

7. Josiah smashed the worship center at Bethel that Jeroboam built.   T   F

8. Josiah celebrated the first Passover since the days of Joshua.   T   F

D. WHAT'S THE POINT?

Even though Josiah served the LORD wholeheartedly, _____ was still coming

to Judah because the people didn't change from the _____. The LORD said He

would take His _____ from Judah just as He had from Israel.

Across

7. Who was the longest reigning king of Judah?

8. God made a covenant with _____, and promised a Savior would come.

9. The LORD said He'd take His _____ from Judah because of their sin.

10. God made a covenant with _____, and promised never to destroy the earth again with a flood.

Down

1. With whom did God make a covenant promising His presence and giving the Law?

2. To whom did God promise a son, land, and blessing?

3. "For assuredly, I say to you, till _____ and earth pass away, one jot or one tittle will by no means pass from the law till all is fulfilled." (Matthew 5:18)

4. Josiah celebrated the Passover for the first time since _____.

5. To whom did God promise an everlasting kingdom?

6. After Josiah turned to the LORD, he began a reformation by repairing the _____.

Chapter 23 Quiz

A. MEMORY VERSE: "The LORD is slow to _____ and great in

_____; the LORD will not leave the _____ unpunished."
(Nahum 1:3a, NIV)

B. KEY FACTS: Write the initial of the prophet in the blanks.

O – Obadiah   N – Nahum   J – Joel   H – Habakkuk   Z – Zephaniah

_____ Prophet of God's grace   _____ Prophesied about Edom

_____ Asked God two questions   _____ Name means "comforter"

_____ Spoke about God's vengeance   _____ Spoke about a locust plague

_____ Descendent of King Hezekiah   _____ Prophesied against Assyria

_____ Prophet of God's wrath   _____ Prophet of faith

_____ Means "worshipper"   _____ Spoke about betrayal of Judah

C. STORY FACTS: Circle the **correct** answer.

1. Obadiah reminded God's people that God was _____.

       jealous   supreme King   good

2. Zephaniah said God's judgment was like a _____.

       plague of locusts   strong tornado   purifying fire

3. Nahum prophesied against Assyria, but wrote the words to _____.

       Judah   Babylon   Edom

4. Joel called people to repentance and told them to have _____.

       torn garments   pleasing sacrifices   broken hearts

5. Nahum's prophecy against Assyria was a _____.

       gleeful gloating   righteous reaction   angry revenge

D. WHAT'S THE POINT?

Habakkuk learned that he could trust God even in _____ circumstances.

Across

2. Zephaniah was a descendent of King _____.

4. Joel was a prophet of God's _____.

6. "The LORD will not leave the guilty _____." (Nahum 1:3a)

8. The theme of Nahum was the downfall of _____.

9. The name "Zephaniah" means "Jehovah _____."

10. The Book of Obadiah is a prophey against the nation of _____.

Down

1. The name "Obadiah" means _____.

3. "The LORD is slow to _____ and great in power..." (Nahum 1:3a)

5. Who was a prophet of faith?

7. What prophet's name means "comforter"?

Chapter 24 Quiz

A. MEMORY VERSE: "My people have committed two _____: They have _____ me, the spring of _____ _____, and have dug their own _____, broken cisterns that cannot _____ _____." (Jeremiah 2:13, NIV)

B. KEY FACTS: Circle "T" if true and "F" if false.

1. The broken cistern is a picture of the destruction of Jerusalem.   T   F
2. God shapes nations and people like clay on a potter's wheel.   T   F
3. The ruined linen belt described the wicked rulers.   T   F
4. God used a picture of a field to show that the exiles would return.   T   F
5. The smashed pot was a picture of a person's spiritual thirst.   T   F
6. The good figs are a picture of faithful prophets.   T   F

C. STORY FACTS: Match the things on the left with the description on the right.

_____ Gedaliah	1. King who burned up Jeremiah's scroll
_____ 50 years	2. Nation where Jeremiah died
_____ Baruch	3. Vision God gave to Jeremiah
_____ Almond tree branch	4. Years exiles would be in Babylon
_____ Zedekiah	5. Jeremiah's scribe
_____ 70 years	6. Picture used to describe the exiles
_____ Babylon	7. Years Jeremiah was a prophet to Judah
_____ Jehoiakim	8. Jerusalem's last governor
_____ Egypt	9. Judah's last king
_____ Baskets of figs	10. Nation who destroyed Jerusalem

D. JEREMIAH'S MESSAGE: Even though Jeremiah prophesied about Jerusalem's destruction, his message gave God's people hope. Write down one hopeful thing Jeremiah said.

_____

Across

3. Who was Jeremiah's scribe?

6. Egypt and _____ had control of Judah in the years after Josiah died.

9. Jeremiah wrote Lamentations to describe Jerusalem's _____.

10. The last king of Judah was named _____.

Down

1. "My people have committed two sins: They have _____ me, the spring of living water..." (Jeremiah 2:13)

2. King Jehoiakim _____ up the scroll with God's words.

4. Jeremiah's image of a field of _____ indicated that God's people would return and buy fields.

5. Jeremiah was a prophet for _____ years during the reign of five kings.

7. Jeremiah said the exiles would return to Jerusalem after seventy _____.

8. "...and have dug their own cisterns, _____ cisterns that cannot hold water." (Jeremiah 2:13)

Chapter 25 Quiz

A. MEMORY VERSES: Connect the parts of these verses.

Beginning:	Ending:
The LORD knows…	…the spring of living water
One jot or one tittle…	…to walk humbly with your God
They have forsaken…	…will not leave the guilty unpunished
The LORD is slow to anger…	…the way of the righteous
What does the LORD require…	…till all is fulfilled

B. STORY FACTS: Circle "T" if true and "F" if false.

1. In 1 and 2 Chronicles you can read stories about Elisha. T F
2. Manasseh reigned longer than any other king in Judah. T F
3. Jehoiada hid baby Joash to protect him against the Assyrians. T F
4. Rehoboam, the first king of Judah, ruled over two tribes. T F
5. People didn't like Jeremiah because he preached God's truth. T F
6. The LORD promised that the people would return in forty years. T F
7. Judah's worst sin was forgetting God's covenant. T F

C. WHO AM I? Write the **correct** name in the blank.

Obadiah   Joel   Habakkuk   Isaiah   Zephaniah   Micah   Jeremiah

1. I said the Messiah would be born in Bethlehem. _____

2. I asked the LORD two difficult questions. _____

3. I talked about a swarm of locusts. _____

4. I said judgment was like a purifying fire. _____

5. I saw a vision of seraphim singing, "Holy." _____

6. I prophesied against the nation of Edom. _____

7. I saw pictures of baskets of figs and smashed pots. _____

Across

4. Hezekiah trusted _____ when the Assyrians attacked.

5. Which prophet smashed pots and baskets of figs?

7. The theme of the book of Chronicles is God's _____ and holiness.

8. Who was the third king to rule after King Solomon?

9. The LORD requires you to "walk _____ with your God." (Micah 6:8)

Down

1. Uzziah got leprosy, and his son, _____, became king.

2. Who was the first king to rule after King Solomon?

3. Zephaniah proclaimed judgement like a purifying _____.

6. Which prophet had a vision of seraphim praising God?

10. Josiah read the Book of the _____ to the people.

Chapter 26 Quiz

A. MEMORY VERSE: "The soul who _____ is the one who will

_____.... 'For I take no _____ in the _____

of anyone,' declares the Sovereign LORD. '_____ and _____!'"
(Ezekiel 18:20a, 32, NIV)

B. KEY FACTS: Match the description with its meaning.

_____ Two sticks

_____ Packed bag and journey

_____ Dry bones

_____ Living creatures and wheels

_____ Lying on his side

_____ Scroll eaten

_____ Windstorm and rainbow

1. Ezekiel must speak God's words.
2. The nation will one day be united.
3. People will suffer when judged.
4. The exile will last a long time.
5. God judges and God gives grace.
6. God is everywhere and sees all.
7. God breathes life into His people.

C. STORY FACTS: Cross out the **wrong** answer.

1. Ezekiel was a (priest/prophet) before he was exiled.

2. Ezekiel was exiled to Babylon with the (first/second) group of people.

3. Life in exile was (not too bad/worse than living in besieged Jerusalem).

4. Before the fall of Jerusalem, Ezekiel's message was that (Jerusalem would be destroyed/

   the people would be going home soon).

5. Anyone who sins and does not repent will (receive mercy/die).

6. The city of the future is named ("the LORD is there"/ "the LORD lives").

7. In Ezekiel's vision, the people in the temple were (worshipping the sun/

   offering sacrifices to the LORD).

D. WHO WAS EZEKIEL? Fill in the blanks.

Ezekiel, the Prophet of _____, preached to the people in _____.

Across

1. Ezekiel's image of a bag and a journey indicated that the _____ would last a long time.
3. God's glory left the temple because of the people's great _____.
5. Ezekiel was a _____ before he became a prophet.
6. The final destruction of _____ happened in 586 BC.
9. Ezekiel's image of two sticks indicated that God would unite the two _____.

Down

1. Daniel and his friends were captured four years after the _____ killed Josiah and defeated Judah.
2. When Ezekiel prophesied to the dry _____, they became alive.
4. " 'For I take no pleasure in the _____ of anyone,' declares the Soverign LORD. 'Repent and live!'" (Ezekiel 18:32)
7. "The soul who _____ is the one who will die..."(Ezekiel 18:20a)
8. When Ezekiel ate the scroll, he was showing that he must speak God's _____ to the people.

Chapter 27 Quiz

A. MEMORY VERSE: "But the _____ of the LORD is from everlasting

to everlasting On those who _____ Him,… To such as keep His

_____ , And to those who remember His _____ to do them."
(Psalm 103:17a, 18)

B. KEY FACTS: Draw a line from the **historical period** to the **reason** that matches it.

The God of Miracles
God did miracles in four historical times for four reasons.

Historical Period	Reason
Exodus/wilderness journey	Protection from idolatry
Elijah and Elisha	Establishment of the spiritual kingdom
Babylonian exile	God's establishment of His nation
Jesus and the early church	Protection from pagan influence

C. STORY FACTS: Circle the **correct** answer.

1. Daniel and his friends were different from the other men because they _____.

    worshipped the LORD   liked to eat vegetables

2. Before interpreting the king's dream, Daniel asked his friends to _____.

    give him advice   pray for him

3. The statue in Nebuchadnezzar's dream represented four _____.

    great nations   plagues from God

4. Nebuchadnezzar's dream meant that God's kingdom would _____.

    last four hundred years   destroy other great kingdoms

5. Daniel's three friends were thrown into the fiery furnace because they _____.

    refused to worship the image   wouldn't eat the king's food

Across

5. Before Daniel interpreted Nebuchadnezzar's dreams, he asked his friends to _____.

6. During the time of Elijah and _____ God did many miracles.

7. Nebuchadnezzar dreamed of a _____ make of gold, silver, bronze, and clay.

8. "To such as keep His _____, And to those who remember His commandments to do them." (Psalm 103:18)

9. Daniel didn't want to eat the royal food because he didn't want to _____ himself.

10. The statue in Nebuchadnezzar's dream represented four _____.

Down

1. Daniel and his friends were different from the other men because they _____ the LORD.

2. A rock not made with _____ hands smashed the statue in Nebuchadnezzar's dream.

3. "But the _____ of the LORD is from everlasting to everlasting On those who fear Him" (Psalm 103:17a)

4. Nebuchadnezzar's dream meant that the Lord's kingdom would _____ other great kingdoms.

Chapter 28 Quiz

A. MEMORY VERSE: "But without _____ it is _____ to

_____ Him [God]." (Hebrews 11:6a)

B. KEY FACTS: Fill in the blanks.

1. When Daniel refused to eat the king's food, he was standing up for what

   God said was _____.

2. When Daniel prayed for the interpretation of the dream, he believed

   that God would _____ him.

3. Daniel spoke the _____ even if it meant bad things would happen.

4. Daniel obeyed _____ _____, not _____

   _____.

C. STORY FACTS: Circle "T" if true and "F" if false.

1. When Nebuchadnezzar got his sanity back, he acknowledged
   God as King of heaven.   T   F
2. Belshazzar laughed when he saw the handwriting on the wall.   T   F
3. Officials in Darius's court could find no fault in Daniel.   T   F
4. Daniel obeyed the king's decree and didn't pray to the LORD.   T   F
5. King Darius regretted the decree he made about prayer.   T   F
6. A law of the Medes and Persians could never be changed.   T   F
7. God sent an angel to shut the lions' mouths.   T   F

D. FOUR MIGHTY KINGS: Match the nations with the kings. Use one answer twice.

Babylon   The Medes   Persia

Darius _____   Belshazzar _____

Cyrus _____   Nebuchadnezzar _____

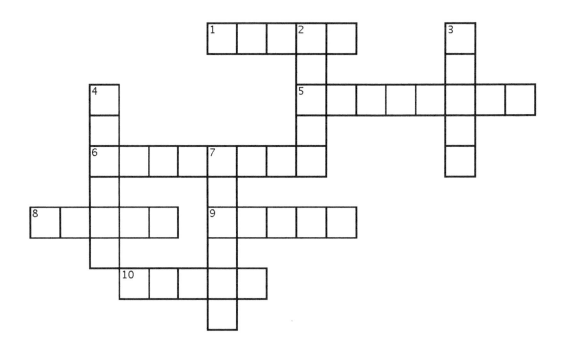

ACross

1. What was left of the tree in the dream?

5. God judged Belshazzar because he defiled the LORD by _____ from sacred goblets.

6. Faith obeys God's _____ instead of man's rules.

8. God judged Nebuchadnezzar because he boasted about how _____ he was.

9. How many years did Nebuchadnezzar act like an animal?

10. Who shut the lions' mouths?

Down

2. Darius was king of what country?

3. "But without _____ it is impossible to please Him [God]." (Hebrews 11:6a)

4. Darius made a _____ that couldn't be changed.

7. Faith prays and believes that God will _____ according to His will.

Chapter 29 Quiz

A. MEMORY VERSE: "They will call on My _____, And I will

_____ them. I will say, 'This is My _____'; And each one will

say, 'The _____ is my _____.'" (Zechariah 13:9b).

B. KEY FACTS: Number the events in the **correct** order.

_____ Cyrus decrees that God's people can return to Jerusalem.

_____ Daniel is taken captive and goes to Babylon.

_____ The rebuilding of the temple is completed.

_____ Zerubbabel and Jeshua return to Jerusalem.

_____ Ezra and Nehemiah return to Jerusalem.

_____ Ezekiel is taken captive and goes to Babylon.

_____ Haggai and Zechariah prophesy about rebuilding the temple.

C. STORY FACTS: Circle **all** the **correct** answers.

1. The men who led the first group of people back to Jerusalem were _____.

      Cyrus   Zerubbabel   Jeshua

2. God's people were in exile for _____ years.

      15   40   70

3. Artaxerxes believed the letter accusing the Jews and told them to _____.

      keep building   stop building   get permission to build

4. Haggai made a connection between being faithful to God and _____.

      God's grace   God's blessing   God's power

5. Zechariah had visions about _____.

      a flying scroll   spinning wheels   chariots

6. Zechariah's visions relate to us today because he talks about _____.

      the Messiah   God's presence with us   God's wrath

Across

5. "...I will say, 'This is My _____'; And each one will say, 'The LORD is my God.'" (Zechariah 13:9b)

7. "They will call on My name, And I will _____ them..." (Zechariah 13:9b)

8. One prophet taught that there is a connection between being faithful and receiving God's _____.

9. Zechariah prophesied about the _____ and future glory for God's people.

10. Who was taken into exile to Babylon in 605 BC.?

Down

1. For _____ years the people forgot about the temple and did nothing.

2. God moved the heart of _____ to let His people return home.

3. Zechariah's visions were about God's reaction when people _____.

4. Jeshua and _____ led the first group back to Jerusalem.

6. The prophets _____ and Zechariah encouraged the people to rebuild the temple even when it was hard to do.

chapter 30 Quiz

A. MEMORY VERSE: "Who can _____ and have it _____

if the Lord has not _____ it? Is it not from the mouth of the Most High that

both _____ and _____ _____ come?"
(Lamentations 3:37-38, NIV)

B. KEY FACTS: Circle "T" if true and "F" if false.

1. It was wrong for Queen Vashti to refuse the king's request.   T   F
2. Haman required that everyone kneel down and honor him.   T   F
3. Mordecai refused to kneel before Haman because he hated him.   T   F
4. The king held out his scepter and welcomed Esther.   T   F
5. The king believed the lie that all Jews were dangerous.   T   F
6. The king delighted in Mordecai and wanted to honor him.   T   F
7. The second decree said that Jews could defend themselves.   T   F

C. STORY FACTS: Draw a line from the word to its description.

Esther	Feast to celebrate God's protection
Mordecai	A mighty king
Purim	An unchangeable command
Decree	Jewish girl who became queen
Providence	Cousin of Queen Esther
Haman	Land where Jews were exiled
Persia	An enemy of the Jews
Xerxes	God's wise governing of everything

D. WHAT'S THE POINT? God's message to His people in the book of Esther was

that even though His people were not _____ to Him, He would still

_____ them from _____ .

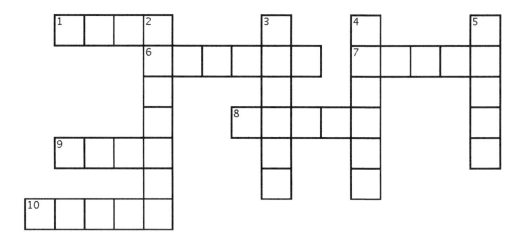

ACross

1. "Is it not from the mouth of the Most High that both calamities and _____ things come?" (Lamentations 3:38)
6. King Xerxes chose _____ to be his new queen.
7. Who was hanged on the gallows he made for Mordecai?
8. How many days did the king's banquet last?
9. Mordecai saved the king's _____ by uncovering a conspiracy against him.
10. Even though His people weren't faithful, God _____ them from destruction.

Down

2. "Who can speak and have it happen if the Lord has not _____ it?" (Lamentations 3:37)
3. The king's second decree said that Jews could _____ themselves.
4. Once the king had made a decree, he could not _____ it.
5. What would Mordecai not do?

Chapter 31 Quiz

A. MEMORY VERSE: "You have kept your _____ because you are

_____." (Nehemiah 9:8b, NIV)

B. KEY FACTS: Put these events in the **correct** order from 1-6.

_____ God's people rebuilt the temple.

_____ Ezra read God's Word to the people, and they renewed the covenant.

_____ Ezra led the second group of Jews to Jerusalem.

_____ God's people in Jerusalem repented of marrying foreign wives.

_____ Nehemiah finished building the walls despite many obstacles.

_____ Jeshua and Zerubbabel led the first group of Jews to Jerusalem.

C. STORY FACTS: Cross out the **wrong** word.

1. Ezra took (Jews/Levites) with him so the people could worship God.

2. On the journey, the people were protected by the (king's army/LORD).

3. Sanballat ridiculed the people, saying the wall was (weak/crooked).

4. When enemies threatened, Nehemiah (stopped working/posted guards).

5. Nehemiah got Sanballat's letter and then (talked to him/prayed to God).

6. When the people repented, Nehemiah told them to (weep and grieve/

   have joy in the LORD).

D. MALACHI, PROPHET OF PREPARATION—HIS MESSAGES:

1. The LORD God _____ His people.

2. God does not _____, so _____ of your sin.

3. Look for God's _____. The day of the _____ is coming.

ACross

3. Levites went with Ezra to _____ so that the people could worship God.

4. In the book of Ezra God said, "I want My people to meet together and _____ Me."

6. In what book was the message that God promised, "I am the supreme King, and I protect My people?"

7. The people wanted to stop building the wall to harvest their _____.

9. Who ridiculed Nehemiah and the workers?

Down

1. The first thing Nehemiah did when the king saw his sad face was _____ to the Lord."

2. "You have kept your _____ because you are righteous." (Nehemiah 9:8b)

4. In the book Nehemiah God said, "Listen to my _____ and confess your sin because I am your God."

5. When the people repented of the sin, Nehemiah told them that God's joy was their _____.

8. Nehemiah gave the workers _____ to hold while they worked.

Chapter 32 Quiz

A. MEMORY VERSES: Match the parts of these verses.

Beginning:	Ending:
But without faith...	...I will answer them
The soul who sins...	...because you are righteous
They will call on My name...	...it is impossible to please Him
But the mercy of the LORD...	...is the one who will die
You have kept your promise...	...is from everlasting to everlasting

B. STORY FACTS: Cross out the **wrong** answer.

1. (Ezekiel/Zechariah) saw a vision of dry bones that came back to life.

2. Daniel said his ability to interpret dreams came from (wise men/God).

3. Belshazzar was frightened by (handwriting on the wall/visions of spinning wheels).

4. Judah was conquered by the nation of (Assyria/Babylon).

5. Haggai told the people it was time to rebuild (the city walls/the temple).

6. Haman wanted Mordecai to (bow down to him/plot against the king).

7. Daniel was thrown into the lions' den because he (ate vegetables/prayed).

C. WHO AM I? Match the name with the description.

_____ Malachi	1. Decreed that exiles could return home
_____ Ezekiel	2. Saw a vision of two temples
_____ Zechariah	3. Interpreted a dream about a large statue
_____ Haggai	4. Married the Jewish girl Esther
_____ Cyrus	5. Wrote the last Old Testament book
_____ Xerxes	6. Left Jerusalem in second group of exiles
_____ Daniel	7. Encouraged people to build the temple

Across

4. Who declared Elijah as God's messenger?

8. Who was the prophet of future glory?

9. What king married Esther?

10. Who decreed that the exiles could go home?

Down

1. Who was the prophet of God's sovereignty?

2. Who was the prophet of encouragement?

3. Ezra was ashamed of the people in Jerusalem because they were unfaithful in their _____.

5. Who threw Daniel into a lions' den?

6. Whose army was defeated by Egypt?

7. Who had visions of dry bones?

Notes

Notes

Welcome, Detective.

Are you looking for an engaging first step to learning Greek? In *The Greek Alphabet Code Cracker*, understanding the Greek alphabet is the key to decoding clues and recovering the stolen Urn of Achilles!

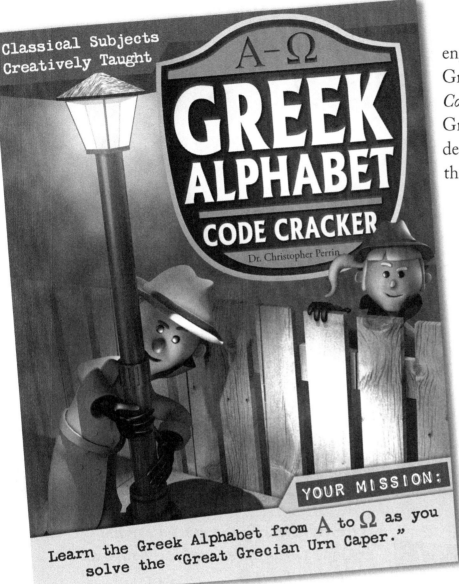

Classical Subjects Creatively Taught

A – Ω

GREEK ALPHABET

CODE CRACKER

Dr. Christopher Perrin

YOUR MISSION:

Learn the Greek Alphabet from A to Ω as you solve the "Great Grecian Urn Caper."

Learn all of the Greek letters from Alpha to Omega, and their phonetic pronunciation. Practice writing the letters, gather the clues from witnesses, and trace the path of the thief! You will first learn to sound out simple English words with the Greek alphabet, and then will go on to learn Greek words as well! This workbook text is an excellent introduction to Greek for students of all ages.

- Full color workbook text
- 8 chapters, to be completed approximately one chapter per week, considering the age of the student
- Learn all of the consonant and vowels sounds, as well as consonant blends, and diphthongs (vowel blends or combinations) by systematic, phonetic lessons
- An excellent preparation for *Song School Greek* or *Greek for Children*

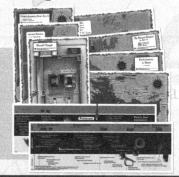